Compiled by
Chris Milner

Consultant editor
Nick Pigott

Design
Tim Pipes

Reprographics
Jonathan Schofield

Sub-editor
Nigel Devereux

Editorial assistant
Sarah Wilkinson

Group production editor
Tim Hartley

Production manager
Craig Lamb

Publisher
Dan Savage

Commercial director
Nigel Hole

Managing director
Brian Hill

Chief executive
Ian Fisher

Published by
Mortons Media Group Ltd, Media Centre,
Morton Way, Horncastle, Lincolnshire LN9 6JR
Tel: 01507 529529

All material copyright
Mortons Media Limited, 2013.
All rights reserved.

The Railway Magazine address: as above

Printed by:
William Gibbons & Son, Wolverhampton

ISBN 978-1-909128-08-8

A *Railway Magazine* Publication

CALEDONIAN RAILWAY EXPRESS LOCOMOTIVE. No. 766.
DESIGNED BY MR. JOHN F. McINTOSH, LOCOMOTIVE SUPERINTENDENT.
DIAMETER OF DRIVING WHEEL 6 FT. 6 IN.   WORKING PRESSURE (PER SQ. IN.) 175 LBS.
WEIGHT OF ENGINE AND TENDER, IN WORKING ORDER, 94 TONS.

Contents

**Above: A colour plate of
'Dunalistair II' No. 766 from
the October 1899 issue of
The Railway Magazine.
See feature on page 69.**

Welcome to the best of

A very warm welcome to volume two of *The Best of The Railway Magazine*. I'd like to thank readers who bought volume one, and those who took the time to write or email some useful feature suggestions for future inclusion.

The format for this volume is very much in the same style as volume one, a selection of the unusual, interesting, and in some cases, what are still topical features, all taken from past issues of *The Railway Magazine*.

With a 116-year history, more than 1,350 issues of *The Railway Magazine* have been published, and the hard part is deciding what to leave out.

Several readers asked for some foreign articles, and this has been achieved with a feature on the 'Hiawatha', plus a picture spread on the GM EMD 'E' & 'F' series locomotives. We've also included a little Irish feature on the erstwhile Tralee & Dingle railway.

A number of the features relate to lines or subjects that are now history – lines have been closed, and locomotive classes scrapped – so I hope they rekindle memories with readers.

Since publication of volume one, additional research has been undertaken within our photographic archive and this has, in a number of cases, allowed us to scan the prints that accompanied original features. Together with improved technology, it has allowed us to achieve a more improved reproduction quality than the original printed magazine.

In addition, our close working with many of the commercial railway photographic libraries has permitted the use of some colour images, rather than all black and white, together with new material, some of which is seeing the light of day for the very first time.

Many readers of *The RM* will remember that it was not until the late 1980s that magazines enjoyed greater flexibility to the positioning and wider use of colour images, and to be fair, many still remember the halcyon days of steam as a 'black & white' era.

Delving back into our archives evokes memories and has filled me with admiration as to what lengths previous editors, staff and correspondents went to bring readers news and features from other railways around the world. These features contain information that was researched, often through personal travel or first-hand experience as a railway

employee, all rather different to the internet age of today.

Past issues of *The RM* have shown what a golden age of railways we had before the decline of the late 1950s and early 1960s. It is said things go in cycles, and we are currently enjoying a new golden era of rail, with rising passenger numbers and travel at speeds our forefathers could only have dreamed of.

The Railway Magazine

The frontispiece from the July 1934 issue is reproduced and shows GWR 'King' No. 6018 *King Henry VI* emerging from Parsons Tunnel between Dawlish and Teignmouth with the 'Cornish Riviera Express'.

Suggestions for features from the past issues are welcome for a possible third volume, and you can send emails to railway@mortons.co.uk or write to us at the address on page 3.

My thanks to designer Tim Pipes, and team leader Kelvin Clements, as well as reprographics technician Jonathan Schofield, editoral assistant Sarah Wilkinson, Jayne Clement for scanning the text, and sub-editor

Nigel Devereux.

I sincerely hope you enjoy volume 2.

Chris Milner
Horncastle, October 2013

Doncaster-built electric locomotive E5015 passes Shortlands with a down 'Golden Arrow' Pullman service in the summer of 1960. COLOUR RAIL

Forty years of the 'Golden Arrow'

Pullman 'Continental Express' renamed in May 1929, to match its French counterpart

By A HASENSON

O N May 15 the 'Golden Arrow' celebrates its 44th anniversary in this country. Heralded as one of the luxuries of its time, it is essentially a product of the heyday of the Pullman era, now unfortunately nearing its close.

From small beginnings on the Midland Railway in 1874, Pullman cars flourished, principally in the south of England in the 19th century. They were adopted enthusiastically by the London, Brighton & South Coast Railway, which ran its first Pullman car in 1875 and its first all-Pullman train in 1881, long before any other railway in the country.

The first Pullman to run in a Continental boat train between London and the Kent coast – an ex-Midland car named *Jupiter* – was put on by the London, Chatham & Dover Railway in 1882. It was not a great success, partly perhaps because of the deep-rooted

aversion of the public to paying a supplement, over and above the normal fare, and was withdrawn in 1884.

Nothing daunted, five years later both the Chatham and the South Eastern put on a special train of luxury vehicles for a first class-only afternoon service to Paris at the time of the International Exhibition in 1889. All cars for these were supplied by the Wagons-Lits, the SER never countenancing Pullmans until after the retirement of Sir Edward Watkin. In spite of all efforts the 'Club Trains', as they were called, were not a paying proposition either. In fact, there were hardly enough passengers for one train after the exhibition was over, let alone two and at the end of the summer season of 1893 they were withdrawn.

On the other hand, the Brighton Company had better luck. In 1891, the directors launched the first commercially successful Pullman to run in a Continental boat train to the South Coast. It plied between Victoria and Newhaven, and – although not, strictly speaking, on the short sea route – its success, both financially and in the number of years it continued to run, make it of some interest.

Spurred on no doubt by the example of these Brighton Pullmans, notably the 'Southern Belle' in 1908, the South Eastern & Chatham Railway – a fusion of the old LCDR and SER – started its own services in 1910. On March 21 of that year the company launched its new Pullmans in several of the Continental boat trains between London and Dover, using six cars specially built for the occasion. They were an immediate success, and from these early beginnings expansion increased rapidly. By the end of the year Folkestone, too, had its own Continental Pullman service, four more new cars having been placed in use, and by the summer of 1914 there was hardly a boat train to the Kent coast which did not have at least one Pullman in its set, and often as many as three. The acceleration in December 1913 of the 4.30pm afternoon express from Charing Cross, first introduced six months previously, gave the fastest-ever service from London to Paris, a mere 6½ hours.

On the French side, too, although there were no Pullmans, there were comfortable bogie coaches, restaurant cars and usually a carriage containing two coupe-lit-toilette compartments for greater comfort. On the Nord, these compartments, advertised as Lits-Salons, were usually found at each end of an ordinary first-class carriage. They contained three seats which could be pulled down to form a couch, and there was also a private toilet.

The First World War interrupted the steady growth of these services as it interrupted so much else, but by the mid-1920s, all was back to normal, the Southern Railway now firmly established after the Grouping of 1923.

Having for too long been overshadowed by the magnificence of the Wagons-Lits sleeping-car trains before the war, Pullmans now proceeded to create some of their own glory. Luxury travel was no longer just confined to millionaires and the nobility, and many ordinary citizens of means demanded better than was hitherto provided. On the Continent, the Wagons-Lits initiated a whole series of all-Pullman trains and lesser such services from 1925 onwards, while in Britain the first all-Pullman train in south-east England – the 'Thanet Pullman Limited' from Victoria to Ramsgate – was started on July 10, 1921.

So far as international services were concerned, however, it was not until November 1924, that the Southern Railway put on what

Unrebuilt 'Merchant Navy' No. 35028 *Clan Line* on the down 'Golden Arrow' passing a splendid array of semaphore signals at Beckenham Junction on March 27, 1954. S CREER/TRANSPORT TREASURY

was to all intents and purposes an all-Pullman boat train between Victoria and Dover. This was composed of seven Pullman cars, and also had one or two ordinary corridor firsts, and a brakevan. Originally a relief, departure was 10.50am from Victoria, arriving at Dover at 12.32, and it was closely followed by the 11am ordinary train. This latter arrived at Dover at 12.40pm where passengers from both trains caught the 12.55 boat, arriving in Calais at 2.10pm and Paris at 6.15pm. Motive power was provided by one of the new 'King Arthur' class 4-6-0s.

In September 1926, the 'Golden Arrow' at last appeared officially on the railway scene, not in this country, however, but in France, where it was called 'La Flèche d'Or'. It was organised by the Northern Railway of France, under the prodding of Lord Dalziel who was president of the Wagons-Lits and who also had a controlling interest in the Pullman Car Co

Ltd. He was enthusiastically backed by Sir Herbert Walker, general manager of the Southern Railway. The train was composed exclusively of first-class Pullman cars, all built in this country, and looking to all intents and purposes like their British counterparts, although somewhat larger.

A trial run was made between Paris and Calais on September 11 for railwaymen and journalists, when a 10-coach train hauled by a Nord Super-Pacific left Paris at 10.25am and reached Calais Maritime at 1.30pm. The return journey was one hour later, leaving Calais at 2.30pm and arriving back in Paris at 5.40pm. Full normal service began two days later, on September 13. An agreement, unfortunately only with French customs, made it possible for all baggage and passport formalities to be carried out on the train itself while en route, a great time saver and much appreciated.

At the same time in England, the Southern Railway put on a matching all-Pullman train, the 'Continental Express'. This was our old friend of 1924 suitably poshed up, and composed exclusively of first-class Pullman cars. It left Victoria at 10.45am, 15 minutes before the ordinary train, and enabled passengers to secure the best seats on the boat at Dover. Calais was reached at 2.10pm and Paris at 5.40pm. These arrangements lasted until 1929, when in May of that year the 'Continental Express' was renamed the 'Golden Arrow' to match its French counterpart. The service had arrived!

There was more to it than mere name-changing, however. The "Arrow" was given its own steamer, the *Canterbury*, specially built, so that there was no danger of contamination with other passengers. Furthermore, by agreement with customs at Dover arrangements were made for 'Golden Arrow' passengers to be ▶

BR 'Britannia' class No. 70004 *William Shakespeare* heads the down 'Golden Arrow' on the approach to Bickley on April 11, 1952. At the time the loco was slightly more than a year into its BR service. JOHN G CLICK

passed through onto the ship as quickly as possible. The new train also left Victoria before the ordinary service, though at 11am instead of 10.45, arriving at Dover at 12.30, Calais at 2.10pm and Paris at 5.35pm, 20 minutes faster than hitherto. An all-inclusive fare of £5 was charged for the complete journey which included first-class travel by Pullman in England and France, and also on the boat.

As a further boost to the service, eight refurbished Pullman cars were added to the train in July 1930. By now, however, the icy blasts of worldwide economic recession were setting in rapidly, and money for luxury travel became strictly limited. In contrast, cruising enjoyed a tremendous boom: it was considered patriotic in so far as it saved foreign currency. As a consequence, patronage on the Pullmans dropped, forcing first a reduction in the number of cars used, and later the addition of ordinary second-class coaches of Southern Railway stock in 1932. By 1939, the number of Pullman cars on the 'Golden Arrow' had

been reduced to a mere four. Other measures included common use of the *Canterbury* from May 1931 onwards, when first- and second-class passengers from the ordinary train combined with the passengers on the 'Golden Arrow' at Dover for the run to Calais.

On the French side too, all was not well. As in England, the number of first-class Pullmans was gradually reduced early on. Later, unlike in this country, second-class Pullmans were added. As well as this, through Wagons-Lits sleeping cars were introduced later, so that by the outbreak of the Second World War all these cars were running regularly in the train. As a further economy, the inward journey was diverted in October 1935 to go via Boulogne-Folkestone, thereby enabling the Nord to use only one rake of cars for the 'Flèche d'Or' instead of two as before.

Then, as 25 years previously, war halted all civilian cross-channel services in September 1939, and it was not until April 15, 1946, that a newly inaugurated train set off once

more from Victoria for its first postwar journey to Dover, hauled by one of the comparatively new Bulleid Pacifics, 'Channel Packet'. At the quayside the *Canterbury* was waiting, ready to resume a civilian role after distinguished war service. Brightly painted, her Oerlikon guns removed, and equipped with radar, she moved proudly off at 12.30pm and entered Calais 1hr 20min later.

As in so many other parts of France there was devastation everywhere, partly because of the fighting in 1940, and partly subsequent bombing and sabotage. Nevertheless, a temporary station of one-storey huts was ready for the inaugural service and, though inadequate, continued to serve for some years. Already a massive programme of reconstruction was getting under way in France. The railways had been shattered during the war and all the Channel ports ruined. Both Calais and Boulogne Maritime stations were rebuilt as quickly as possible, in view of their importance to cross-channel traffic, the former being reopened in 1952 and Calais Maritime in 1958. A postwar London to Paris timing of 8hr 45min was gradually whittled down over the years to 6hr 35min, partly thanks to electrification, which was proceeding apace in the 1950s, in Britain as well as in France.

The first phase of the Kent Coast electrification scheme was inaugurated on June 15, 1959, when electric trains started running to Ramsgate via Gillingham, Faversham and Margate, and to Dover via Gillingham, Faversham and Canterbury. Phase two was brought into operation on June 12, 1961, when electric traction was inaugurated from Victoria to Folkestone and Dover via Sevenoaks, Tonbridge and Ashford, the last steam-hauled 'Golden Arrow' running the day before, hauled by 'West Country' class Pacific *Appledore*. Finally, on June 18, 1962, it was also possible to

'Flèche d'Or' arriving at Paris Nord on July 12, 1967, behind SNCF loco No. BB-16056 bearing a special headboard for the electrically worked section south of Amiens. The solitary Pullman car is at the rear, and later was shunted round to Gare de Lyon A HASENSON

**Left and right:
Final days of steam
on the 'Golden
Arrow' in Britain
and France:
Leaving Victoria
(left) on June 11,
1961, hauled by
'West Country'
Pacific No. 34100**
Appledore; **and
passes the
outskirts of
Boulogne (right)
behind Pacific
No. 231.E.21**
A HASENSON

travel by electric train between Maidstone East and Paddock Wood, and also Maidstone East and Ashford.

In France, electric traction on the northern region of the SNCF was inaugurated between Paris Nord and Lille via Creil, Longueau, Arras and Douai on January 7, 1959. The 'Flèche d'Or' continued to be steam hauled throughout from the coast to Paris until Amiens, three miles further north from Longeau, was also electrified more than a year later, and after considerable rebuilding. In May 1960, the high-speed AC overhead electric traction between Amiens and Paris was inaugurated, and steam haulage then ceased south of Amiens on the 'Flèche d'Or'. It stopped altogether on January 11, 1969, when a 'K' class Pacific, No. 82, brought the last northbound steam-hauled train into Calais Maritime. From then on diesel locomotives have provided the usual motive power for the 'Flèche d'Or'.

Most passengers passing through Boulogne since the opening of the new Ville station in 1962 are unaware that the station is situated in what was the middle of a river! One of the many schemes of reconstruction in Boulogne involved straightening the course of the Liane, filling in the old river bed, and using this for housing and for the site of the new station.

In 1952, the 'Golden Arrow' morning departure was changed for the first time to an afternoon one, thereby enabling French Railways to run only one set of carriages for its train, just as before the war, from 1935 to 1939. However, the new timing proved most unpopular, and the ordinary morning service continued to be well-patronised. Eventually, the departure time was changed back to a morning one in May 1960.

In Britain, the 'Golden Arrow' remained nominally all-Pullman until 1965. From its re-inception in April 1946, it was all first

class, except for an initial period of about a year when it had two or three second-class Pullmans in addition. In October 1949, however, second-class Pullmans were again introduced, as there simply were not enough first-class passengers and, besides, the relief was attracting too many second-class travellers, causing overcrowding in the height of the season. It was hoped some could be persuaded to pay a supplement and travel second class on the 'Golden Arrow'.

A reprieve in the decline was offered when the old train was replaced during the Festival of Britain, in June 1951. Consisting mainly of new Pullmans and a few refurbished cars, they were distinguished from older Pullmans by

"In Britain, the 'Golden Arrow' remained nominally all-Pullman until 1965."

having the traditional oval sidelights at the ends replaced by square lights.

By 1954, the charms of the 'old lady' were no longer so obvious, and the Southern Region was quietly slipping in ordinary second-class carriages of Southern Region stock until, in May 1965, the 'Golden Arrow' became officially part-Pullman only, from then on comprising just four first-class Pullman cars, the rest of the train being of ordinary second-class carriages.

In France, the 'Flèche d'Or' suffered a similar fate. Although only part-Pullman in 1946 and including at that time also ordinary SNCF stock, it became once more all-first all-Pullman in July 1947. By this time, too, the *Invicta* had taken over from the *Canterbury* on the Dover-Calais run. As in England, however,

air travel was making increasing inroads on luxury travel, and the 'Flèche d'Or' was forced to abandon its original first-class-only concept just as before the war, and introduce second-class Pullmans in October 1949, as on the 'Golden Arrow', and finally ordinary carriages of the SNCF in 1950.

When third class was reclassified second class on most European railways in June 1956, all second-class Wagons-Lits Pullmans were withdrawn, many to be rebuilt for other purposes such as restaurant cars. In Britain, on the other hand, second-class Pullmans continued on the 'Golden Arrow' for another 11 years until withdrawn in May 1965.

The economics of running Pullman cars in France has led to an even more drastic reduction in their numbers than in England.

By the mid-1960s, only one Parlour Pullman (or at the most two) were in service on the 'Flèche d'Or', meals being provided by the nearby restaurant car. In December 1967, this was further reduced, when a Parlour Pullman in the southbound train was replaced by a Kitchen Pullman serving only light refreshments, and the wagon restaurant by a voiture bar. Finally, on June 1, 1969, the last claim of the 'Flèche d'Or' to be a luxury train will cease when the Pullman cars are withdrawn altogether.

It is now doubtful whether the 'Golden Arrow' or its Pullman cars will continue to run for much longer in this country. The advantages of the all-purpose electric multiple units are such that, unless special Pullmans are built, they may soon be taken off altogether. Over the years Pullmans have given a wonderful service, pioneered many technical features relating to railway safety and comfort, and although since 1967 only a division of British Rail Catering, the name deserves to be perpetuated. Perhaps a Channel tunnel, when built, will give this train a new lease of life. ∎

The Callander and Oban Section of the LMSR

'Black Five' No. 45158 *Glasgow Yeomanry* (one of only four named) stands at Callander at the head of an Oban to Glasgow service, on April 3, 1961. J & J COLLECTION/SID RICKARD

By O S NOCK,
BSc, DIC, AMIMech E

SOMETIME about 5am, a northbound traveller, still wakeful from station noises at Stirling, hears the rhythmical tattoo of the wheels punctuated by the sound of rushing water, not once but several times. The beat of the engine becomes louder and more echoing in the ascent of Dunblane bank, and keen ears will note, too, that this beat is not that of a 'Royal Scot', a compound, nor yet any of the Stanier types. Then sleep comes again, and our traveller probably is not fully roused until dawn is riding the Highland sky. It does not matter if the day be fair or foul, nor whether it be Loch Lubnaig under a lemon-yellow sky, or the steep mountainsides of Glen Ogle, vague in driving rain; his first glimpse from the carriage window will be one to be remembered.

Such is many an Englishman's first introduction to the Oban line, the first railway to penetrate the West Highlands. The Callander

& Oban was indeed incorporated as a distinct company as long ago as 1865, the same year as the Dingwall & Skye Railway was authorised. But, whereas trains were running through to Strome Ferry in 1870, it was not until 10 years later that the whole of the Callander & Oban line was opened to traffic. Unlike other routes through the Highlands, there were definite prospects of a remunerative tourist traffic in the summer, and with Oban's growing importance as a port a fairly steady business all the year round seemed probable.

By the year 1860, David Hutcheson's steamer business had grown to such an extent that the frequency of service was almost equal to that now provided by the famous firm he

founded, David Macbrayne Limited. In addition to the through service from Glasgow to Inverness via the Crinan and Caledonian canals, there were sailings to Mull, Skye, and the Outer Hebrides. The mails from Glasgow and the south were all carried by water, which Hutcheson rightly claimed as the swiftest conveyance in the West Highlands, and the journey from Glasgow to Oban took 9½ hours. The so-called 'Charing Cross of the Highlands' could also be reached by road coaches, on some of which circular tours were operated in conjunction with the steamers, and altogether there was quite a brisk business centred upon Oban.

So, it was not surprising that railway promoters got busy. Unlike the West Highland Railway, of which I wrote in *The Railway Magazine* just a year ago, a fairly obvious route presented itself. From Strathyre, there leads north at first and then westwards a chain of glens that for centuries before had provided one of the main highways to the west; it was greatly improved by General Wade after the Jacobite rebellion of 1715, but although the course would not appear to include any serious obstacles, the difficulties of construction were evidently underestimated.

To a present-day traveller, the only place east of Dalmally that would seem likely to cause trouble is the ascent of Glen Ogle, but nevertheless the company was soon in financial difficulties. The line was opened as far as Glenoglehead, then called Killin, in 1870; in the next three years only 15 miles were completed. The contractor for this section, Glenoglehead to Tyndrum, was Mr Easton Gibb, the father of Sir Alexander Gibb, this year's President of the Institution of Civil Engineers. But even before Tyndrum was reached, the company's resources apparently were running out, for in 1870 an Act was passed abandoning the extension westwards from that point, and reducing the Caledonian Railway's contribution from £200,000 to £162,000.

Oban, however, was far too great a prize to be let slip in this way, particularly as there were rival schemes on foot; and so, after considerable negotiations, the Caledonian Railway came to the rescue. The new extension from Tyndrum to Oban was authorised in 1874 and work was pushed rapidly forward. On July 1, 1880, the line was opened throughout to Oban. Although it was legally a separate company, the bulk of the shares were owned by the Caledonian, and that company operated the traffic from the outset. Very soon it became the busiest of all railways in the Highlands, though for many years the receipts were not up to the rather sanguine expectations of the promoters.

From the operating point of view it ranks second only in difficulty to the West Highland;

Former Caledonian 'Oban' 3P No 14621 arrives at Killin Junction with the 1.40pm summer service from Glasgow to Oban in the early 1930's. *RM* ARCHIVE

the ruling gradient is indeed 1-in-50, but the longest banks are generally not so severe. An even greater handicap are the curves, which not only preclude anything in the way of fast running, but are so sharp in places as to restrict the types of locomotive that can be employed. Almost from the time of opening, the Caledonian worked the line with special engines found nowhere else in the system, and it is only in recent years that any 'strangers' have appeared.

The locomotive department, then in charge of Mr Brittain, seemed rather at a loss as to how to work this very heavy road. First of all they borrowed a Webb 2-4-2 radial tank engine from the LNWR. This little engine must have acquitted itself well, for a new design based on the Crewe locomotive was prepared at St Rollox, and 15 engines of the type were ordered from Neilson & Company and put to work in 1881. They also were 2-4-2 tanks, but with outside cylinders, stove-pipe chimney and the characteristic Brittain appearance. They lasted a very short time on the Oban road. There was something radically wrong with their

radial axleboxes, and after many failures and much rough riding they were transferred to a less exacting route.

The old ungainly looking 0-4-2 mineral tender engines, examples of which were at work on various parts of the Caledonian till quite recently, took their place as a stop-gap measure, and then in 1882 Mr Brittain's very successful 'Oban bogies' were put to work. These engines, which might be described as a Caledonian version of the celebrated 'Skye bogies' of the Highland Railway, but minus the heavy double framing at the front end, had an almost complete monopoly of the route for nearly 20 years. At that time, the Oban engines did not work south of Callander, or Stirling at the farthest, whereas nowadays most trains are worked through from Oban to Glasgow by the same engine.

Although the line as authorised in 1865 does not begin till Callander & Oban junction box is reached, three-quarters of a mile east of the present Callander station, Stirling is a much more clearly defined frontier point between Lowlands and Highlands, and here the interest and charm of a journey to Oban begins. As the train crosses the Forth and speeds across the level meadows towards the gorge of Allan Water, away to the north-west at the head of the broad valley of the Teith is Ben Ledi; this most prominent outpost of the Highlands lies immediately to the west of Callander, and although it is hidden from view during the ascent of Dunblane bank, from the moment one leaves the main line it serves as a kind of guiding star, especially so from the footplate, during the twists and turns of the road past Doune and Drumvaich where a sense of direction can be lost.

We are now on the track of the Dunblane, Doune and Callander Railway, which starts off in great style as a double line, but which somewhat surprisingly changes to single at Doune after about one-third of its length – a curious state of affairs on a railway only 11 miles long. One can only suppose that funds were running short, and did not permit of a ▶

Eastfield B1 No. 61396 stalls on damp rails in the Pass of Leny as it climbs from Callander to Stratheyre with a westbound freight, August 23, 1960. WWW.RAILPHOTOPRINTS.CO.UK/HUGH BALLANTYNE

double track throughout. The country is such as one sees south of Beattock, rolling upland pasture land; but as Callander is neared the prospect on the north of the line becomes steadily wilder, and ragged outcrops of rock begin to show on hillsides where bracken is ousting the heather. This introduction to the Highlands is indeed much more gradual than on the neighbouring LNER route, at any rate until Callander is reached.

By this time the train is nearing Callander & Oban Jct, where the line to the original Callander terminus branched off; the ticket platform is passed and then, at just 16 miles from Stirling, the present Callander station is reached. This is a neat and pleasant layout characteristic of the Caledonian Railway, to which a large clock, mounted on top of the footbridge spanning the tracks, adds a touch of the unusual. Here, the Glasgow-Oban trains attach or detach their Edinburgh portions, which are usually brought into Callander by 4-4-0 locomotives; on these duties can be seen 'Dunalastairs' of the second and third batches, and sometimes also the big McIntosh superheater 4-4-0s. A noteworthy point about locomotives working between Dunblane and Oban is that one never sees a standard LMSR type; not even the Class 4 Midland 0-6-0s, nor the 0-6-0 shunting tanks have penetrated into this region.

This leads me on to the Oban engines proper, and the need for special types will be apparent before we have travelled many miles beyond Callander. Brittain's 'Oban bogies' were superseded in 1902 by the McIntosh 55 class, which also, most curiously, had undisputed possession of the route for exactly 20 years. These powerful engines, with their 5ft diameter coupled wheels, and their 19in x 26in

On August 24, 1960, Stanier 'Black Five' No. 45468 leaves Strathyre with the 7.50am Glasgow to Oban, 45359 will follow with the Stirling to Oban daily goods.
WWW.RAILPHOTOPRINTS.CO.UK/HUGH BALLANTYNE

cylinders, made short work of the 1-in-50 banks with the loads of those days, but Caledonian enterprise was not content to run branch-line stock on so fascinating a tourist route. So, luxurious bogie coaches, built in the style of the crack Aberdeen express of that time – the 'Grampian Corridor' – were put on to the Oban line, thereby adding to the engines' burden. Yet it was not until almost the close of their career that any of the type were modified.

Then, in 1930, No. 14607 was provided with a large boiler, formerly carried by No. 17901 of the McIntosh 918 class, which latter engine was scrapped about the same

time. No. 14606 was similarly treated in 1931, in this case receiving the boiler from No. 17904. These two engines, however, did comparatively little passenger working in their altered condition, for very soon afterwards the 'Clans' were transferred from the Highland line.

With the load now made up to seven or eight of the latest LMSR bogies we get away from Callander for the real business, and less than a mile out, after the River Leny has been crossed, the railway strikes out over green meadows for what appears to be a solid wall of mountains, a majestic entry to the Highlands proper.

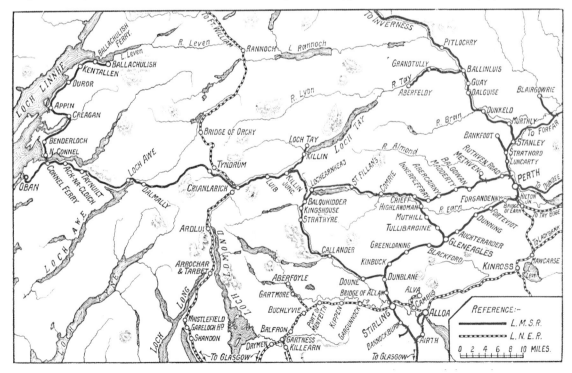

"The railway literally wiggles its way up the boulder strewn, thickly wooded flanks of Ben Ledi"

Map of the Oban to Callandar line, and connections with other routes.

The heights crowd so closely round the Pass of Leny that it is only when the hills are close at hand that the gap can be descried. Then the railway literally wriggles its way up the boulder strewn, thickly wooded flanks of Ben Ledi, along a track that from the footplate looks more like a sylvan country lane, and where the silver birches would surely meet overhead but for the blasting exhausts of engines toiling up the first piece of 1-in-50 ascent.

Speed is rarely more than 20mph up this bank, and the Pickersgill 4-6-0s, in particular, make very heavy weather of it when loaded to their maximum tonnage. On my last down journey No. 14625 of this class, with 223 tons tare – only seven tons inside maximum – went up at a steady 18.3mph; but this type, although built as recently as 1923, has always seemed to me effete for so heavy a road as the Callander & Oban. The cylinders, it is true, are larger than those of the McIntosh engines, but with a small boiler, no superheater, and the unusual provision, in post-war days, of 'D' slide valves, from the very start of their careers they have had their work cut out to keep time. They were, of course, designed as a light-weight short-wheelbase engine, and here, at the head of the Pass of Leny, we come to the principal cause of weight restriction. Twice within a quarter of a mile the railway crosses the wild, brawling river, and each time on the slenderest of bowstring girder bridges.

Over the second of these bridges the defile is seen to broaden out. Then comes a glimpse of the foot of Loch Lubnaig, a series of reedy bays from which the River Leny flows lazily away, with little suggestion of the torrent it becomes in a few hundred yards. Here, at the foot of the loch, is passed the ancient ruined chapel of St Bride, dramatically pictured by Scott in The Lady of the Lake; today, the place where the Fiery Cross was handed from one runner to the next is almost exactly marked by the crossing loop and signalbox of St Brides.

Now comes the unusual luxury, in the West Highlands, of a level run, a well-aligned five miles along the western shore of Loch Lubnaig. The track runs at the water's edge for

An up special goods train formed of hopper wagons and hauled by McIntosh 0-6-0 No. 17599, pauses at Strathyre to pass another service.

practically the whole way. This is one of the very few scenes on the route that is not usually seen to the best advantage from the train, though curiously enough my own first sight of it was entrancing beyond description: under the blazing noonday sun a heavy mist which had filled the glens since dawn was just lifting; great banks of cloud were floating up the green hillsides, leaving the sparkling water an almost Mediterranean blue.

Just beyond the head of the loch the train reaches Strathyre, a charming village lying in the narrowest part of this deep valley; at most seasons, both village and station seem garlanded from end to end with flowers. On the up platform there is an exquisite figure of a heron, made entirely in granite quarried from Ben Cruachan; in its upraised bill a gas burner is concealed, and this striking ornament makes a strangely beautiful lantern at night. The easy grading continues for a mile or so beyond Strathyre, and the brisk restart soon brings us in to very historic country, where every stream, almost every tree, and certainly every hidey-hole is venerated as the scene of some daring exploit of Rob Roy.

One cannot travel between Callander & Oban without remarking on the extent to which all the operating staff are 'up' in the scenic and historical attractions of the route. Guards

would seem to make it part of their job to point out places of interest, though one such man distributing those remarkably comprehensive handbills which describe the route, seemed almost apologetic when he came to a compartment full of mountain enthusiasts, and saw the seats strewn with large-scale ordnance maps, and camera and binoculars at the 'ready'. This handbill is prepared in the style of the route books dealing with famous trains, and is presented gratis to all passengers no matter how short their journey may be. The outside bears the following happily worded inscription: "The LMS present this Guide to Travellers in the hope that even a little knowledge of the story and romance of the continuous sequence of bens, glens, lochs and old castles will add to their enjoyment of the journey".

By this time we are running into Balquhidder, one of the most important intermediate stations on the route. Before the extension from Crieff was constructed along the north side of Loch Earn, this station used to be called Lochearnhead, although it lies almost exactly halfway between the latter place and Balquhidder. While the engine is taking water in readiness for the tremendous climb up Glen Ogle it is a good opportunity to write something of the fine work being done by the 'Clan'- type locomotives since their transference from the Highland section.

To any Scottish enthusiast who feels moved to pipe a coronach in lament of the anglicising of the former Highland Railway, a trip over the Oban line can be a most stimulating experience, for here the 'Clans' are working harder than ever before. They are rostered to take 255 tons without assistance – a remarkable figure over a route of such grading. But even this tonnage appears to be well within their maximum capacity; during the past summer one of them took a tare load of 295 tons forward from Callander unpiloted, and reached Oban barely two minutes late.

The palm, as far my knowledge goes, must ▶

Oban station presented a wonderful sight in the 1930s.

however be awarded to No. 14766 *Clan Chattan*, which worked the 12.15pm ex-Glasgow to time on an occasion when the load westwards from Balquhidder was 302 tons tare. On this run, speed was steadily maintained at 17mph up the 1-in-60 of Glen Ogle bank. How far from all-out the engines were being worked on these notable trips I am not able to say, but from my experience on the footplate with the normal loads of 230 to 250 tons the 'Clans' appear to be linked up to decidedly shorter cut-offs than are customary on the neighbouring West Highland line.

The ascent to the 940ft altitude of Glenoglehead summit actually begins just south of Balquhidder station, but the real tug-of-war comes on restarting. To the accompaniment of a thunderous beat from the engine the train is fairly lifted up the hillside, while far below there gradually opens out a fascinating view of Loch Earn. The village of Lochearnhead, and the graceful curving viaduct of the railway to Crieff seems but a stone's throw, a hundred feet or so down the hillside.

The tranquil beauty of this scene is greatly enhanced by the altitude of our travelling viewpoint, the loch itself is surprisingly regular in shape. Then little by little the fair prospect is cut off, as the train winds round a spur of the mountain into the wild morain of Glen Ogle. The Gaelic word, of which 'ogle' is a phonetic rendering, means 'terrific', and as the engine pounds away up the almost impossible ledge cut in the hillside, the tumbled array of vast boulders, and look of utter desolation, certainly make a picture as savage as it is contrasting with the placid vista of a few moments ago. So, at 17 miles from Callander, we come to Glenoglehead, at one time the terminus of the line, and then called Killin.

Caledonian 0-6-0 No. 57571 waits at Kentallen for the road to clear with Ballachulish branch freight, in August 1960. RAIL PHOTOPRINTS COLLECTION

The situation is not unlike that of Lochearnhead, for the village lies some miles away to the north-east, at the head of Loch Tay; it was only when the branch line from Killin Junction to Killin was opened, four miles of precipitous descent, that the summit point of the main route received its present name. Now it is no longer a station, but curiously enough it shares with the still lonelier summit of the West Highland line, Corrour, and with Achnasheen on the Dingwall and Skye railway, the distinction of being a place where engines are re-manned. On the LNER this procedure is adopted only in certain cases of pilot engine working, but on the Callander and Oban during the summer the 5.12pm from Buchanan Street, and the 5.15pm from Oban regularly exchange engine crews at Glenoglehead.

While on the subject of Glenoglehead and the ascent from Balquhidder, mention must be made of the scenic excursions operated jointly by the LMSR and the LNER, from Glasgow to Crianlarich and back outward via Callander and home by the West Highland line. Mr D S Barrie has given me details of one such journey, which is of particular interest in that the engine was a Great Eastern 4-6-0, No. 8548. In spite of having 6ft 6in coupled wheels, the "Hiker" did splendidly up the banks with her 160-ton load; indeed Dunblane, 4.9 miles from the start at Stirling, was passed in the most unusual time of 7min 28sec. The 27¾ miles to Balquhidder were completed in 47½ minutes, and then came a smart ascent to Glenoglehead, in just 16 minutes; the fastest I have noted personally for this 5¼ miles, with a 'Clan' and 240 tons, is 17¾ minutes. The engine was worked by an LNER crew accompanied by an LMSR pilotman.

And now, having passed the summit, I must hasten on in harmony with the increased speed of the train. A brisk run, downhill at 1-in-69, brings us to Killin Jct; this station, set in a ring of fir trees, is an oasis indeed in the

vast expanse of purple-brown moorland. On the run down from Glenoglehead, quite half the length of Glen Dochart can be scanned from the right-hand window, and at the extreme eastern end lies Killin and the head of Loch Tay, with Ben Lawers making a noble background. Good connections to and from Killin are provided with all main line trains at the junction, and when travelling to Oban it is well worthwhile to break one's journey and make the short trip down the branch. Until quite recently this line was worked by a Drummond 0-4-4 tank engine, but during the past summer one of the 5ft 9in McIntosh 0-4-4s, No. 15210, has been on the job; she is housed in the one-engine shed at Loch Tay terminus.

Soon we are down to the level of the River Dochart; Luib is passed, and along a practically level course there follows some of the fastest running of the journey. The hills, packed around on every side, are wild and bare, and it is the river here that provides the finest scenery; there are some charming glimpses alongside the little lochs Tubhair and Dochart, and then, almost before there is time to recognise the locality, the West Highland viaduct is seen stretched across the strath and we are stopping at Crianlarich.

This little hamlet, which looms so large and important as 'half-way house' between Glasgow and Fort William, is no more than a wayside station on the LMSR route. There are no advertised connections with the LNER, but the connecting loop from Crianlarich junction to the West Highland line provides not merely a means of interchange of goods traffic, but also, as I described in *The Railway Magazine* for last January, a double crossover loop for LMSR trains.

It is rare for trains of both companies to be on view at the same time, but last summer when I was travelling by the first of the Glasgow-Oban Sunday excursions, the 9.55am

The stilted signalbox at Luib. S RICKARD

ex-Buchanan Street, we had a most exciting race with the 9.58am from Queen Street to Mallaig. As we came round the curve past Loch Dochart I caught sight of the steam of the rival, well away up the 1-in-60 bank to Tyndrum; but we ran through Crianlarich at almost full speed, slacked to somewhere about 30mph to exchange tablets at the junction loop, and then our two engines, a 'Clan' piloted by a Drummond 0-6-0 goods, got away with great zest up the more moderate grades on the south side of Strathfillan. In a very short distance we had gained sufficiently on the LNER train to recognise the engines, and a few minutes later were almost abreast just a mile away across the valley. But when nearing Tyndrum the Oban line, in following the lie of the land, swings away in a V-shaped salient to the south, and by the time we had negotiated this, and were panting up the 1-in-44 into Tyndrum station, the two 'Glens' with their 350 ton load were disappearing over the ridge towards the Horseshoe Bend.

Passing through Tyndrum today it is not easy to visualise the little place at the height of its glory. Before the coming of the railway it was an important coaching station lying at the junction of the routes to Fort William and Oban. Its importance was enhanced by the construction of the railway, for when funds ran out, Tyndrum became the railhead at which the bulk of West Highland tourist traffic was handled. Now, the remains of the old terminus can be seen in what looks like a surprisingly large goods yard, lying below the present station, and to its right going westwards, and the greatest activity to be seen today is that of holidaymakers in the caravan coach. For a space of four years Tyndrum played its unforeseen role. In the meantime, the new Act had been passed authorising the extension of the line, and in 1877 the Tyndrum-Dalmally section was opened.

The restart from Tyndrum is on a grade of 1-in-49, and for nearly a mile the railway toils upwards to the Perth-Argyll County March. Here, beneath the tremendous screes of Beinn Laoigh, is the watershed between east and west flowing rivers, and the train is soon romping away down the gently graded upper part of Glen Lochy. After negotiating the Glenlochy crossing loop the descent steepens to an average inclination of 1-in-55, indeed the eastbound climb from Dalmally to the County March forms the hardest locomotive proposition on the whole route.

The 'Clans' appear to make light of it, and Mr W Rowing Coleby has given me details of a run on which the redoubtable No. 14766 *Clan Chattan* took a 215-ton load up the 1-in-50/60 portion at a steady 31-32mph and covered the 6¾ miles from Dalmally to Glenlochy crossing in 15¾ minutes start to stop. Travelling on the footplate in the reverse direction is an extraordinary experience, for,

BR Standard 4MT No. 80092 waits at Killin Junction with the 10.20am to Killin. The 07.55 Glasgow Buchanan St-Oban leaves with observation car at rear on July 12, 1965. JOHN R HILLIER

looking through the cab glasses, you seem to be literally falling downhill, and the driving skill needed to keep a steady even pace can be well appreciated.

Long before Dalmally is reached the mighty Cruachan is dominating the whole scene ahead; this most distinctive mountain, monarch of all Argyll, whose name was for many years the battle cry of Clan Campbell, has five distinct peaks and is seen at its finest from the train descending Glen Lochy. Dalmally lies a little to the west of where the glen is joined by Glen Orchy, and from the railway, running high up the southern slope, there is a glimpse of the octagonal church of

"The grades are quite moderate, not exceeding 1-in-100"

Glenorchy, and the village of Dalmally, close by. The station, which is 46¼ miles from Callander, is a little farther on, and here a stop of three to four minutes is scheduled on all trains, for taking water. In cases of double heading the pilot engines are sometimes watered at Taynuilt to save an extra-long stop at Dalmally.

From here, a brisk restart brings us, in two miles, at the north-east corner of Loch Awe, to a scene as beautiful as it is unlike the usual conception of a West Highland loch.

There is an astonishing variety of country on this route, and here, where one might expect to find a wild desolate sheet of water, is a lake with the quiet charm of Windermere. The first sight of it from a westbound train comes on crossing the River Orchy a short

hundred yards from where it debouches into the loch; here are the ruins of Kilchurn Castle, very prettily situated on a small island.

Then the railway swings round in a full right angle to run just above the water's edge on the wooded lower slopes of Ben Cruachan. Less than a mile from the viaduct over the River Orchy is Lochawe station and pier, whence it is a very pleasant sail up the loch. During the summer a special day-tour train leaves Oban at 9.30am for Lochawe; the return working is provided, during the height of the season, by the 1.40pm from Glasgow, but in early September when the latter train does not run a special is worked leaving Lochawe at 5.25pm. The engine for this train works up from Oban as pilot to the 3.40pm Edinburgh and Glasgow express.

The student of geography will by this time have noticed a curious point about Loch Awe – the highest surrounding hills are at the foot of the loch instead of at its head. One might naturally expect its outlet to be at the far end among the quiet low-lying woodlands instead of in the wild pass into which the railway is now climbing. The grades are quite moderate here, not exceeding 1-in-100, and we get along in fine style high above the north-western arm of the loch where it narrows to the Pass of Brander. The opposite shore is one long line of rough crags beneath which the cliff face is covered with loose scree.

Falls of Cruachan platform is passed and soon we come to the foot of the loch where some old piers are a reminder of the combined coach and steamer route to Oban in pre-railway times. Through the courtesy of David Macbrayne Limited I was able to study an old bill of 1867 on which it was stated that the coaches would run "each lawful day", a vivid ▶

reflection of the Sabbatarian attitude of the time. It makes an interesting contrast with the conditions of today, when by using the splendid Glasgow-Oban excursion trains so many Scots can enjoy a long Sunday in the West Highlands.

These trains make the quickest overall journeys on the route, and the second portions in each direction make the longest non-stop runs. A particularly fine booking is that of the 6pm up from Oban, which runs from Taynuilt to Balquhidder, 46¼ miles, in 92 minutes inclusive of three stiff banks. These trains are usually very heavy and are piloted by the handy little Drummond 0-6-0 tender engines.

The remarkable day excursion trips from London to Staffa and Iona, run occasionally in the summer, with the joint LMSR and LNER scenic excursions, are the only trains that pass Callander without stopping; the usual stops at Balquhidder and Dahnally are made to take water, and sometimes a halt is also necessary at Loch Awe for crossing purposes. On the last trip of the season this year, by a curious coincidence not likely to be repeated often, of the pair of engines used, one was designed by Dugald Drummond and the other by his brother Peter. The pilot was a Caledonian 0-6-0, and the train engine a Highland 4-6-0 No. 14686 *Urquhart Castle*; the latter is stationed at Balornock, and frequently works over the Oban line.

In the Pass of Brander travellers may have noticed a series of unusual-looking signals; each post has two arms, one facing in each direction of running, and both arms at 'all clear'. These are not connected in any way with the block signalling, but are installed on this wild stretch as a precaution against falling boulders. Some little distance up the slopes of Ben Cruachan is a fence of wires, and should any one of these wires be broken by falling rock all the special signals below would automatically be put to danger.

By now the train has emerged from the pass and we are nearing Taynuilt, with the blue waters of Loch Etive ahead. A brief halt, and then the line winds its way through the green countryside of Lorne; it is a region of low but rugged hills, vertical-sided rock cuttings and switchback grading at 1-in-50 or so. Loch Etive and the far hills of Benderloch are rarely out of sight, and at Ach-na-Cloich the shore is brilliant with saffron-yellow seaweed.

Looking ahead, the graceful steelwork of Connel Ferry viaduct soon catches the eye, and out beyond is the Firth of Lorne and a first glimpse of the mountains of Morven. From Connel Ferry Jct, the last stopping place of Oban trains, the Ballachulish branch runs northwards along the eastern shore of Loch Linnhe; through the Stewart country of Appin, and so to Loch Leven and the foot of Glen Coe.

In the meantime, the engine of the main

Above: In typical scenery and working towards Balquhidder on July 27, 1957 is 'Black Five' No. 44724.
COLOUR RAIL

Right: With a stormy sky approaching, BR Class 4MT No. 80028 waits at Killin to depart for Killin Junction in August 1965.
K N HARRISON

line train is rousing all the echoes on the gruelling 1-in-50 ascent to Glencruitten summit. Here, as on the other stiff banks, the 'Clans' appear to be quite master of the situation, and I have timed No. 14767 *Clan Mackinnon* to cover the 3¼ miles in 10min 7sec start to stop, with a full 275 tons.

From the passing loop at the summit the railway makes a spectacular descent into Oban. It first of all swings round due south, and runs down the face of a hillside so green that it might be in Ireland; while from the right-hand carriage window there opens out a bird's eye view of Oban bay with its piers, its miniature capes, and the blue hills of Mull, distant and appealing over the island of Kerrera.

Then, on nearing the foot of the bank, the line turns almost completely round to the north, and we come to the ticket platform: this latter is used only for the 10.45pm mixed train from Glasgow, which reaches Oban at 4.31am and calls at the platform three minutes earlier.

Just beyond the ticket platform, on the up side of the line, are the locomotive sheds. Here, at almost any time of the day, is to be seen a veritable gathering of the 'Clans'. These engines are held in high esteem by the Oban men, and it is good to hear them referred to by their names rather than by mere numbers. In speaking of them the prefix 'Clan' is omitted, and instead of the usual 'fourteen-seven-sixty-

five' and so on, one hears shed staff and enginemen alike talk of *Fraser*, *Stewart*, or *Mackinnon* just as if they were fellow workmates.

Less than a minute from passing the engine sheds the train has cleared a deep cutting and is swinging round into Oban terminus, which lies on the water front. The 71-mile journey from Callander takes a little under three hours by most trains, though one of the Sunday excursions, making only two stops, has the fastest booking, namely 2hr 27min.

In the height of the summer there are seven passenger trains in each direction, but this number is reduced to three from the end of October till Easter. Oban station has quite a spacious layout, and all of its four platforms can accommodate trains of 350 to 400 tons.

The LMSR has continued the Caledonian tradition in the matter of station adornment, and at Oban the concourse is decorated with hanging baskets of flowers. Oban itself is one of the most beautiful seaports in Scotland, a place that combines most skilfully the sophistry of Torquay with the wistful haunting air of the Hebrides. The sight of its lovely bay, with a fleet of drifters at the jetty, yachts at anchor, and against some dark background the scarlet funnel of a Macbrayne ship, is a pleasing end to a journey that is of the greatest charm throughout. ■

A little bit of posing by the footplate crew as Gresley A4 No. 22 *Mallard* heads the down 1.30pm Paddington-Penzance service through Sonning Cutting on April 26, during the 1948 Locomotive Exchanges. M W EARLEY

Results of the 1948 Locomotive Interchange Trials

DURING 1948, the Railway Executive sponsored a series of intensive locomotive interchange trials between the various regions of British Railways, with a view to trying out representative locomotive types of the former railway companies with standard loads.

As far as possible, identical conditions were selected, both over the routes on which the locomotives were designed primarily to work and on other routes in various parts of the country. These trials aroused a good deal of interest, and a report has now been compiled on them. It is not intended to make copies available to the public because of the cost of large-scale production. It consists very largely of tabular matter, descriptions of the test arrangements, loads, coal and water consumption, and so forth.

On its formation in 1948, British Railways inherited four series of modern locomotive types, one from each of the former main line

companies. Although each of these series was highly standardised within a single company, hardly any features or details were common from one company to another. In pursuance of its general policy of engineering standardisation, the Railway Executive decided that it would not continue to build four varieties of locomotives for each traffic duty. It proposed a single series of about 12 standard types, each of which would contain the best features of existing designs, and which could have added to them improvements and developments as experience and the ingenuity of the design

> "Fourteen types of locomotives were tried on selected routes on each of five regions"

staffs should indicate.

Of the various methods of locomotive testing, that which gives the quickest general survey of passenger and economy is the dynamometer car, which measures draw-bar pull, speed, and horsepower. The indications so given, related to the coal and water consumed, are a fair measure of the overall efficiency of the locomotive.

Fourteen types of locomotives were tried on selected routes on each of five regions, ranging as far north as Inverness and as far west as Plymouth. The test covered the period from April to December, 1948, and the results fill 131 pages of the report. The tests were not intended to be a contest between locomotives of similar types, which it was appreciated had been designed, for the most part, to fulfil the requirements of their particular regions. The results, therefore, do not disclose any dramatic or unexpected features, nor is it possible to declare that one ▶

Former streamlined LMS Duchess No. 46236 *City of Bradford* **starts a train for the West of England from Paddington in July 1948.** *RM* ARCHIVE

type of locomotive is 'the best'.

From the outset it was realised that these indications would be of a very broad kind, as the trials were carried out under the normal operating conditions obtaining at the time of each test run and without any special preparation of the locomotives. It was agreed that the locomotives used should be taken direct from traffic, having run between 15,000 and 20,000 miles since last general repair and there was consequently some variation in mechanical conditions, particularly in the case of freight locomotives.

It was also realised that, in the existing circumstances, inequalities which are liable to be experienced in any variable speed testing on the track would be present. Traffic delays and temporary speed restrictions may be mentioned as examples of these inequalities and, whilst the traffic delays tended to cancel out over a number of tests, the number and siting of temporary speed restrictions affected some locomotives more than others. It was appreciated, however, that further testing would subsequently have to be undertaken on the Rugby and Swindon testing plants and with the mobile testing plant when such limitations would not apply.

The Western Region locomotives had grate and smokebox arrangements specifically designed to suit Welsh coal, and these, together with the firing technique to which the Western Region enginemen had been trained, differed from what is customary with the types of coal used on the trials. In view of these conditions it was arranged that, on completion of the trials, additional tests should be made on the Western Region using Welsh coal.

The greatest care was taken to make the test runs as nearly comparable as possible. Every controllable factor was controlled; and unpredictable conditions such as weather, signal and permanent-way checks, and late running are all recorded, so that their influence can be borne in mind. As the engines concerned were not all fitted with continuous blow-down, the apparatus was put out of action on the locomotives which normally carried it.

West Country Pacific No 34006 *Bude* **reverses out of Marylebone station with a dynamometer car during the 1948 Loco Exchanges. Note the loco is running with a Stanier tender.** *RM* ARCHIVE

All the three dynamometer cars which were used were calibrated on uniform lines at Derby before the trials began. Coal used for lighting-up was separated from that used during actual runs; and care was taken to see that the quantity of fuel remaining in the firebox at the end of a test was about the same as at the start. Similarly, tenders were calibrated beforehand; and then at the end of a run the water level in the boiler was brought to the same level as at the beginning of the test.

At the beginning of the report, some extremely interesting figures are given, to convey, in the briefest way, the summarised results. They show the ratios of All coal/All work for the various engines, and are derived from the grand totals for all engines of the class throughout the whole series of tests over all applicable routes. The coal ratios are expressed in total weight (lb) divided by work done (hp/hr). Water ratios are also given to show the evaporation secured on the different locomotives; in this case the figures are: water (total weight, lb) divided by work done (hp-hr). These results are given in the accompanying table.

The general plan of the report is to present, first, dimensions and other relevant data of the types of locomotives concerned, followed by folding tables, showing details of the test results, including coal and water consumption. Later pages give the performance figures over selected portions of the routes (speed, horsepower, cut-off, and regulator position), notes on adhesion and slipping and draw-bar pull characteristics, and diagrams showing the oscillations encountered with the various locomotive classes are included, followed by dynamometer car records illustrating the coasting tendencies of the freight engines. The methods of working the various locomotives then are given, followed by a five-page appraisal of the mechanical condition of the engines, with notes on the defects which developed during the trials. Finally, there is an appendix devoted to the additional tests carried out on the Western Region.

In recent issues of *The Railway Magazine*, Mr Cecil J Allen has published his own observations of these trials, made from the point of view of a passenger. It is interesting to examine some of the performances recorded during the trials and to see how the test data compare with Mr Allen's impressions.

On May 14, the 'Merchant Navy' engine *Belgian Marine* put up an excellent performance between Penrith and Preston with a train of 503 tons tare (525 tons full), gaining six minutes (eight minutes net) over the schedule time of 86 minutes for this 72.2 mile run, which includes the ascent, from the north, of the notorious Shap incline – 9½ miles in all, at gradients varying from 1-in-106 to 1-in-142. A recorded drawbar horsepower figure of ▶

Heading an Exeter to Paignton service, West Country No. 34009 *Lyme Regis* runs along the sea wall at Teignmouth during the 1948 Loco Exchanges. W S RUMBOLD

Region	Class	Coal consumption ratio = Coal (total wt., lb) Work done (h.p.-hr.)	Water consumption ratio = Water (total wt., lb) Work done (h.p.-hr.)
Western	4-6-0 "King"	3.57	28.58
Eastern	4-6-2 "A4"	3.06	24.32
London Midland	4-6-2 "Duchess"	3.12	27.08
London Midland	4-6-2 "6P"	3.38	25.81
Southern	4-6-2 "Merchant Navy"	3.60	30.43
Western	4-6-0 "Hall"	3.94	29.97
Eastern	4-6-0 "B1"	3.59	27.64
London Midland	4-6-0 "5"	3.54	27.99
Southern	4-6-2 "West Country"	4.11	32.64
Western	2-8-0 "2800"	3.42	26.80
Eastern	2-8-0 "O1"	3.37	25.73
London Midland	2-8-0 "8F"	3.52	27.26
	2-8-0 "Austerity"	3.77	28.75
	2-10-0 "Austerity"	3.52	28.05

The exchanges saw a GWR 'King' working on the East Coast Main Line, and on May 19, 1948, No. 6018 *King Henry VI* emerges from Hadley Wood tunnel with the 7.50am King's Cross-Leeds Express. M W EARLEY

GWR 'Modified Hall' 4-6-0 No. 6990 *Witherslack Hall* passes Harrow-on-the-Hill with a Manchester-Marylebone express. *RM* ARCHIVE

1,629 was obtained, at 49.7mph (equivalent to 1,920 hp on level) which is even higher than Mr Allen's estimate of 1,700 (assuming that he was also working on the 'equivalent' figure). The cut-off was 33 per cent; the boiler pressure 255lb per sq in and the steam-chest pressure 2254lb per sq in. The notes on the engine working record that a better performance seemed to be obtained when it was being worked fairly hard. The regulator was usually ¼ to ⅓ open on rising gradients, when the cut-off was normally 23-25 per cent, the increase to 33 per cent being required, evidently, to get the heavy train up Shap. The

coal burnt per mile, over the whole trip (Carlisle to Euston) averaged 50.22lb – i.e. 0.079lb per ton-mile (including engine) or 3.86lb per drawbar horsepower/hour. The corresponding water consumption was 31.80lb per drawbar horsepower/hour.

Another Bulleid engine, the 'West Country' class Pacific *Bude*, did brilliantly on runs between Marylebone and Manchester. Mr Allen noted a climb up the 1-in-105 to Amersham after the earlier part of the run had been spoilt by a series of checks. The train was 360 tons (380 tons full), and speed rose from 27 to 45mph up this gradient; while later, climbing

from Great Missenden to milepost 31½ speed only fell from 71½ to 60mph.

The report shows recorded drawbar horsepowers, at various points en route, as varying between 1,266 and 1,574 (equivalent to 1,600 to 1,962hp) with a cut-off varying between 25 and 30 per cent. Coal consumption was 4.07lb per dbhp/hr over the whole run, and water consumption 31.43lb per dbhp/hr.

The Western Region 'King' class worked under difficulties in regard to fuel when engaged on the King's Cross and Leeds trains. There was much smoke, and it was difficult to keep the fire in good condition. The engine, nevertheless, got away well, and cleared Finsbury Park very swiftly. The load was 525 tons full (495 tons tare) yet the coal consumption, in spite of the nature of the fuel, was only 3.43lb per dbhp/hr (53.93lb per mile over the whole trip). Water consumption was 28.35lb per dbhp/hr. Recorded horsepower amounted to 1,480 (equivalent) at Wrenthorpe with regulator half-open and cutoff 35 per cent. The boiler pressure then was 240lb per sq in. The report states that "the black smoke indicated that the firing rate was too high, and this condition led, on occasions, to steam being wasted at the safety valves".

However, special additional trials were held on Western Region metals, using the Welsh coal normally supplied to Western Region engines. The average coal consumption using the Welsh coal was about 6½ per cent less, in lb per dbhp/hr, or 9.2 per cent, in lb per train-mile. These figures make due allowance for the difference in calorific value between the two kinds of coal. With the 'Hall' class the difference was far more marked, the figures being 17.7 and 19 per cent respectively.

The Eastern Region A4 class 4-6-2s gave

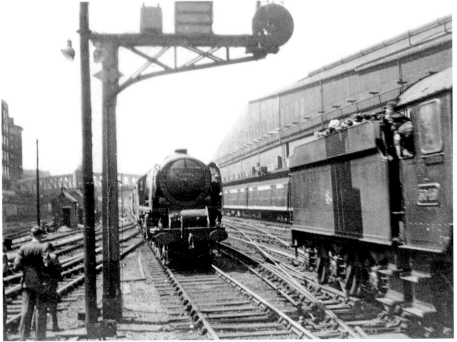

The arrival at Paddington on June 3, 1948, is No. 46236 *City of Bradford* with an express from Plymouth. Watching are young trainspotters and the crew of 'Castle' No. 5049 *Earl of Plymouth*. BRIAN BRAMALL

From *The Railway Magazine*, September/October 1949

perhaps the best figures of any of the engines concerned in regard to low coal consumption per drawbar horsepower/hour; on May 7, No. 60033 *Seagull* took a 330-ton train (345 tons full) over the mountainous route from Plymouth to Newton Abbot and thence to Paddington. In spite of a heartbreaking permanent-way restriction to 15mph at Plympton, which made it impossible to attack the 1-in-41 Hemerdon Bank in good style, *Seagull* lifted the train over the top at 18½ mph. On this run, coal consumption averaged 44.87lb per mile, or 3.19lb per dbhp/hr. Water consumption was 23.82lb per dbhp/hr. The recorded horsepower up Hemerdon Bank was 1,111 (equivalent to 1,598, with an equivalent drawbar pull of no less than 12.75 tons). Cut-off was 53 per cent with full regulator; boiler and steam-chest pressures were 245 and 235lb per sq in respectively.

Among the most memorable revelations of the locomotive interchange trials was the capability and general excellence of the 'Royal Scot' class, as rebuilt with taper boiler. These three-cylinder 4-6-0s weigh only 83 tons without their tenders, and yet showed that they could more than hold their own against the much larger Pacifics.

This was particularly noticeable on the runs to and from Waterloo. On June 18,

Testing of the performance of locomotives included running 'Merchant Navy' No. 35017 *Belgian Marine* over Shap with the 'Royal Scot', with 14 bogies in tow. ERIC TREACY

No. 46154 *The Hussar*, running from Exeter Central to Waterloo, showed a drawbar horsepower of 1,548 (1,782 equivalent) at Crewkerne, with cut-off 30 per cent and regulator a quarter open. The boiler pressure was then 242lb per sq in. Other very high powers were also recorded during this run. The coal consumption was 3.46lb per dbhp/hr, the corresponding figure for water being 25.46lb. Over this run the coal used averaged 50.65lb per mile, with a load of 482 tons (515 tons full).

On the same route, the 'Duchess' class, with the same load on June 25, showed figures ▶

Rebuilt 'Royal Scot' No. 46162 *Queen's Westminster Rifleman* leaves Reading with a Paddington-Plymouth service on May 17, 1948. M W EARLEY

A large gathering of 'top brass' in bowler hats have turned out to see A4 No. 22 *Mallard* emit some uncharacteristic black exhaust on departure from London Waterloo with a down 'Atlantic Coast Express' in 1948. ERIC TREACY

of 3.00 and 25.87lb per dbhp/hr for coal and water respectively; the equivalent power recorded for Chard-Crewkerne was 1,600, the cut-off being 25 per cent and regulator first valve being full open. The boiler pressure then was 230lb per sq in.

The 'Merchant Navy' coal and water figures were 3.49 and 30.6lb per dbhp/hr. At Chard, the recorded horsepower was 1,550 (equivalent), cut-off being 25 per cent, and boiler and steam-chest pressures being 260 and 200lb per sq in respectively.

These are but a few examples taken from this voluminous report. The use which the Railway Executive will make of the mass of data which has been accumulated can be summarised under two main headings:

(1) As all the locomotives demonstrated their ability to operate the selected trains to the booked timings when operating on 'foreign' routes, differing widely in character from the 'home' routes, the Railway Executive is satisfied that no limit need be placed on its proposals for standardisation by reason of suitability of particular locomotives for the routes over which they will have to work.

(2) The tests have indicated many features of design worthy of consideration for the new standard types, and the drawing offices are now examining closely their possible application. Examples are:

(a) Use of the largest boilers which weight limits will allow to give ample reserve of power for all circumstances.

(b) Use of wide fireboxes in the larger

engines for highest combustion efficiency.

(c) Firebox and ashpan arrangement to give best results with varying qualities of coal.

(d) Adoption of design features to promote good riding and minimum wear and tear on the track

The conclusions which have been reached as a result of the trials show that for comparable conditions and duties locomotives with wide fireboxes had a higher overall efficiency than those with narrow fireboxes, but the effect of differences in other design features reversed this in some cases.

The importance of correct firing technique in relation to the type of coal used, and the

> ## "The greatest care was taken to make the test runs as nearly comparable as possible"

necessity for adjusting details of design, such as spacing of fire bars, to suit the type of coal used, were especially evident in connection with the higher power outputs.

There was a clear indication, too, of the advantages of high boiler output and large thermal capacity to give a reserve of power and margin for rapid recovery without an appreciable decrease in overall efficiency.

Steam temperatures were not recorded, but there were indications that an increase in

the degree of superheat effected an improvement in efficiency in the case of express passenger and mixed-traffic locomotives. In the case of freight locomotives the improvement was much less marked.

The performances of the different locomotives with regard to slipping were variable, and it is recognised that further investigation is desirable. In view of the irregular draw-bar pulls recorded in certain cases it is considered that further investigation should be made into the effect of balancing, valve setting, and other relevant factors on the smoothness of draw-bar pull.

The express passenger and mixed-traffic locomotives with the smaller diameter coupled wheels experienced no difficulty in attaining the speeds necessary to maintain schedules, and on all routes it was noted that the average power required from the locomotives was low in relation to maximum power required.

Whereas individual tests of this kind have been carried out from time to time by all the former companies, this is the first occasion on which so comprehensive a series has been run. It has given the Railway Executive the opportunity of basing its locomotive design policy on known and recorded facts.

It must be appreciated, however, that the tests outlined cover only operating and performance features. These have to be supplemented for each locomotive by data on building and repair costs and on availability in daily service. ∎

Too little, too light and too late

A survey of British Railways diesel railbuses

By J M TOLSON

IT is now more than 10 years since the British Transport Commission decided to buy about 20 diesel railbuses for use on rural branches in various parts of the country.

Even then, serious doubts were raised as to the wisdom of ordering lightweight vehicles which could not haul a tailload, so that a separate traction unit would be required for freight haulage, or if passenger traffic increased sharply at peak periods. Railwaymen were none too confident of their success, and the public was warned not to expect too much of them as a means of saving unremunerative branches from closure. Protagonists of road transport pointed out the disadvantages of buying small quantities of non-standard vehicles at high capital cost, compared with the use of mass-produced road vehicles of the same capacity which could far more effectively connect rural areas with the railhead. Many of these fears were realised, as the railbuses have not had a very happy career, and the majority have now been withdrawn.

Twenty-two railbuses – numbered 79958-79 in the BR diesel railcar fleet – were ordered from five manufacturers which were allowed considerable latitude to develop their own ideas within certain basic requirements; these prescribed a single underfloor engine of 112-150hp, providing a maximum speed of 55mph for a vehicle seating 46-54 passengers.

Two were built by Bristol Commercial Vehicles Ltd and five each by Park Royal Vehicles Ltd, AC Cars Ltd, D Wickham & Co Ltd, and the German firm of Waggon und Maschinenbau. It was decided to allocate five to the Eastern Region, three to the London Midland, four to the Western and the remaining 10 to the Scottish Region.

The first vehicle – No. 79979, destined for the Scottish Region – was delivered by AC Cars in February 1958, but the remaining four vehicles of the same design – Nos. 79975-8, which were to work on the Western Region – were delayed for some time because of a fire at the works. These were extremely light, weighing only 11 tons, but

A Waggon und Maschinenbau No. E79960 stands at Haverhill having arrived from Audley End. COLOUR RAIL

were provided with a single underfloor BUT 150-hp engine which was a standard BR power unit, giving a high power/weight ratio of 13.6hp per ton and very smart acceleration from rest.

Seats for 46 passengers were provided in two saloons – one on each side of a centre entrance vestibule – which was fitted with automatic doors and retractable steps

> "Railbuses have not had a very happy career, and the majority have now been withdrawn"

operated by the driver, whose controls were housed in a small-windowed cubicle, originally open to the passenger accommodation, but later fitted with folding wooden doors.

The five vehicles from Waggon und Maschinenbau – Nos. 79960-4, delivered in April 1958 – were larger than the AC Cars and

weighed 15 tons, with an overall length of 41ft 10in. They were able to seat 56 passengers and provided standing room for another 40, but although seating arrangements were similar to those of AC Cars' vehicles, the interior fittings of polished wood were more luxurious and curtains were fitted at each window. The controls differed from the BR pattern in that the 'deadman's handle' was a plunger on the driver's left which could be depressed by his elbow and, as the throttle was a footpedal, driving in open country had a curious 'no hands' appearance because the right hand was required only to change gear or apply the brake.

Another unusual feature was the provision of one flat and one convex buffer at each end, with buffers of similar shape on opposite sides of the car to help in the negotiation of curves if two vehicles were coupled together, although, like other railbuses, they were not capable of hauling an unpowered tailload. The engines, which were of the Buessing type rated at 150hp at 1,900rpm, were new to BR and after a few years began to give trouble, so because of the high cost of importing

▶

replacements from Germany, railbuses Nos. 79961/3/4 were fitted, in 1962/3, with AEC 'A220X'-type 150-hp engines.

The Park Royal railbuses – numbered 79970-4 – were powered from the outset by the standard BUT horizontal 150-hp engine, like the AC Cars vehicles. Although they were longer by two inches than the German vehicles, they provided seats for only 50 passengers in the usual two saloons, separated by a centre vestibule, and had few features worthy of note.

On the other hand, the two vehicles constructed by Bristol Commercial Vehicles, with bodies by Eastern Coachworks – Nos. 79958 and 79959 – produced several novel ideas.

The construction was based on principles used in the combine's road vehicles and the upholstery and decoration were standard with these. The railbuses were powered by a single underfloor Gardner 112-hp diesel engine with a fully automatic gearbox incorporating overdrive and giving a maximum speed of 50mph. Seats for 56 passengers were provided in the usual two saloons, but as the floor when fully laden was only 7in above the standard platform height, steps were required only for low-level halts.

Special resilient wheels, to reduce shock and noise on rail joints, were supplied by Svenska Aktiebolaget Bromsregulator of Sweden, and the air-operated braking system was developed by Dunlop to eliminate wheel locking while maintaining optimum braking. This was achieved by a monitor brake shoe which initiated and controlled the main braking effort through disc-type brakes, while each vehicle was fitted with a bus-type mechanical handbrake acting on all four wheels, of sufficient power to allow the bus to continue in service in the event of air-brake failure.

The last design to appear was by Wickhams of Ware, which specialises in the production of self-propelled lightweight rail vehicles. The bodies of the five buses – Nos. 79965-9 – had all-welded frames of square-section steel tubes giving a light but immensely strong construction. Seats for 48 were provided by 22 bus-type seats in each of the usual saloons and two tip-up seats at each end. They were powered by a Meadows six-cylinder engine rated at 105hp at 1,800rpm which drove through a Wickham-Freeborn automatic coupling, a multiple clutch device acting like a fluid coupling when the engine was idling, but locking into firm engagement when normal running speed was reached.

Two of the Wickham railbuses had additional experimental features. No. 79968 was fitted with CAV automatic gear change, a dashboard device enabling the driver to select automatic or manual control of his

Park Royal railbus No. 79970, one of five built, stands at Alloa station on February 7, 1960, having worked along the old Caldeonian route from Larbert via Airth, which closed on January 29, 1968. COLOUR RAIL

gears, while No. 79969 was fitted with Andre Westinghouse pneumatic suspension in place of the standard semi-elliptic axlebox springs.

The Eastern Region was the first to place its railbuses into revenue-earning service.

The five German vehicles were allocated to it and based at Cambridge to facilitate the working of a four-day cyclic diagram, with one bus spare. The lines concerned in this were those to Mildenhall and Saffron Walden in the Cambridge area, and the branches from Witham to Braintree and Maldon in the London Division, with workings over the Colne Valley line to take the buses to and from the two southern branches.

Services began in earnest on July 7, 1958, and, although operation was

reasonably successful, difficulty was experienced in carrying any large quantity of parcels and luggage, but more especially the bicycles and perambulators which rural travellers had been accustomed to take with them. Despite the fact that, in the first year of railbus services, operating costs were reduced by £66,000, only one branch was proving a profitable venture and the services as a whole were still losing about £4,000 a year.

Traffic on the Braintree branch soon proved too much for the railbus, which was replaced by a two-car set, and even today the future for passenger services on this branch is reasonably healthy. However, on the other branches the position was far from rosy and

One of two vehicles built by Bristol Commercial Vehicles, with bodies by Eastern Coachworks, railbus No. SC79959 was fitted with resilient wheels and had upholstery and interior decorations common to road passenger vehicles of the Tilling Group. It stands at Gleneagles in October 1963. COLOUR RAIL (DE1117)

not long after the closure of the Colne Valley line, from January 1, 1962 – which caused the transfer of the railbuses to Witham to be made over the Stour Valley line to Marks Tey – passenger services were withdrawn from the Mildenhall branch from June 18, 1962.

Services on the Audley End-Saffron Walden-Bartlow and Witham-Maldon branches survived for another two years, but were both withdrawn from September 7, 1964, and the railbuses were then put into store at Cambridge.

In May 1965, No. 79964 was sent to the North Eastern Region for trials on the Haltwhistle-Alston branch, where it was joined in August by No. 79963 – the latter soon returned south, but No. 79964 remained there until early 1966.

The trials were unsuccessful for a variety of reasons, including problems with refuelling which could only be carried out at South Gosforth. Its inability to haul parcels vans when required proved a further disadvantage, and winter conditions brought fresh problems including trouble with the heating system.

After a further period in store at Cambridge, Nos. 79961-4 were transferred to Buxton, on the London Midland Region, in July 1966, as replacements for Park Royal vehicles on the Millers Dale services.

Four AC Cars vehicles – Nos. 79975-8 – were allocated to the Western Region for use on the branches from Kemble to Cirencester and Tetbury. Operation began on February 2, 1959, with a greatly increased service.

New halts were opened at Chesterton Lane on the Cirencester branch and at Church's Hill and Trouble House on the Tetbury line, where the closed station of Culkerton was also reopened as an unstaffed halt.

It had been intended to provide through trains to Swindon from both branches, but as the lightweight buses would not operate the track circuits this was not possible, and some difficulty was experienced in maintaining good connections from each branch with both up and down trains at Kemble. Still, most problems were soon resolved and the services were initially very successful. Another new halt at Park Leaze on the Cirencester branch was opened on January 4, 1960, and traffic increased to such an extent that overcrowding on this line became a serious problem. It was suggested that a single railcar of the 55XXX series might be more suitable, although this would increase operating costs and interfere with the cyclic working on the two branches. Despite this promising start, the services

Examples of AC and Park Royal railbuses stand side by side at Grangemouth station in June 1967, and were used on duties to Falkirk Grahamston. Services on the route ceased six months later. GEORGE M STADDON/COLOUR RAIL (DE1804)

Railbuses were trialled deep in Cornwall, and here No. W79978 is at Boscarne Junction in June 1966. DAVID A LAWRENCE/COLOUR RAIL

ultimately proved unremunerative and were withdrawn on April 6, 1964.

All four vehicles then gravitated to former Southern Railway branches now forming part of the Western Region. Two were soon found employment on a shuttle service to Bodmin North from June 14, 1964, connecting with trains from Wadebridge to Bodmin Road at newly opened exchange platforms at Boscarne Junction. This service, which also incorporated certain trips to Wadebridge, was withdrawn on January 30, 1967.

The other two started work on the Yeovil Junction-Yeovil Town branch on December 28, 1964. After this service had survived several attempts at withdrawal, Yeovil Town station was closed on October 3, 1966, and the railbuses ran to Pen Mill Station, although they were still used to carry parcels between Town and Pen Mill stations.

Soon after this the railbuses were replaced by larger railcars and in February of last year all four vehicles were transferred to the Scottish Region.

The London Midland Region's experience with railbuses has been relatively short and far from happy. Three Park Royal vehicles – Nos. 79971-39 – were allocated to Bedford for use on the branches to Northampton, and Hitchin.

> "In the first year of railbus services, operating costs were reduced by £66,000, and only one branch was proving a profitable venture"

Operation began on August 11, 1958, and accelerated, with augmented services being introduced at the start of the winter timetable, but despite a great increase in traffic, continual mechanical failures dogged the vehicles. They were replaced for long periods by steam push-and-pull trains and by the end of 1959 had departed to Wolverton, after which they were sent to the Scottish Region where they seem to have been more successful.

Two of these – Nos. 79972/3 – returned to the London Midland Region in December 1965, for use on the Millers Dale-Buxton branch, where they began work on January 3, 1966, but once again numerous difficulties were encountered and they spent much of the time out of use.

The two German railbuses – Nos. 79961/4 – which arrived to assist in these workings in July 1966, did not see a great deal of use and services were withdrawn on March 6 of last year.

The Scottish Region has been by far the largest user of railbuses and has had experience of all types except the German vehicles. At one time there were no fewer than 13 railbuses allocated to it and at present all the surviving vehicles are to be found there. Four lines to the north of Glasgow and Edinburgh were chosen for railbus operation and services started between Gleneagles, Crieff and Comrie on September 15, 1958, using AC Cars No. 79979, with a more frequent weekday service of 10 trains to Crieff and three to Comrie.

New halts were opened at Strageath and Pittenzie and the services brought a marked increase in traffic despite the fact that connections at Gleneagles with mainline trains were not too good. However, the services ultimately proved unremunerative and were withdrawn from July 6, 1964, after a long period when steam trains were again used on the branch.

The next branch to receive a railbus was the former Great North of Scotland Speyside line between Craigellachie and Aviemore, on which services began on November 3, 1958, with three trains in each direction and an extra train on Saturday. One return journey was extended to Keith Junction and one to Elgin, and services were at first carried out by a Bristol railbus (which covered more than 300 miles each day) although, in due course, Wickham and Park Royal vehicles were also used on this line. On July 15, 1959, four new halts were opened: Imperial Cottages, Gilbey's Cottages, Dalvey Farm and Ballifurth Farm.

Drivers were warned of their approach to these by white boards stating 'Request Stop 200 Yards Ahead'.

The frequency of services was further

Five German-built railbuses from Waggon und Maschinenbau were trialled, including No. 79961 seen approaching Audley End on a working from Bartlow in May 1964. This vehicle was one of two with AEC engines. DAVID PERCIVAL/COLOUR RAIL (DE1338)

improved and overall journey timings reduced by up to 15 minutes, but despite this, and the fact that a fine view of the beautiful scenery was to be had from the railbus, patronage did not greatly increase. Passenger traffic was particularly sparse on the section between the tourist centre of Grantown-on-Spey and Aviemore, but receipts from the whole service were poor and it was withdrawn from October 18, 1965.

The third branch on which railbuses were introduced was the Devon Valley line with its delightfully named stations of Dollar, Rumbling Bridge, Crook of Devon, and Balado.

Two Wickham vehicles began work on this route on May 4, 1959, and one through

journey in each direction between Perth and Stirling enabled the buses to be stabled overnight at these points. Frame trouble caused the Wickham vehicles to be replaced by Park Royal buses and these two types dominated the services, which again were relatively poorly patronised and withdrawn from June 15, 1964. A Wickham railbus took over the Craigendoran-Arrochar shuttle service along the Glasgow-Fort William line from the celebrated C15 4-4-2 tanks in November 1959, although steam did not completely disappear until the following April. The closed station of Rhu was reopened as an unstaffed halt in conjunction with these services. Park Royal vehicles and two-car sets were also used on this line but

Wickham railbus No. M79967 waits at Comrie in July 1962 on its way from Gleneagles to Crieff. The station clock says 07.59, but it is actually 6.45pm. These units were fitted with Westinghouse pneumatic suspension in place of standard semi-elliptic axle-box springs. The Crieff-Gleneagles line closed to passengers on July 6, 1964, and to goods traffic from November 2, 1964. R HERBERT/COLOUR RAIL (DE533)

From *The Railway Magazine*, January 1968

the shuttle service was withdrawn on June 15, 1964.

Railbuses were to find a more intensive use on lines on the Glasgow & South Western section, particularly around Ayr. Services began on the Lugton-Beith branch on April 6, 1959, using a Bristol vehicle, which was later replaced by an AC Cars railbus, but despite the increase in revenue the service proved unremunerative and was withdrawn from November 5, 1962. Railbuses were also found employment from Hamilton on workings to Holytown, Strathaven and Coalburn, but soon achieved a reputation for unreliability and were gradually replaced by two-car sets.

Concentration in Scotland

The most concentrated use of railbuses in Scotland was around Ayr, and from April 6, 1959, most services on the Ayr-Dalmellington branch were entrusted to these vehicles, which even ran certain trips to Kilmarnock.

Their use gradually increased and from February 5, 1962, further reorganisation brought about the use of railbuses for most trains on the Kilmarnock-Ardrossan-Ayr services, as well as certain workings over the Darvel branch; services over the Dalmellington and Darvel branches, as well as the Kilmarnock-Ardrossan services, were withdrawn from April 6, 1964, but they continued to be used on the Kilmarnock trains, despite an ever-growing number out of use.

By November, 1966, a mere handful remained in service and the Ayr-Kilmarnock services were being covered by two Park Royal vehicles – Nos. 79970/1 – most of the others being out of use. It had been hoped to start a diesel railbus operation in the Larbert-Alloa and Falkirk Grahamston-Grangemouth branches from November 7, 1966, but the withdrawal of no fewer than

An AC Cars railbus arrives at Cirencester Town from Kemble on May 13, 1961, sadly all too little to save the service which ceased on April 6, 1964. COLOUR RAIL

six of the Scottish vehicles meant that this had to be postponed until the transfer of the four AC Cars vehicles from the Western Region early last year, when two were allocated for these services and the other

> ## "Their operation has not been successful, not at least being their unreliability and inability to haul trailers"

two sent to assist on the GSW section, as only one Park Royal vehicle was in active use. Since then the Park Royal bus has also been employed on the Alloa-Larbert service.

It would appear that the interesting experiment in small rail vehicles will soon be at an end, for 17 have been withdrawn at the time of writing.

Their operation has not been successful due to a number of reasons, not least being their unreliability and inability to haul trailers if traffic demanded, while their rough riding, particularly at speed, earned them such disparaging nicknames as "four-wheeled bicycles" and "bucking broncos".

The first to be withdrawn was Wickham vehicle No. 79969 – in December, 1963 – and two more of the same type were withdrawn in the following year. Although no further withdrawals occurred for another two years, towards the end of 1966 no fewer than 12 were taken out of service, rendering both the Wickham and Bristol types extinct. Although all the German vehicles have been ▶

Saloon interior and driving position of railbus No. E79961, built by Waggon und Maschinenbau, Germany, and delivered to British Railways, Eastern Region, in April 1958.
BRITISH RAILWAYS

Passengers boarding the 12.14 Aviemore-Elgin railbus at Imperial Cottages Halt, on the Speyside Line, on June 16, 1964. This former Great North of Scotland Railway line was closed from October 18, 1965.
ROBERT H DARLASTON

Park Royal railbus No. SC79973 leaves Dunfermline Upper in February 1964, a location that appears to be a railway modeller's paradise. The destination blind is blank, but the unit is heading east. GEORGE M STADDON/COLOUR RAIL (DE1535)

withdrawn, two have been sold to the M & GN Joint North-Norfolk Railway Limited and two to the Keighley & Worth Valley Railway.

Only one Park Royal and four AC Cars vehicles remain in service and their life may well be limited, as the services on which they work are scheduled for withdrawal in the near future.

We may yet see the service on the Smallbrook Junction-Newport-Cowes line in the Isle of Wight taken over by a private company and operated by rather luxurious four-wheel vehicles built by the Sadler Rail Coach Company of Southampton. These rail coaches, which are 43ft in length, can seat 50 passengers at first-class spacing, or 75 in more cramped surroundings. With a top speed of 58mph, auto-air temperature control and air suspension, these may prove of interest, but it seems doubtful if they could achieve more than their more austere predecessors in the economy-conscious atmosphere of British Railways, as the type of lines for which they are most suitable are usually those most prone to early extinction.

In conclusion, I would like to thank the Public Relations Officers of the Eastern, London Midland and Western Regions for their generous help in the preparation of this article. ∎

BRITISH RAILWAYS DIESEL RAILBUSES

No.	Manufacturer					Weight (tons)	Body length	Seats	Engine	Withdrawal date
79958	Bristol/E.C.W.	...	...	...	...	13½	42 ft. 4 in.	56	Gardner 112 b.h.p.	10/66
79959	"	...	...	...	...	"	"	"	"	10/66
79960	Waggon und Maschinenbau		...	...	15	41 ft. 10 in.	56	Buessing 150 b.h.p.		11/66‡
79961	"	...	...	...	...	"	"	"	" *	8/67
79962	"			...	...	"	"	"	"	11/66§
79963	"			...	...	"	"	"	" *	11/66‡
79964	"			...	...	"	"	"	" *	4/67§
79965	Wickham	...	...	...	...	11¼	38 ft. 0 in.	48†	Meadows 105 b.h.p.	6/64
79966	"	...	...	...	...	"	"	"	"	6/64
79967	"	...	...	...	...	"	"	"	"	10/66
79968	"	...	...	...	...	"	"	"	"	10/66
79969	"	...	...	...	...	"	"	"	"	12/63
79970	Park Royal	...	...	...	...	15	42 ft. 0 in.	50	B.U.T. (A.E.C.) 150 b.h.p.	3/67
79971	"	...	...	...	...	"	"	"	"	—
79972	"	...	...	...	...	"	"	"	"	8/67
79973	"	...	...	...	...	"	"	"	"	8/67
79974	"	...	...	...	...	"	"	"	"	11/66
79975	A.C. Cars	...	...	...	...	11	36 ft. 0 in.	46	B.U.T. (A.E.C.) 150 b.h.p.	—
79976	"	...	...	...	...	"	"	"	"	—
79977	"	...	...	...	...	"	"	"	"	—
79978	"	...	...	...	...	"	"	"	"	—
79979	"	...	...	...	...	"	"	"	"	11/66

* Replaced by A.E.C. "A220X" 150-b.h.p. engine in 1962-3.   † Includes 4 tip-up seats.   ‡ Sold to M. & G.N. Joint North Norfolk Railway Limited.   § Sold to Keighley & Worth Valley Railway.

A summary of the diesel railbuses order by British Railways.

Grass roots

A look back more than 30 years to some early scenes from the preservation era.

Standing at Park Halt, this May 1983 view at the Middleton Railway shows Borrows 0-4-0WT *Windle,* with a wagon and brakevan to carry the passengers, about to depart for Moor Road.

Many of us are old enough to remember Dinting Railway Centre, established around the single-road Great Central shed. In this 1978 view is an unrestored No. 6115 *Scots Guardsman*, 0-6-0T No. 1704 *Nunlow* and 'Jubilee' No. 5596 *Bahamas*. The centre closed in 1991 after a dispute with the landlord, and as recently as two years ago the site was overgrown, but the shed was still extant.

A three-car Derby DMU stands at Fairlie Pier on September 18, 1965, preparing to return to Glasgow St Enoch. Fairlie Pier closed on July, 31, 1972. ALL PICTURES: TRACKS NORTH COLLECTION

End of the line

There was always something fascinating about the terminus station at the end of the line. Here's a few memories.

In poor condition is Middleton station, north of Manchester, where a two-car DMU waits to depart to Manchester Victoria on August 24, 1963. Services were withdrawn on September 7, 1964.

A pair of three-car DMUs tick over at Barry Pier forming a connecting service for a Campbell's steamer sailing to Weston-super-Mare on August

The fishing port of Mallaig is where B&RCW Class 27 No. D5387 waits with the 6.25am to Fort William on September 1, 1964.

'Blue Train' No. 084 stands at Balloch Pier on July 3, 1964, before returning empty to Balloch for its next working. The station closed in September 1986.

A single car DMU leaves Abingdon for Radley on August 22, 1963. The station, which retained much Great Western character, was closed on September 9, 1963, just over a fortnight after the photo was taken.

Empty stock working at London termini

Coaches for a Shrewsbury train near Westbourne Park being hauled into Paddington by 2-6-2 tank engine No. 6135 on August 3, 1958.

By ALAN RANNIE

WHEN the average traveller arrives in London, he cares little about what subsequently happens to the train which brought him there. Similarly, when he is beginning an outward journey, he expects to find a clean, warm carriage awaiting him at the appropriate platform at least 20 minutes before starting time, again without troubling how it got there. But much happens to a long-distance train between the end of one journey and the beginning of the next, and although the advent of electric and diesel traction will doubtless bring great changes, the elaborate arrangements for dealing with steam stock, which originated, for the most part, before the Grouping of 1923, present an interesting field of study.

If one looks at an old plan or print of a station such as Euston or Paddington, one sees that in early days platforms were few and widely separated. Between them were numerous tracks, often with turntables for transferring vehicles from one line to another.

In those days, when trains were infrequent and marshalling quite simple, the station itself served for a carriage shed and any cleaning or remarshalling could be performed within its limits. But as the 19th century advanced great changes took place.

The stations, once on the edge of the town, became closely hemmed in by other buildings, and the huge growth of main line and suburban traffic made it necessary to instal the maximum number of platforms. At King's Cross there were still six lines between the two main departure platforms until about 30 years ago, but this was already a somewhat curious survival. Moreover, however many platform lines had been contrived, it was still impossible for any train to occupy one for long, while the successive introduction of lavatories, sleeping cars and restaurant cars made the servicing of rolling stock a far more complex affair.

Carriage depots had to be established where room could still be found, in some cases a good way down the line, and to them an ever-increasing number of trains had to be sent out empty, only to be brought in again later, ready for their next down journey to the provinces. The supply of engines raised a similar problem, though a smaller one, of course, as they move under their own power and occupy tracks and points of intersection for a minimum of time.

Thus, the running lines outside the termini became burdened, over and above the trains shown in the public timetables, by light engines working to and from the sheds and by empty carriage trains in connection with sidings which might be situated in several different places. The latter alone may amount to about 40% of the actual number of arrivals and departures, and in some cases special tracks have been provided. The difficulties are increased by the fact that empties necessarily leave from the arrival side and vice versa.

If we analyse the problem a little more closely, we find that, though most of the termini have just a few long-distance trains which are sent back to their points of origin without leaving the station precincts, in normal working it is only suburban or medium-distance trains which are so treated, as far as steam working is concerned. And even so, the 'rush hour' period results in there being many local train sets, not in service during the middle of the day, which must be stored somewhere away from the terminus until they are wanted again in the evening. These may often be seen in widely scattered sidings throughout the suburban area during the midday period.

Long-distance trains fall into three categories:
1) Those based in provincial depots and receiving their main servicing there. These are usually scheduled to spend from two to five hours at the London end, and during this period they must to some extent be cleaned and re-equipped.
2) Trains based in London, leaving chiefly in the morning or at night, which require a thorough overhaul, especially if sleeping cars are included.
3) Special trains of every kind, such as reliefs to ordinary services, boat trains, football excursions and so on. For these a large reserve of suitable rolling stock must be maintained, not least on summer Saturdays, which are tending to assume greater importance in the eyes of operating officers.

The large carriage depots are indeed vital places in the railway economy, and a mishap, such as a derailment at a focal point, can have serious consequences, especially where (as is too often the case) only one entrance and exit is available. Hence, if there is room to stable a spare train or two in the immediate neighbourhood of a big station, it is a most desirable thing to do.

Special 'pilot' engines are largely used for handling empty trains and many well-known classes of passenger tanks have ended their days in this way, but in some cases tender engines in ordinary service are found on the job as well, especially where, as at Old Oak Common and Stratford, engine sheds and carriage sidings are close together.

The following outline of what happens to a train after its arrival at a London terminus is of fairly general application, and might equally apply to many large provincial stations. Let us imagine that an express has come to rest in a main arrival platform at or near its booked time.

The passengers rapidly disperse and the fireman, or a shunter, uncouples the big engine, which then waits patiently for release to turntable or shed. Within a quarter of an hour or less a tank engine, which has probably brought in an empty train to another platform,

Empty coaches of the up 'Mancunian' waiting to leave Euston, with Class 8F 2-8-0 locomotive No. 48122 on August 3, 1958, at the same time as an Oerlikon EMU leaves for Watford Junction. ALL PHOTOS BRIAN MORRISON

will be coupled on at our tail end.

Meanwhile, platform staff will have cleared the vans, picked up discarded newspapers and shut the windows, for the inside of the carriages must not be allowed to get chilly or wet. Some of the restaurant car staff will have gone off to check accounts and stores (for most of these vehicles depend for supplies and some cooking on terminal hotels or special kitchens) while others remain with the train, tidying up or laying the next meal. The express guard will have gone off duty, but his place will be taken by another, for no train, even if it is empty, is allowed to proceed without one.

Presently, the signalman will be informed, by telephone or plunger, that we are ready, and as soon as a suitable interval occurs in the

"Special 'pilot' engines are largely used for handling empty trains"

regular traffic, we unostentatiously move out on to our appointed line. This is not a casual business, for in the working books, scheduled times and paths are laid down for every movement: but late arrivals or other causes may lead the signalman or local controller to use his discretionary powers. Only when we have gone will the express engine be free to move, except in the rare cases where a crossover near the buffer stops enable it to escape to an adjoining line.

The distance we have to cover may be less than one, or more than seven miles, and our journey will probably not be a particularly rapid one. It will certainly be in the general interest to have us out of the way, but we have, of course, a low priority where conflicting traffic

paths occur, and we may be kept waiting some time at the entrance to the depot while a previous train is being disposed of. Probably we shall be finally pushed in by a diesel shunter, to avoid our tank engine being imprisoned and to allow it to be attached to the next outgoing train. We shall be impressed with the fact that everything is quiet and highly organised.

Exactly what is done to our train will depend on its character and on whether it has finished its day's work or not. It will, in any case, be coated with a special solution and passed slowly through the carriage washing plant, if there is one, emerging externally clean. In some depots this work is still done by hand. Then every coach will be boarded by an internal cleaner, male or more probably female, the lavatories will be tidied and flushed, water-tanks replenished, compartments swept and dusted, and clean antimacassars fitted in first-class compartments. When there is a worker available for each vehicle this process takes about three-quarters of an hour.

If the train has finished for the day, vacuum-cleaning normally takes place and at intervals of a week or a fortnight carpets are thoroughly cleaned on both sides. Sleeping cars need special treatment: sheets, pillows and blankets have to be changed and beds made up, special laundries sometimes being provided. The wheels and undercarriages are also subject to inspection and electric batteries may need to be 'topped up' by connecting them to the mains through special plugs.

Much of this work will be done under cover if a large enough carriage shed is provided, but before going back to the terminus our train will probably be parked in an open siding, which ▶

may have to be selected carefully with a view to its length or to its priority on the departure list. Some of the older sidings cannot take the whole of a modern train. It may also require re-marshalling, or a defective vehicle may need to be shunted out. The sidings must be brightly lit at night, for work will continue during most, if not all, of the 24 hours. In winter, hot steam must be available from pipes to keep the coaches warm in the absence of a locomotive; sometimes an old engine-boiler serves for this purpose. Finally, the depot must have staff facilities, including, probably, a canteen, and offices to which instructions for extra trains, seat reservations and so forth are sent.

On the return journey, once again our train will have its scheduled path, designed to bring it alongside the departure platform, fully staffed and duly equipped and labelled, at an appropriate time, varying from 20 minutes to an hour or more in the case of night expresses. Only if the weather is very bad, or some mishap has occurred, is it likely not to be there when required.

It will also be clean, and it is the travelling public rather than British Railways that often should be blamed for shortcomings in this respect. Such is the general picture, but local peculiarities lead to a variety of methods at different stations, and lend additional interest to this important side of traffic operation.

Paddington now receives and despatches

more long-distance trains than any other terminus in this country, if not in the world. Forty-seven restaurant and five sleeping car trains leave daily in the present winter service, and there are about 70 departures to places more than 60 miles away. To the total departure list of 140 advertised trains (excluding the Hammersmith electrics) must be added 14 for parcels traffic only and 90 empty stock workings, rising to 115 on Saturdays in summer.

Fortunately, the Western Region is well-equipped for dealing with this enormous traffic, especially since the improvements of 1929. There is a special down empty carriage line, to the north of the relief lines, all the way to Old Oak Common (3½ miles out), where the main engine and carriage depots have been situated since 1902. To reach this line from the arrival platforms involves no interference with down working except in the case of local trains from the Bishops Road platforms (Nos. 14 and 15) to the relief lines, but these are not very numerous.

There is also a double-line flyover bridge connecting Old Oak yards with the down side of the main lines, and empty trains or light engines which may have been sent out of Paddington on the down main can diverge at Portobello box (just west of Westbourne Park) onto the line leading to this bridge. All up empty trains use the flyover and then an up

Stanier 2-6-2 tank No. 40172 at St Pancras with stock of a Sunday train from Leicester in August 1958. The loco was withdrawn at the end of 1959.

An 0-6-0 pannier tank, No. 8754, passing Westbourne Bridge signalbox, opposite Royal Oak station, with empty stock to form a Paddington to Swansea train.

carriage road south of the main lines right into Paddington itself, provided that they are destined for platforms 1 to 4, from which most of the expresses start.

For the last half-mile or so (from Subway Junction) there is a second up carriage road on the opposite side of the down main, from which all platforms can be reached. Also between the up and down main lines is Paddington Yard, with four terminal sidings in which local stock is stored, and for turning engines which do not need to go to Old Oak between duties there is the Ranelagh yard, about a quarter of a mile out on the down side.

Ten pilot engines are normally at work between Paddington and Old Oak, but main line engines also are used, in which case they bring in the empties of an earlier train than the one they are booked to work out of the station, sometimes adjourning to Ranelagh in the interval. Another local feature is the occasional 'trailing' of the train engine behind outgoing empties.

Old Oak Locomotive Depot is one of the largest in the country, and the adjacent carriage yard, with its 56 sidings of generous length, takes the premier place. There is room for about 1,200 coaches, and the turnaround on exceptionally busy days has been known to reach 2,500. No less than 30 of the sidings are under cover and the sheds have all services, including vacuum power, laid on by

pipe, though in the absence of a mechanical washing plant all external cleaning is done by hand. Sleeping car linen is laundered at Swindon and restaurant car stores come from the station hotel at Paddington; the crews generally join the trains at Old Oak.

There is another and much smaller yard known as West London Sidings on the down side, a little nearer London than Old Oak. This has nine roads and is used chiefly for non-corridor stock.

The long-distance traffic at Euston is quite

"Sleeping cars need special treatment: sheets, pillows and blankets have to be changed and beds made up"

as important as that at Paddington, for though rather fewer trains are involved some of them run much further afield. There are some 75 movements of empty stock in each direction, but about half of these are but elongated shunting movements.

In spite of its rambling and old-fashioned appearance, successive improvement schemes have given Euston quite a good layout from a

traffic-working point of view. The engine shed has always been a mile away at Camden, though the original roundhouse, still visible on the up side, has long been devoted to other purposes. The more modern shed, which is none too big, is on the down side of the main line. The carriage sheds at Willesden Junction, now used chiefly for storage purposes, were the main ones until they were superseded in 1953 by the magnificent new depot near Stonebridge Park.

Before 1903, two of the four running lines on the Camden bank had to be devoted to engine and carriage working, but in that year the Euston and Camden widening was completed. This gave separate engine lines to and from the sheds at a slightly lower level on the west side, and two carriage depots, one on each side, less than half a mile outside the terminus. Moreover, a subway was provided, leading from the arrival platforms to the larger, or western, of these two yards, which deals with the 'short turnaround' expresses scheduled to spend only a few hours at the London end. Trains can be backed out by their own engines through the subway and can be subsequently shunted into the departure platforms without fouling the main lines. The shed on this side has 11 roads, is about 800ft in length, and there are other, open sidings.

Thus, it is only those trains which need to be serviced at Stonebridge Park, or stored at ▶

Train of empty carriages from Euston, hauled by Fowler Class 3 2-6-2 tank engine No. 40070, passing Camden motive power depot (on the right). Having topped Camden Bank, it is heading down the underpass to Primrose Hill tunnel.

Willesden, that come on the main lines at all. In the down direction they mostly take the inner or 'slow' line up the bank and the series of flyovers at Camden, completed in 1922, ensures that no conflicting movements with up traffic occur there. For up empty trains a special deep-level connection, from the slow line near the east end of Primrose Hill Tunnel, to the west carriage yard outside Euston, was made at the same time.

At Harlesden, a mile beyond Willesden, the approach roads to the new depot leave the slow lines. Though situated at Stonebridge Park, more than seven miles from Euston, it is often referred to as the Willesden depot. In spite of the distance out, room was found for it with difficulty, a fact that illustrates the growth of London forcibly.

This depot represents the last word in scientific equipment for the thorough servicing of trains, and has been visited by many delegations, including a party of Russian railway officials. The shed in which all work except external cleaning is carried out has a length of 1,120ft, but contains only four lines, along which the coaches are moved by an ingenious system of 'mules' as the work progresses. All services, such as steam- or vacuum-cleaning power, are available at numerous points from overhead pipes, while pits facilitate work on the underframes. The staff totals 250, of which 17 are in the

laundry, which deals with huge quantities of sleeping car linen.

Alongside the shed are seven stabling and 15 marshalling sidings, and the yard is accessible from both ends, though the northern approach is needed only in emergencies. The new depot deals with all sleeping car trains, of which 11 leave Euston nightly, even in winter, and also with the other London-based expresses, including the West Coast postal express and the Anglo-Scottish day trains, together with stock required for

"The number of trains to be dealt with varies from 30 to 40 daily, the majority require to be remarshalled"

extra services, such as Liverpool boat specials. The number of trains to be dealt with varies from 30 to 40 daily, and the majority of them require to be remarshalled. Tank engines are used between Euston and Stonebridge Park, with diesel shunters in the depot itself.

The electric service to and from Euston has its own depot at Stonebridge Park, and spare steam trains for stations between Watford, Tring and Bletchley are accommodated in the

east carriage shed outside the terminus: this has five roads.

The former Midland Railway terminus of St Pancras deals with about 40 down empty trains daily, including sleeping cars and Scottish expresses, divided more or less equally between the two main carriage depots, and a similar number in the opposite direction. The layout is somewhat old-fashioned and cramped, so that very careful organisation is needed to make things work smoothly. For passenger working there is only a plain double line most of the way to Kentish Town, though fortunately there are separate goods lines, available for empty coaching stock, on the west side.

Engine sidings, with turntable, are close at hand, but many light engines must use the main lines as far as Islip Street signalbox (1¼ miles) on their way to and from Kentish Town depot. Long-distance trains with a short turn-round period are dealt with in 10 open terminal sidings adjoining the Cattle Dock, a short distance beyond Kentish Town on the down side. These sidings are rather short and lacking in modern facilities: moreover, they can only be entered or left by way of the down goods line, a back-shunt being involved, with use of a crossover in the up direction. Empty passenger trains thus severely limit the ordinary use of the goods lines at this point and obstruct the route from all parts of North and East London towards Brent Sidings, while between Cattle Dock Junction and St Pancras the goods lines are used for these empties as much as for their original purpose.

The up goods line gives an easy run into the departure platforms at St Pancras, but the down goods is, of course, more difficult to reach. When down empties cannot be got across conveniently just outside the station, they can use the main up line (which is to this extent worked as a single line) for about 400 yards as far as the site of the old Cambridge Street signalbox. Beyond this point they can wait in a special down carriage road on the up side of the main lines, until it is practicable to put them onto the down passenger or goods roads at Dock Junction, which now marks the end of the first block section out of St Pancras.

The main carriage depot, at which trains based on London, as well as all sleeping cars and reserve stock for extra trains, are stored, was placed by the Midland Railway five miles out on the up side, just beyond Cricklewood station. Here are 15 sidings – about half of them under a shed – accessible only by a back-shunt from a shunting neck, apart from one which has direct egress to a running line. Cricklewood boasts a washing machine, but sleeping car linen is sent to Willesden (Stonebridge Park). Among the extras that the depot has to provide are 'Starlight Specials', and boat trains to Tilbury, of which 15 sometimes leave St Pancras in a week.

Cricklewood depot is on the opposite side of the layout from the goods lines proper, and down empty trains must proceed along the slow line from Watling Street junction box, whichever road, goods or passenger, they may have followed so far. There is, however, a 'second up goods' behind the up slow platform

J50/3 class 0-6-0T No. 68983 emerges from the gloom of Copenhagen Tunnel into the spring sunshine on April 30, 1955, working to Finsbury Park carriage sidings.

at Cricklewood, extending about a mile to Watling Street and handy for empty trains. They can cross to the ordinary up goods line in two stages between Watling Street and West Hampstead station, or follow the slow line to Finchley Road and thence the main passenger to St Pancras.

Diesel shunters are used in the sidings

themselves, but main line engines share the rest of the stock-working with powerful modern tanks, the old Midland 0-4-4s having long since disappeared. The engines bringing empties in give a helpful push to departing trains, when the road is sufficiently clear.

Traffic working at King's Cross has always been attended with great difficulties, largely because of the short distance between the platform-ends and the mouths of Gasworks tunnels. All three up lines are on the east side and the three down ones are on the other, a fact which causes many conflicting movements in the confined space, especially as local trains coming from the up slow have to be crossed over all the other lines between Belle Isle and King's Cross to reach the suburban station (platforms 11-15). The engine sidings and turntable on the west side can be reached only by two reversals, and if the increased number of expresses since the Second World War had not been offset by a marked diminution in local trains the situation would have been more difficult still. It is significant that a flyover is to be built outside King's Cross before electric services are introduced on the East Coast route.

The present layout is such that empty stock trains (of which there are more than 50 each way daily) must use the original pair of lines in the middle Gas Works Tunnel, crossings to or from the slow roads being made at Belle Isle or further afield. Light engines for King's Cross motive power depot, which is ▶

N1 class 0-6-2T No. 69469 and Class J50/4 0-6-0T No 68985 combine forces on September 20, 1953, to haul a rake of 14 coaches from an arrival from Newcastle, up the incline towards Finsbury Park carriage sidings.

curiously situated on the far (west) side of the goods yard, diverge up an incline at Belle Isle, while those coming into the terminus reverse into a siding between the up and down main lines at Copenhagen Junction, waiting there for a path into King's Cross. The signalboxes of Belle Isle and Copenhagen Junction are close together beyond the north end of Gas Works Tunnel, and there are only four tracks from here to Holloway.

The nearest carriage sidings are on the down side, near the site of Holloway station and about 1¼ miles out. These are 17 in number and though there is no shed they are fairly well equipped with essential services, including mobile vacuum cleaners. The 20-odd trains dealt with account for about 1,050 coaches weekly and they include the short turnaround trains from such places as Leeds, Cleethorpes, Peterborough and Cambridge, as well as the night van trains, of which the number tends to grow. The buffer stops at Holloway are at the London end and trains are drawn out on to a 'high-level' shunting road, but they have to cross the other main lines at ground level to reach the up slow.

There are two groups of sidings for suburban stock in the neighbourhood of Finsbury Park, but it is between Hornsey and Wood Green, nearly five miles from King's Cross, that the largest of the old Great Northern depots is situated. On the down side are the six 'Waterworks' sidings, used chiefly for vehicles needing attention, but on the up side there are three yards in succession, known as Hornsey Nos. 1, 2 and 3, with a total of 32 sidings open towards the south. Here are stabled the sleeping car and other trains serving Scotland and the North East coast, involving a minimum of 1,300 vehicles weekly, and requiring two shunting engines throughout the day and night. It is strange that the only shed provided is a small affair with four roads, all the main servicing being carried out in the open air. Laundry work is sent to York, and a 10-ton truck is filled with litter from the coaches every week.

It would obviously be impracticable to work the empty trains destined for Hornsey yards, numbering more than 30 daily, across the whole expanse of eight running lines which comprise the main line at this point. Hence, it is the custom to run them past Wood Green on the down slow or goods roads and over the flyover leading to the Hertford line. A little further on they are reversed and taken through a further set of sidings known as Bounds Green, where there is a washing machine, thus entering Hornsey yards from the country end. Bounds Green has a carriage repair shop and 12 double-ended sidings, used chiefly for reserve stock and outer suburban trains. In spite of the apparently liberal accommodation in these various groups of sidings, enough for 850 coaches in all, it is necessary to borrow

Stock for a West of England train makes a cautious approach to London Waterloo hauled by M7 class 0-4-4 tank engine No. 30123 on August 7, 1958.

some of the Ferme Park freight sidings at busy times in summer, a practice which occurs also at Old Oak and Cricklewood.

Empty trains between Hornsey and King's Cross have exceptionally easy schedules in the working book, sometimes as much as one hour up and two hours down. The latter allows for passing through the Bounds Green washing plant at 3mph. The engines used are drawn

"Empty trains between Hornsey and King's Cross have exceptionally easy schedules in the working book, sometimes as much as one hour"

from the stud of sturdy tanks which work the suburban service; main line engines are not used at all. Normally eight express trains (including the new Sheffield Pullmans) are turned at King's Cross itself, but on summer Saturdays this method is used on a large scale, to the extent, indeed, of returning a Leeds train to Newcastle or vice versa. On these occasions a section of the Holloway staff comes up to King's Cross to do the necessary cleaning.

Holloway, Hornsey and Bounds Green have recently been placed under one depot master, who has under him a staff of 220, rising to 260 in summer. There is a prevalence of

electric cooking on ex-LNER restaurant cars and these vehicles can be connected for battery recharging to the mains at Holloway, Hornsey or King's Cross; at King's Cross there is a large kitchen under the inner end of platforms 6-10.

In the case of Liverpool Street, there are 10 platforms in the middle of the station available for main line work, and about 14 expresses are daily turned round in the terminus, a much higher figure than elsewhere. This is facilitated by the fact that no runs on the old Great Eastern much exceed 100 miles, and many are far shorter. In spite of this, there are not less than 47 empty workings out of the station daily, in connection with steam and diesel trains, nearly all of which use the main lines (now the middle pair as far as Bethnal Green) till they reach Bow Junction, a mile short of Stratford. Here, they diverge onto other lines, north of the main tracks, which give access to the various depots.

First there is Thornton Field, which is at right angles to the main line and has recently been modernised and enlarged to a total of 51 sidings. But many expresses, including all those with restaurant cars, are dealt with in the 18 sidings (some through roads) alongside the Cambridge line platforms at Stratford. Both yards are fitted for pre-heating trains, and Thornton Field has a washing machine. The remaining sidings, alongside Channelsea curve, are chiefly used for reserve stock.

As the engine sheds are at Stratford too, extensive use is made of express engines, usually run tender first, for working empty trains. For engines not needing to go to Stratford there is a central turntable at

Liverpool Street, and a siding between the main and electric lines just outside. The up working closely corresponds to the down.

The handful of long-distance trains at the former LNER terminus of Marylebone, are catered for by a small carriage shed close by on the up side, and by sidings at Neasden, where the Aylesbury and Wycombe routes diverge. Here, also, is the engine shed, reached by a spur on the down side. Over the five miles between Neasden and Marylebone there is only a plain double line, but colour-light signalling permits of close headway between trains.

Though, so largely electrified, Waterloo retains a good deal of long-distance steam traffic. The winter service gives 25 expresses to the Exeter or Bournemouth lines, but on August Saturdays this number swells to more than 60. There are also steam locals to Basingstoke or beyond, and frequent Southampton boat trains which may reach double figures on exceptionally busy days.

The Nine Elms engine shed is reached by a back-shunt from a terminal spur on the down side at Locomotive Junction, near Queens Road. This is connected by a crossover with all the eight running lines between this point and Waterloo, but the favourites for light engines are the up main through and down main local. There is a good deal of coming and going, as space outside Waterloo is very limited and the only turntable is remotely situated on the Windsor side.

The carriage depot is at Clapham Junction (four miles out) between the separate wings of the station serving the main and Windsor lines. There are 48 terminal sidings, some of them covered by a large shed, and there is also a repair shop. The whole yard covers 10 acres and will hold 600 coaches. The approach lines pass through a two-track washing plant which helps to maintain the high standard of cleanliness usual on the Waterloo expresses.

Many of the main line stopping trains (and those of the Portsmouth electric service) are reversed at Waterloo, but there is a minimum

On July 6, 1951, an unusual combination of Drummond locomotives departs from Waterloo with a heavy empty coaching stock working destined for Clapham Junction carriage yards. Yet to be fitted with a smokebox numberplate, T9 4-4-0 No. 30710 pilots M7 0-4-4T No. 30322, the crew of which were no doubt grateful for the assistance provided by the larger engine.

of 32 winter workings to Clapham sidings and the same number back. The down Windsor local line lies handy to the main arrival platforms, but beyond Locomotive Junction there is a short bottleneck with only one down Windsor line. The electric service over this section amounts to 14-18 trains hourly, but the colour-light signalling, which permits of a two-minute headway, reduces delays to a minimum. Only 10 minutes are usually allowed for empty trains between Waterloo and West London Junction, where the Clapham approach roads begin. In the opposite direction, the busy up main through line is joined by empties at this point. This line is duplicated for the last three-quarters of a mile into the terminus, so that trains awaiting entrance to a platform need not delay other traffic. Eight Drummond 0-4-4 tanks are normally set aside for the work, but Feltham shed contributes

one large 4-6-2 tank.

Among the other Southern Region termini, the 'Chatham' side of Victoria achieves distinction by handling Continental traffic via Dover and Folkestone, as well as expresses to the Thanet resorts. There is a fair-size carriage shed just outside the station, while the engine shed and a further carriage depot are at Stewarts Lane, about a mile further on. Light engines and empty trains can keep off the two main lines by using the two outer tracks on Grosvenor Bridge and a burrowing junction beyond. The line rises steeply onto the bridge and heavy trains are pushed as well as pulled out of the terminus, with rousing echoes from the roof. The Stewarts Lane carriage shed, which services the 'Golden Arrow' and the 'Night Ferry' sleeping cars, was formerly a Pullman car depot. As reconstructed by the Southern Railway about 25 years ago, it has a washing plant and 19 sidings, some very short. The capacity is 117 vehicles.

The remaining termini have interesting features, but the number of steam workings is small. Consideration of the arrangements at the larger stations indicates the magnitude of the operations involved in the storage and servicing of passenger rolling stock, and will quicken the interest of many travellers who must often see an empty train, possibly with famous nameboards, chugging gently along on a parallel track behind anything from a tender-first Pacific to a little pannier-tank.

In conclusion, the writer would like to express his thanks to officers of the British Transport Commission, at headquarters and in the Regions, who have assisted him with information for this article. ∎

Class K3/2 2-6-0 No. 61810 passing Bethnal Green with empty stock for a train from Liverpool Street as a local service departs for Hertford East.

The scene at Glaisdale after the September 1931 washout.

A double washout

THE striking photograph, by Mr F Ingham, reproduced above, shows the two-span girder bridge erected by the LNER to replace that over the River Esk, near Glaisdale, on the Battersby and Whitby line, which was washed away in September, 1931.

It will be recalled, moreover, that this was the second replacement.

The first washout took place in July 1930, when the original stone bridge was carried away by flood-water. A new single-span girder bridge was then almost erected, when, in September 1931, some days of rain of almost tropical severity resulted in the river changing its course, and cutting through a cliff 100ft high, in a way which this photograph clearly shows, with the result that the right-hand abutment of the new bridge was carried away.

The present two-span bridge was then designed and erected, and was opened in 1932. As will be seen, the right-hand abutment of the right-hand span has been erected at a point well behind the shelter of the cliff, leaving ample space for the most furious flood-waters of the future.

From the November 1934 issue

Electric to diesel on South Tyneside

THE North Eastern Region of British Railways has taken interim measures to reduce the losses on the Tyneside electrified services.

The first major step has been from January 7, with the replacement, by diesel multiple units, of the electric trains on the South Tyneside line between Newcastle and South Shields (11 miles).

The frequency of service has been increased from 30min to a 20min interval; two trains in the early morning and two in the late evening in each direction have been withdrawn. The overall journey times of trains have been increased by four minutes.

The number of passenger journeys made on this line fell from 3½ million in 1956 to 2½ million in 1961. Factors contributing to this decreased demand are stated to be the excess of available public transport in relation to demand, housing developments moving population to areas further away from the railway, and the expansion of private transport.

At the same time, railway operating costs have increased, and the high incidence of fixed cost associated with electric traction made it impossible to continue the services in their previous form with their present level of use.

These changes have involved certain modifications to the Sunderland-South Shields service.

Reorganisation of the North Tyneside electric services is being considered.

From the February 1963 issue

Collecting locomotive numbers

AT Tamworth Juvenile Court recently several Birmingham youths, who collect locomotive numbers, were accused of railway trespass.

The boys, between waiting for trains, had run about the permanent way and put coins on the metals, which they had collected after the passage of trains as souvenirs. Some caustic comment on the practice was made from the Bench.

The collecting of locomotive numbers is a perfectly legitimate hobby for railway enthusiasts and pursued intelligently may serve useful and instructive purposes.

Many of the railway companies, perhaps particularly the LMSR, afford special facilities for the pursuit of this hobby.

It would be a pity if, because of the irresponsible actions of certain of those who indulge in the hobby, it were to fall into disrepute.

Not all the reports which appeared of the Tamworth case in the press made it clear that the strictures of the Bench were directed against trespass on the line and the danger resulting therefrom, and not the collection of engine numbers, as such.

From the January/February 1945 issue

London level crossings

IN a letter from Mr G T Moody, attention is drawn to the remarkable fact that the electrically operated suburban lines of the Southern Railway between Barnes and Richmond are intersected by no fewer than four level crossings, at Vine Road, Barnes, White Hart Lane, Mortlake, and North Sheen.

At Barnes there are two separate crossings, one over the Richmond line and the other over the Loop, each with its own control cabin.

Although none of these crossings is a main road, there is a fair amount of vehicular traffic, which has to get across between trains averaging 20 to the hour.

There has been some agitation locally to abolish the crossings, but as the line here is on the same level as the adjacent land, raising or lowering the roads to cross by overbridges or underbridges would be an expensive business.

From the September/October 1945 issue

Tralee & Dingle Nos. 1 & 2 attack the 1-in-35 incline at Camp after leaving Castlegregory Junction en route to Dingle with a cattle train on April 29, 1938. W A CAMWELL

The Tralee & Dingle Railway

By CYNRIC MYTTON-DAVIES

ONE of the most westerly lines in Europe will no longer be available for passengers by the time that this issue of *The Railway Magazine* appears, for the announcement was made on March 15 that the Tralee & Dingle Light Railway is to be closed to passenger traffic on April 17.

The main line from Tralee to Dingle will continue to convey goods traffic, but the branch line from the junction to Castlegregory is being closed entirely.

The Dingle peninsula, which this railway serves, is the northernmost of the four arms of land that stretch out into the Atlantic from the south-west corner of Ireland. The line had its origin in the Tralee & Dingle Light Railway Co Ltd, which was incorporated on June 4, 1884, under the Tramways & Public Companies

(Ireland) Act, 1883. Under the original powers and those granted by the Tralee & Dingle Light Railway Order of 1888, 371 miles of 3ft-gauge single track were built, and opened on March 31, 1891. Baronial guarantees were given to enable the capital to be raised, and, owing to continual deficits in working, the line was transferred in 1896 to the Grand Jury of the County of Kerry and thereafter controlled by a Committee of Management.

In 1925, at the time of Grouping in Eire, the Tralee & Dingle Railway was merged into the Great Southern Railways, but up to that time it had its own works and repair shops at Tralee, the headquarters of the undertaking.

Since then, locomotive repairs have been effected at the company's works at Inchicore instead of in the shops at Tralee, and carriage and wagon repairs undertaken at Limerick.

Naturally, this narrow-gauge railway has its own station at Tralee, which stands some few hundred yards distant from the (Irish) standard-gauge station; the track, however, actually runs on through the streets right into the sidings of the main station in order to facilitate the transfer of merchandise and parcels from the narrow- to the standard-gauge vans and wagons and vice versa, but passengers are not carried on to the main station. When the Tralee & Dingle Railway was described in *The Railway Magazine* for May 1898, in an article by Mr T J Goodlake, there were two standard-gauge stations in ▶

Tralee, as both the Great Southern & Western Railway and the Waterford, Limerick & Western Railway had separate termini at Tralee adjoining each other and were connected end to end. After the amalgamation of the WL & WR and the GS & WR in 1901, however, the WL & WR station was closed and all standard-gauge trains transferred to the GS & WR station.

The configuration of the Dingle peninsula is roughly that of a long mountainous backbone, which rises to a crest at about one-third of the way westward and roughly halfway along the main line, so that from Tralee to Dingle the trains are climbing all the time for the first half of the journey and then descending for the remainder of the way, although there are, of course, inclines and declivities on both sides of the crest. This crest is the culminating point of a 3¾-mile bank between Castlegregory Junction and Glenagalt, which has a gradient of 1-in-30; the highest point is reached at Glenagalt, 680ft above sea level. The track is of the flat-bottom type, and single line working obtains throughout, but there are passing loops and sidings at Castlegregory Junction and Annascaul. Since, however, there are now only two trains daily in each direction, the loops are not normally required.

There are seven locomotives, numbered 1 to 6 and 8, in service on the line at the present time. They are all English built, six having been constructed by the Hunslet Engine Company's works at Leeds, and one by Kerr, Stuart & Co Ltd.

The first three engines were 2-6-0 tanks, with outside cylinders (13in x 18in) built by Hunslet in 1889. Nos. 1 and 2 were rebuilt in 1903, and No. 3 in 1902. No. 4, a Hunslet product of 1890 – a much smaller locomotive – was an 0-4-2 intended for the Castlegregory branch. In 1892, the Hunslet Engine Co supplied No. 5, a somewhat larger tank engine of the 2-6-2 type, but with No. 6, supplied by the same maker in 1898, the railway reverted to the familiar 2-6-0.

Dingle station plays host to a passenger train for Tralee waiting in the platform, while a cattle special waits on the right to follow.

Kerr, Stuart & Co Ltd supplied Nos. 7 and 8 in 1902 and 1903 respectively, and these also were of the 2-6-0, with outside cylinders. In 1908, No. 4 was scrapped, and the Kerr, Stuart No. 8 was renumbered as 4. The other Kerr, Stuart engine was scrapped in 1928, leaving the number 7 vacant. The railway reverted to the Hunslet Engine Company for its last order, which was placed in 1910, and was for the present No. 8, a 2-6-0 tank, generally similar to the original three.

All the locomotives are fitted with cow-catchers, since the track runs for the most part along the side of the main road, where cattle and sheep frequently wander at large. In many places there is no dividing wall or fence between the road and the rails, and level crossings are frequent, and sometimes unprotected. Each locomotive is also fitted with a large and powerful acetylene headlamp at the base of the chimney.

All cars and freight wagons are built with bogies, passenger cars are eight-wheeled and straight-sided, and the finish gives a match-boarding effect; the doors open inwards.

The interiors are divided into two compartments, one of which is about twice the length of the other. In the long section the seats run along the sides of the car, and in the small one across the car. The third-class coaches have wooden seats, and the first class upholstered of the same design as is standard for first-class rolling stock throughout the Great Southern system. All windows in both classes are fitted with two bars, so that it is impossible to lean outside.

There are 13 stops, most of which are optional, between the main line terminals, and six between Tralee and Castlegregory. Most of these are 'flag' stops, having neither platforms nor buildings, and are marked only by a gate and a nameboard inscribed in both English and Irish characters. Only Lispole, Annascaul, Camp, and Castlegregory Junction have platforms, and these are also the only stations at which there are booked stops. At Camp and at Annascaul locomotives take in water, as it is between these two points that the steepest section of the line is situated.

It was only to be expected that there should have been a certain amount of opposition to the inception of the line, on the part of the inhabitants of the Dingle peninsula, who felt that their happy, self-contained little world was being invaded and linked up with the great world of commerce, stress and trouble, and that its peculiar characteristics would soon be lost, and it would become spoiled. Some of these people resorted to active measures against the railway, and local railway officials have some amusing stories to tell of the attempts that were made to discourage the service,

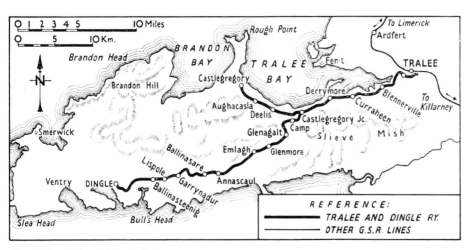

Map of the Tralee & Dingle Railway.

including that of one Paddy Kennedy who, on one occasion, resorted to soaping the rails! This, however, did not achieve the result that Paddy had hoped for, and the railway remained.

It is interesting to compare that original hostility with the present-day affection for the line that is held by most of the people. In spite of the journey time for the 32-odd miles being two-and-a-half hours, a bus service which covered the distance in a much shorter time, and which was inaugurated a few years ago, had to be discontinued owing to lack of support, the people preferring the railway. There are some who assert that the line has been kept open only for the entertainment of visitors, and would themselves welcome its substitution by a regular service of Great Southern buses, but the fact is that it handles a really considerable freight traffic.

Although buses are now to serve the needs of passengers, the main line to Dingle is to continue in use for goods. For this purpose a lower standard of maintenance is, of course, contemplated.

On the non-technical side it may be said that this railway traverses some extremely beautiful country, and the views from the carriage windows are among the best in Eire. Mountain ranges, surprising glimpses of the sea penetrating inland in charming bays, deep valleys, wild heath and bogland, and little green fields on the plains, are all to be seen as the train takes its leisurely way down the peninsula. The terminus of the line at the western end is Dingle station, but the rails continue further – down to the port – and freight wagons are regularly taken to the little goods platform near the pier to be loaded with fish and the merchandise (much of which is coal) brought in by the small steamers that call from Cardiff, Swansea, and other Welsh and west of England ports.

The general direction of the main line is from north-east to south-west. It follows the southern coast of Tralee Bay, which is the northern coast of the Dingle promontory, from Tralee to Castlegregory Junction, whence the branch line continues along the coast, then it strikes inland through the Gleann Na Galt and reaches the southern coast near the Inch Peninsula, slightly east of Annascaul, after which it follows westward for the remainder of the distance, keeping a mile or so inland, behind the foothills of the mountains which are known as the Slieve Mish.

Beyond Dingle there is no transport system whatever, so that the scene before the departure of the trains to Tralee is both fascinating and interesting, with carts, pony traps, jaunting cars, and a few motors all drawn up in the diminutive station yard, unloading parcels, luggage, and passengers. The same is true of Tralee, particularly on Saturdays, the local market day, when every

Hunslet 2-6-0 No. 2 sits at Dingle station with the monthly cattle special, attracting interest from local children on the cattle dock platform.

A cattle special has just arrived at Dingle on a July day behind loco Nos. 8 and 1, and is about to be shunted to the cattle dock.

shop in the town seems to deliver customers' purchases to the train.

The composition of the trains is usually locomotive, goods wagons, composite first- and third-class coach, third-class brake coach, and then another third-class coach, all bound for Dingle. These are followed by

"The journey time for the 32-odd miles being two-and-a half hours"

another set of cars for Castlegregory, and goods wagons for the same destination in the extreme rear. A spare locomotive with steam up is in readiness in a siding at Castlegregory, by the time the train arrives, to haul the rear portion of the train for its last six miles.

Running time is allowed as follows: Tralee to Castlegregory Junction, 10 miles with three optional halts, 40 minutes; Castlegregory Junction to Castlegregory, six miles with two optional stops, 36 minutes;

Castlegregory Junction to Annascaul, 11¼ miles with four optional stops and 3¾ mile bank with 1-in-30 gradient, 65 minutes; Annascaul to Lispole, six miles with two optional stops, 25 minutes; Lispole to Dingle, five miles with one optional stop, 20 minutes. This timing applies both to the morning and afternoon departures from Tralee. In the reverse direction the schedule varies a little.

The 7.30am train from Tralee serves the main line only, the 11.55 serves the Castlegregory line only, maintaining the previously specified schedule, and the 5.30pm serves both main and branch lines.

In the up direction, there is a train from Castlegregory to Tralee at 8.10am from Monday-Friday and 9.50am on Saturday, still keeping the same schedule, and another every weekday at 3.55pm, which connects with the afternoon train from Dingle.

The morning train from Dingle makes no connection at the junction from Castlegregory. There are no trains in either direction on Sundays. ∎

The FL9 series, is an electro-diesel, working from third rail or its diesel unit. Sixty were built for the New York, New Haven and Hartford Railroad. In Metro North livery. No. 2015 nears Crugers, New York state, with a commuter service.

American Classic

There are some things that stand out as iconic symbols of America and one of those is General Motors' EMD E and F series diesel locomotive. It was first produced in 1937, and when the production run ended in 1963, close on 9,000 units had been built. The backbone of the US railroads in those eras, the locos were also bought by railways in Canada, Mexico and Saudi Arabia.

Right: A pair of Mexican 1,750hp FP9 locos, Nos. 7016 and 7025, tick over at Aguascalientes on January 9, 1979. Ferrocarriles Nacionales de México had 25 such locos, built at La Grange, Illinois.

Below: GO Transit FP7 diesel No. 902 runs into to Toronto Union station past Bathurst Street on a wintry February 11, 1983.

Above: Denver & Rio Grande West F9A No. 5771 restarts the 'Zephyr' from Glenwood Springs station, Colorado, on July 30, 1978. This loco is now displayed at the Colorado State Railroad museum, Golden.

Right: Built in 1950, Milwaukee Road F unit No. 72A works over the grade crossing at Iron Mountain, Michigan, on July 31, 1979, with a freight.

Below: The cutely named Soo Line's FP7 No. 502A runs through Marshfield, Wisconsin, in October 1976 with a long freight consist. A second FP7 and an EMD GP30 No. 706 also provide the power.

ALL PHOTOS: TRACKS NORTH COLLECTION

Railway Photography

By CANON ERIC TREACY, MBE

TWENTY years ago, I snapped a moving train from the window of another moving train at Crewe. Surprisingly, the result was recognisable as a train – but only just.

Thus encouraged, I shot hopefully from the end of station platforms, with a series of cameras ranging from a borrowed Leica to an ancient reflex about the size of a piano accordion. My best results were of various railwaymen who were always ready to pose for me! However, I kept at it, and in December 1936, *The Railway Magazine* published one of my photographs of a Liverpool-London express.

Thus rewarded, and considerably helped by the advice of such good folk as Maurice Earley and E R Wethersett, I graduated to the stage when I could produce train pictures which could stand up to the searching, but just criticisms of my fellow members of the Railway Photographic Society.

Came the war, and my departure into the Forces. The war ended, I took up my hobby again with increased enthusiasm, after six years in which I was concerned with more serious things than photography. I receive many letters from enthusiasts on the subject of train photography, and I will now try to deal with the sort of questions that I am most frequently asked in these letters.

Watched by a p-way team, LNER V2 No. 60802 makes a spirited start from Leeds Central.

It is understandable that a photographer will claim that his own apparatus is the best. After years of experimenting, during which I have used every camera from the Leica, with its 35mm film, to the large plate camera using 9 x 12cm plates, I am now convinced that the best camera for this kind of work is the Press fitted with a focal plane shutter and a wire direct vision viewfinder.

The advantages are that the use of plates enables the photographer to develop each exposure separately, thus making it possible for each plate to be developed according to the lighting conditions when the exposure was made; that a fast-moving train is not an easy thing to sight in the small prism view finders fitted to many folding cameras, and a wire frame finder makes it possible to watch the train full-size until the moment of exposure; and that to arrest the movement of a train travelling more than 50mph, a shutter operating as near the plate as possible, and at a speed of not less than $\frac{1}{500}$th of a second is required. Focal plane shutters, consisting of two blinds operated by a spring mechanism, move across the sensitive surface at a speed regulated by the tension of the spring and the width of the slit between the two blinds, with genuine speed down to $\frac{1}{800}$th of a second, which is sufficient to stop all but the very fastest trains for the photographer. One sometimes doubts the accuracy of these shutters when marked at $\frac{1}{2000}$th of a second.

My own camera is a Zeiss Contessa Nettel Press taking a 9 x 12 cm plate, and fitted with a 6in Ross Xpress coated lens with an aperture of f4.5. It is 14 years old, and is as good now as it was in 1936. This is due, I believe, to my custom of sending it every winter to be cleaned and to have the shutter speeds overhauled. It has the disadvantages that it is heavy to carry about, and that plates can be

Working hard up the 1-in-75 gradient from Holyhead station is 'Black Five' No. 45249 with a parcels train in 1949.

loaded only in a dark room, whereas a film camera can be reloaded in the daylight. Be that as it may, it is a camera that I know and treasure; and I naturally think it is the best for the job.

Practically any camera will produce good results in this kind of photography provided that it has a good Anastigmat lens and a reliable shutter; that the case is light proof; and that it is not asked to do more than it is capable of. For instance, a shutter with a maximum speed of ¹⁄₁₀₀th of a second will not stop a train doing more than 25mph. The camera must be held quite still when the exposure is being made; by far the most common reason for unsatisfactory results is camera-shake at the moment of exposure. Due regard must also be given to the strength of the light at the time of the exposure, and the shutter and aperture adjusted accordingly.

There is not much to choose between the lenses of any of the leading makes. I have used the following lenses at various times in the last 20 years: Zeiss Tessar, Cooke Aviar, Ross Xpress, and Dallmeyer Pentac, and the results have been excellent. In spite of the reputation of the Continental lenses, it is my opinion that no better lenses are made than those of Ross, Taylor Hobson, and Cooke. My Cooke Aviar was a lovely lens, and so is my Ross Xpress.

The focal length of the lens is important. If it is too short, it will result in distortion of the image. By that I mean that the front of the train will appear disproportionately larger than the back. If the focal length is too long, the depth of focus will be small, and it will be almost impossible to achieve sharp focus along the whole length of the train. This latter problem can be solved by the use of a swing front on the camera, a fitting which must be operated with great care, but which will bring into sharp focus the plane along which it is swung.

My own conclusion is that a lens with a focal length of 6in on a plate 9 x 12cm is about right. It does not distort the image, and it gives a reasonably generous field of sharp focus, although there is not much margin, and one has to focus accurately. Proportionately, a lens with a focal length of 4½in would be suitable for a 3in x 2in negative.

Today there is a vogue for the coated lens. I am not prepared to deny the claims which are made for these lenses; to do so would be to question the results of scientific enquiry. The lens I use at present is coated, I use it both in my camera and in my enlarger, and I get admirable results with it, but I cannot detect that they are any improvement upon the results I got some years ago with my non-coated Cooke Aviar lens.

As a useful second string, I use a Super Ikonta film camera taking a 2¼in x 3¼in negative. This camera is fitted with a Zeiss

A heavy Newcastle-Liverpool train in early 1963 sees 'Jubilee' No. 46631 *Tanganyika* leading rebuilt 'Patriot' No. 45527 *Southport* out of Leeds City past the station pilot.

Tessar lens and a Compur Rapid shutter exposing down to ¹⁄₄₀₀th of a second. It is an admirable camera for photographing in confined spaces (such as on the footplate) as it possesses a range finder. I also find it useful for capturing those more intimate aspects of the railway scene in which the larger camera would be too obtrusive. For instance, I used this camera to take a photograph in York Locomotive Depot, where the light was such that I had to open up to full aperture, and the shorter focus lens gave the greater depth of focus that I needed. One of my favourite pictures, taken in a bright interval between hail storms on Shap Fell, also was taken with

"In December 1936, *The Railway Magazine* published one of my photographs."

this camera.

My advice to anyone taking up railway photography would be to purchase (new or secondhand) a film or plate camera fitted with a lens of aperture not less than f4.5 made by one of the reputable lens makers and a Compur Rapid or focal plane shutter. My own preference would be for a plate camera, but films will be found in many ways preferable. I would suggest that the negative should not be less than 3¼in x 2¼in. I fear that the enthusiastic miniaturists will not agree with this. The Leica and the Contax (if you can

afford them) are lovely cameras, a joy to handle and a joy to use; but I have not found them best for this kind of work. Whatever the experts may say, I do not think that they will produce as sharp a whole-plate enlargement as a 3¼in x 2¼in negative, for the obvious reason that in the latter case the degree of enlargement is less. Moreover, these cameras are very expensive, and beyond the reach of most amateurs. I would say on this point that good results depend more upon the user than on the camera. The photographer must understand how to use the light, how to compose his picture, and how to operate his camera.

I am often asked by those who are starting railway photography how they may obtain lineside permits. It took me about five years to work my passage, and it was only after the Second World War that I was granted the full facilities I required. It is understandable that the Railway Executive should be careful about ▶

'Black Five' No. 5428 is renamed after the author (right) at Tyseley on May 3, 1969.
J W ELLISON

granting permits, as inexperienced visitors on railway property can be a considerable hindrance and worry to the staff. I ascertained recently the policy of the Railway Executive about permits, and cannot do better than quote from the reply I received: "The general policy of British Railways in regard to amateur photography is normally to allow this on platforms and other public parts of passenger stations without a permit, provided that in the case of a 'closed station' the photographer is in possession of a travel or platform ticket. Such an arrangement is naturally subject to a condition that no interference is caused with the working of traffic, and the duties of the staff, and at other busy times it may not be practicable to allow it. (Much depends, of course, on the tactful way in which the photographer goes about his business.)

"As regards photography on line-sides and other parts of railway premises not normally open to the public; primarily in the interests of safety, this is not allowed unless the photographer first obtains a permit through the Public Relations & Publicity Officer of the Region concerned. While British Railways endeavour to give all reasonable and practicable encouragement to bona fide photographers whose work is of a recognised standard, the number of such permits is necessarily very restricted and we would advise applicants to support their case with as good evidence as possible of their qualifications.

"Permits are normally granted only for sections of line or other places free from third-rail electrification, nor are they readily granted in respect of all busy junctions or sections of line having tunnels or lengthy cuttings. A little careful research will nearly always discover suitable over-bridges, embankments, or other vantage points from which good photographs can be obtained without actually entering railway property."

Before the war I used Agfa Isopan Fplates, developed in Pyro Metol, and found them very good. Now that Agfa materials are no longer available, I have discovered an even better combination of plate and developer. Ilford HP3 plates developed in Johnson's Fine Grain Developer are fast and almost grainless.

My usual practice is to expose during the summer months (April to September) at ⅟₅₀₀sec with aperture f11. I develop the result for 12min in the developer at 65deg. The resultant negative is strong and grainless, and usually prints well on 'soft' grade paper. I sometimes use Kodak P1200 plates. With the same exposure, I develop them for 20-25min at the same temperature. In my film camera I use HP3 or Kodak SS Pan films, and obtain admirable results by following the makers' instructions for developing.

It is, I am certain, a bad thing to change from one kind of plate (or film) to another,

One of the classic locations used by Eric Treacy was Olive Mount cutting, Liverpoool, from where 'Jubilee' No. 5603 *Solomon Islands* emerges with a train from Hull in the late 1930s.

A 1959 shot of A4 No. 60007 *Sir Nigel Gresley* climbing away from Leeds Central Station with the up 'White Rose' to London King's Cross.

although necessity sometimes forces this on us. We shall achieve much better results if we standardise on a certain emulsion and developer, the joint performance of which we thoroughly understand.

I do not propose to say anything about dark room technique, as this is dealt with adequately in the standard photographic handbooks. I must, however, outline some of the reasons for spoiled negatives. The most

frequent causes of failure are dirty cameras or plate holders, which produce pin-holes on the negatives; tight packing of slides in camera cases, which causes light streaks on the negatives; lack of constancy in temperatures of the developer, hypo, and washing water, which produce grain or reticulation; and dirty dishes or dusty darkroom resulting in a host of negative defects. All developers should be filtered before use.

"Every photographer has a vision of his ideal picture"

All those who claim to be serious photographers will wish to undertake their own developing and printing. A large proportion of the satisfaction of this hobby is in the processes which follow the exposure. Moreover, we cannot expect the same painstaking treatment of our negatives by someone who knows nothing of our enthusiasms—nor our longing that a particular exposure should receive very special treatment. Therefore, in our budget, we must allow for darkroom equipment, and a reliable enlarger.

Taking the photograph is, of course, the heart of the matter. It is not the slightest use having the right camera and a train in a perfect setting, if one is not able to make a satisfactory picture of it. Every photographer has a vision of his ideal picture; it is something that he will never achieve, and a very good thing that he does not! For it is the hope of one day achieving a study that will satisfy in every respect that is our incentive; and if ever we fulfilled our ideal, I think we should find our incentive gone.

My aim in railway photography is not just to produce a technically flawless picture of a train, sharp all over, and so placed that neither trees nor telegraph poles sprout out of the boiler. What I want to do is to interpret in visual form the feeling that the railway arouses in me. It consists of so much that is intangible – lighting, smells, sounds, relationships, memories, and so on.

The first thing I would say about 'taking the picture' is that we should see the subject not so much as something to record, but as something which we are going to use to symbolise something much bigger than we can see through our view finder.

Let us now consider some practical details. The first is viewpoint. Fully 75 per cent of the effectiveness of a railway photograph is governed by the setting in which the train is placed. It is this which makes the difference between a picture and a record. Therefore we need to precede our photography with some careful planning, for which it is necessary to know details about the position of the sun, the gradients, and the surrounding country.

As we travel by train, we frequently shall spot places which will suit our purposes, and to these we can return when opportunity permits. I would far rather take one picture in the right setting, than half a dozen in undistinguished surroundings.

It goes without saying that we have to arrange our position so that nothing obtrudes ▶

Above: A visit to Paddington in 1953 sees No. 70027 *Rising Star* departing for Plymouth.

Right: 'Royal Scot' No. 46109 *Royal Engineers* heads a Leeds-Bradford train away from Leeds City in 1950.

Below: LMS 4F No. 4153 on an Edge Hill to Crewe mixed goods train is signalled into the loop at Edge Hill.

A view from The Keep at Newcastle-upon-Tyne as Gresley Class V1 2-6-2T No. 67673 departs from Newcastle Central with a local service.

from the background to interfere with the train. I remember once photographing a train at Hellifield without noting too carefully the background, only to find, when the negative was developed, that two cows on a distant hillside appeared to be perched on the top of the engine's boiler.

It will be found that certain engines have a viewpoint which suits them better than others. For instance, the formerly streamlined Class

A rare Treacy shot from the footplate of an LNER B1 near Thirsk while working a Newcastle-Liverpool express.

7s of the LMR are hideous when photographed almost head-on from ground level. They look rather like large black crows with wings outspread, about to 'take off', whereas, taken from a high viewpoint, above the height of the engine, the 'cut-off' smokebox gives an impression of power and thrust.

The rebuilt 'Royal Scots' are, in my opinion, best photographed from an angle of about 60 deg so that the powerful looking double chimney is seen from the side. There will be many opinions about this; and I will say only that even the ugliest of modern engines will be found (like human beings) to have an angle from which they look their best!

There are those who mount their cameras on tripods and focus carefully for each exposure; but my method is to work with a fixed mark scratched on my focusing scale.

By trial and error I have discovered that point of focus which, at an aperture of f 6.3, larger than which I never expose, gives me a sharp image from about 30ft to infinity. For a wider field of focus, I reduce my aperture and make adjustment when developing.

Most of my work is done near large stations and junctions, as in such places one finds a setting more typical of the railway than in the open country. Therefore my trains are not moving very fast, and I find an exposure of ⅟₅₀₀th of a second sufficient for my purposes. In open country, where trains are moving at 60mph or more, I need to use a speed of ⅟₁₀₀₀th of a second to arrest motion. The advantage of my fixed focus method is that I can come into action immediately. Quite often, something unexpected will turn up which would be lost if a tripod had to be set up and focus carefully adjusted. Moreover, there are some spots in which it would be quite impossible to spread oneself in such a way.

The aperture and shutter set, one waits for the moment of exposure. In this, never watch the train; that is fatal. Instead, the eye should be fixed, and kept fixed, on that point on the track at which it has been decided to take the photograph. If the camera is not fitted with open sights (wire frame viewfinder), difficulty may be found in sighting the train through a small glass viewfinder. In such circumstances, it may be advisable to compose the picture through the finder, with the camera mounted on a tripod, and make exposure as one watches the train by direct vision.

While on this point, I would like to add a note of advice on a small matter in which care is amply repaid. Have your slides numbered and keep a careful record of each exposure, noting the number of the slide, and details of the train, place, date, time of day, plate used, light, and exposure. These particulars can be very useful in standardising the method of exposing and processing. Whenever I study my photographic records I find some new fact emerges of great value to my future activities.

The quality and direction of the light are perhaps the most important factors in the production of a good photograph. In these islands, it is by no means easy to ensure the right lighting conditions. At least, that is true in the north, where I do most of my photography. The sun, which is essential for sparkling and lively results, can rarely be relied upon to shine when we want it. Clouds and hills are frequent companions. Perhaps the flatter areas of the south are luckier in this respect.

During a recent holiday, I waited eight days for a gleam of sunshine. Oddly enough, the light is photographically at its worst at midsummer, except in the evening and early morning, when the sun is lower in the sky. The months of spring and autumn give the best lighting conditions. During these months, the cooler atmosphere produces more exhaust from the engine, and the sun is not so high in the sky that it throws such dense shadows. The brittle light of winter can produce some very lovely results, but it is so weak that there is a risk of serious under-exposure in the shadows.

Normally, we should operate with the sun shining from behind us at an angle of not less than 45 deg on the train. This should light up the wheels and motion of the engine. When the sun is right overhead (as it is at midday in the summer) it produces the most disappointing results. Unfortunately, the sun is in this position for all the midday procession of trains to the south as it passes my favourite pitch on Shap.

I would not, however, lay down any hard and fast rules about this, as it is possible to obtain some striking results with the sun slightly behind the engine. In such circumstances, care must be taken that the shadowed front of the engine is not lost in an area of shadow behind it.

In this kind of photography, an exposure

"Most of my work is done near large stations and junctions."

Black smoke for the benefit of the cameraman from 'Royal Scot' No. 6101 *Royal Scots Grey*.

'Jubilee' No. 45726 *Vindictive* passes Greskine signalbox, north of Beattock summit, with a Birmingham-Edinburgh train in 1959.

meter is not much use, as the conditions in which we work dictate our speed and aperture. The speed of the train governs our exposure, and the requisite field of focus governs the aperture. As I have said already, I make my adjustments in my developing dish rather than on my camera. Plates that I know to be under-exposed I give three or four minutes longer in the developer.

One thing I recommend in all lighting conditions is the use of a lens hood. It is most important to cut out all unwanted light from the scene we are photographing. However great the temptation, I never expose in dull weather; the results are always muddy and lifeless. ■

Former LBSCR I3 Class 4-4-2T No. 32021 gets away from Groombridge with 10.52am Tunbridge Wells West to Victoria service on May 21, 1951. The loco was withdrawn in the September of 1951, and cut up at Brighton Works. A J K WADMORE

The British 4-4-2 tank engine

By PETER WINDING

ON the withdrawal of Nos. 30582 and 30584 by the Southern Region last year, the 4-4-2 tank engine became extinct on British Railways, and one more familiar type of locomotive has passed into the limbo of history. That is, with two exceptions – the preserved London, Tilbury & Southend Railway No. 80, *Thundersley*, and the Adams tank No. 30583 (London & South Western No 488), now owned and operated by the Bluebell Railway.

Of all British tank engines, the 4-4-2 type was probably the most elegant. It belonged to an era when locomotive engineers regarded it as a part of their job to produce engines that were aesthetically pleasing, and if their performance was not always on a par with their looks, they are nevertheless still remembered with affection by all who admired the classic symmetry that was the hallmark of British locomotive practice some 50 years ago.

At the time of the Grouping, in 1923, the four main-line companies mustered a total of 454 4-4-2 tanks. As a type, the zenith of its popularity was around 1910, although the maximum number in service was not reached until 1915. Thereafter, the total declined slightly to the 1923 level, and by the advent of British Railways, in 1948, had fallen to a total of 267.

Considering that the 4-4-2 tank was an adaptation of the ubiquitous 4-4-0 type, it is remarkable that it was not taken up before 1880, and then only to a very limited extent. Indeed, for many years it remained the exclusive protégé of one man, William Adams. At a time when the fashionable trend was towards inside cylinders he saw a special virtue in having them outside, and this no doubt explains why he adopted the leading bogie wheel arrangement.

Other designers did not follow his example, partly because they were convinced that inside-cylinder machines set up less severe stresses, and also because the overall size of the 4-4-2 tank must have made it seem something of a luxury compared with much smaller and more compact four-coupled tank engines which performed suburban duties at that time. At a later period, Adams himself adopted the 0-4-4 tank, and one only has to think of the Lancashire & Yorkshire 2-4-2 tanks to realise that the leading bogie was superfluous.

There is an understandable tendency to regard the 4-4-2 tank as an elite type of tank engine intended for express duties. In fact, with the notable exception of the London, Brighton & South Coast Railway 13 class, they were all designed for suburban or local passenger duties, and with the further exception of the Great Western 'County' tanks and the London & North Western 'Precursor' tanks, this is clearly borne out by their somewhat meagre dimensions. The mention of these last two types emphasises that several

4-4-2 tank classes were directly derived from successful 4-4-0 designs, sometimes with no further alteration than a reduction in the diameter of the driving wheels.

Broadly, so far as Britain is concerned, the development of the 4-4-2 tank was commenced in 1880 and concluded in 1915, although new engines were added to existing classes until 1930. When compared with the development of other well-known types, its history is a peculiar one, and this is best revealed by treating it chronologically.

The first railway to use the type was the London, Tilbury & Southend, and, as already mentioned, the design was by William Adams, who at that time was Locomotive Superintendent of the London & South Western Railway. The precise details of how he came to undertake the job are not clear, but the reason he was chosen was certainly because of his former connection with the Eastern Counties Railway, which supplied the motive power to work the Tilbury line. By 1879, Adams had produced for the South Western his leading bogie, four-coupled 'Steamroller' classes, and it is readily apparent that he used the 4-4-0 tank as a basis for the Tilbury 4-4-2 tank.

The latter was a simple, sturdy machine with two outside cylinders and 6ft 1in diameter driving wheels. A total of 36 were built, and they must have given every satisfaction. Under the LMSR renumbering scheme of 1929 they became Nos. 2056-2091; the last was withdrawn in 1935.

Adams, too, must have felt well satisfied, because in 1883 he put a basically similar design into service on the South Western.

This was the famous 0415 class, as they came to be known, and by 1886 he had built 71, plus a further dozen similar engines that he rebuilt from his earlier design of 4-4-0 tank. These engines handled the bulk of the extensive suburban and outer-suburban services on the South Western until the turn of the century, and were, by all accounts, highly satisfactory machines. Although their wheel diameter was only 5ft 7in, they had a good turn of speed, and Ahrons (British engineer and author) states that they regularly worked to

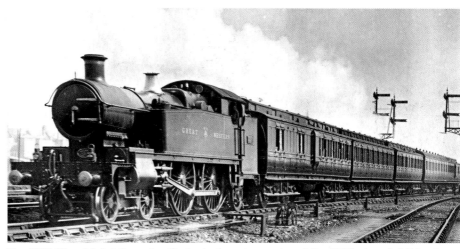

The GWR 'County' 4-4-2 was in effect a tank engine version of the 3800 class 4-4-0 tender locomotives and 30 were built between 1905 and 1912 for London suburban services before being replaced by the 6100 class from 1931. No. 2235 heads a suburban service west from London Paddington in 1930. *RM* ARCHIVE

schedules that required an average speed of more than 40mph.

The 0415 class was the most numerous of 4-4-2 tanks ever built for a British railway, and as a class it was also the most long-lived, spanning a period of 78 years. It is perhaps only fair to point out that all but three of the class had passed to the scrap heap 30 years ago, and that the survivors owed their longevity to the peculiarities of the Axminster branch. It is one of this trio that now has the distinction of being the last working 4-4-2 tank in the country, and surely no engine ever had a more charmed existence!

Commencing life in March 1885, it was withdrawn from service by the LSWR in September 1917, and disposed of to the Government General Salvage Depot at Sittingbourne. By a stroke of good fortune it was resold to the East Kent Railway in 1919 and remained in that service until 1946, when it was purchased by the Southern Railway and entered into stock as No. 3488. With the final reconstruction of the Axminster branch in 1961, its end must have seemed certain, but again it was rescued, this time by a sixth owner – the Bluebell Railway.

In 1888, the 4-4-2 tank appeared for the first time as an inside-cylinder machine, when

Mr Hurry Riches built a class of six engines for the Taff Vale Railway. They had a shorter total wheelbase than the Adams engines, coupled wheels only 5ft 3in in diameter, and a somewhat more generous heating surface and grate area. The class is interesting as the only 4-4-2 tank built for a Welsh company. They were constructed between 1888 and 1892 and survived just long enough to become GWR Nos. 1301-1306. Thus, after 12 years, Adams had only one convert, but the year 1892 was to prove more auspicious!

Francis William Webb, no less, ordained that Crewe should put the type on record, and 10 somewhat-tarnished Metropolitan-type 4-4-0 tanks of 1871 were duly given a respectable bunker and a pair of trailing wheels.

A more regal gesture from an equally unexpected quarter came when the Wirral Railway celebrated its recent amalgamation with the Seacombe-Hoylake & Deeside Railway by taking delivery of a brand new 4-4-2 tank. This engine was an inside-cylinder side-tank with 5ft 3in driving wheels. The dimensions were modest – 16in x 24in cylinders, total heating surface 981.6sq ft and a grate area of 15.75sq ft.

Principal interest attaches to the fact that the engine was a prototype. It was the sole 4-4-2 tank owned by the Wirral and was No. 1 until renumbered 6830 by the LMSR, which scrapped it in 1924.

The years that followed were not auspicious. Adams had abandoned the type in favour of 0-4-4 tanks, other designers were turning over to six-coupled designs, and all interest in the 4-4-2 tank seems to have died a natural death. Indeed, for five years this hiatus is so complete that it serves as a demarcation between what may be regarded as the first and second phases.

In retrospect it seems appropriate that the second phase in the development of the 4-4-2 ▶

TYPICAL BRITISH 4-4-2 TANK ENGINES

Railway	Date		Class	Wheel dia.	Cylinders		Boiler pressure	Grate area	Total htg. surf.	Weight in wkg. ord.	
					dia.	stroke					
				ft. in.	in.	in.	lb.	sq. ft.	sq. ft.	tons	cwt.
L.T.S.	1880		1P	6 1	17	26	160	17.25	1,020	56	3
L.S.W.	1883		0415	5 7	17½	24	160	18.14	1,059	54	2
T.V.	1888			5 3	17½	26	160	19.00	1,209		
G.N.	1898		C12	5 7½	17½	26	170	20.8	1,250	62	6
G.C.	1903	†	C13	5 7	18	26	160	19.59	1,101	66	13
L.N.W.	1906		3P	6 3	19	26	175	22.4	1,939	75	15
L.B.S.C.	1906		I1	5 6	17½	26	170	17.35	1,045	66	10
L.B.S.C.	1908	*	I3	6 7½	21	26	180	23.75	1,500	76	0
L.B.S.C.	1908	*	I4	6 6	20	26	170	17.35	1,098	70	5
G.W.	1905	*	2221	6 8½	18	30	200	20.35	1,348	75	0
L.T.S.	1905	a	3P	6 6	19	26	170	19.77	1,099	71	3
N.B.	1911	‡	C15	5 9	18	26	175	15.8	1,235	68	15
G.W.	1914	*	4600	5 8	17	24	200	16.6	1,271	60	13
Furness	1915	*	—	5 8	18	24	160		1,070	59	15

(Certain detail alterations within classes are not specified)
* Superheated
a L.M.S.R. built engines had a total heating surface of 1,205
† Later rebuilt with superheater
‡ Original boiler 1,309 sq. ft. and 16.6 sq. ft. grate area

tank should have been heralded by the LTSR. This new design appeared in 1897 and was the work of Thomas Whitelegg. It was in most respects simply an enlargement of the Adams type, but with 6ft 6in diameter driving wheels. The class consisted of 12 engines, numbered 37-48. Subsequently, they were rebuilt at Plaistow in 1905-11, and in this form became the basis of the final design which was multiplied by the LMSR to 1930.

This class was followed by a further series of 6ft 6in engines, Nos. 51-68, in 1900-1903. The latter remained in their original condition, and became Nos. 2092-2109 under the LMSR (1929) renumbering scheme. Towards the end of their days they were sent to the Midlands in the hope that some use might be made of them. In fact, very little was, and they spent years lying about at various depots before the last of them was withdrawn in 1953.

The Tilbury's addiction to 4-4-2 tanks probably surprised no one, but when Ivatt of the Great Northern adopted the type for suburban duties quite a few eyebrows must have been raised. The Great Northern suburban services were certainly no picnic, and the tough grades might well have suggested, as they did a few years later, that something more than a pair of four coupled wheels was called for. Not that the Ivatt design was underpowered; it was, in fact, quite a hefty machine weighing nearly 63 tons, and slightly larger than Drummond's contemporary M7 class 0-4-4 tank.

However, despite their very capable performance, they did not long monopolise these arduous duties, as by 1906 Ivatt had put his faith in 0-6-2 tanks. Thereafter, the 4-4-2 tanks were gradually superseded on the London services, and departed for greener pastures, where the majority of them continued to flourish on local passenger and branch-line services until well into the diesel era. The design was derived from his small 4-4-0s, and the class consisted of 60 engines built between 1898 and 1907. They were classified C1 by the LNER and those that went to British Railways took the numbers 67350-95/97-99.

It is difficult to say whether Ivatt's contribution influenced the vogue in 4-4-2 tanks that followed. If one were to draw a parallel with his Atlantics the answer would definitely be in the affirmative. At all events there is no doubt that it had a profound influence on D Earle Marsh, who was his chief assistant mechanical engineer at Doncaster, before accepting the post of locomotive superintendent on the LBSCR in December 1904. Marsh produced his first passenger tank design in 1906, and as it was intended for suburban duties it is very strange that he adopted the 4-4-2 wheel arrangement when his predecessor Robert Billinton, and Ivatt, had already clearly demonstrated the superiority of

A drawing office photograph shows the attractive lines of GNR C12 No. 1509 that dates from 1919. *RM* ARCHIVE

Former Great Central Class C13 No. 5055 stands at Manchester Central on July 29, 1939, with a suburban service. This loco became No. 67429 in BR capital stock. E S RUSSELL

The Taff Vale Railway built six 'C' class 4-4-2Ts from 1888, and were the first of that wheel arrangement to appear in the UK with inside cylinders. They were later rebuilt as 4-4-0s for working autotrains, and scrapped by the GWR between 1925 and 1927. No. 170 sits in the yard at Cathays in the early 1920s. Note the valances on the pony wheels. LPC

the 0-6-2 tank for this type of work. Between September 1906, and March 1908, Marsh evolved four classes of 4-4-2 tank for the Brighton, three of them for suburban traffic, and one for express passenger duties.

The three suburban types were unmistakably based on Ivatt's design, but unlike the latter they proved to be deplorable machines, and notwithstanding three bites at the cherry, there was little to choose between them. They were classified I1, I2 and I4, and

consisted of 20, 10 and five engines, respectively. Between 1925 and 1932, REL Maunsell transformed class I1 by rebuilding them with spare Billinton B4-type boilers. In this guise most of them survived into the era of British Railways, although they did very little work during their last years.

By way of contrast with these failures, the Marsh I3 class express passenger tank was a striking success, and has come to be regarded as a landmark of British locomotive practice.

Yet, in its first form, it was nothing more than a tank engine version of Billinton's excellent B4-type 4-4-0. However, although the prototype, No. 21, had all the qualities of a sound design, Marsh was prevailed on by his chief draughtsman, B K Field, to incorporate a superheater. As redesigned, the second engine differed considerably from No. 2 and subsequently, the whole class, consisting of 27 engines, was brought into line with the second specification, except that No. 21 retained her larger 6ft 9in diameter driving wheels.

The general history of this class is well known, but it is worth emphasising that it was the only class of 4-4-2 tank that was specifically designed for express passenger duties, and certainly the only one that seriously challenged the ubiquitous 4-4-0 on its own ground.

The performance of these superb engines may be roughly summarised by the fact that for many years they handled trains of approximately 245 tons between London and Brighton to the crack schedule of one hour, and sometimes achieved start-to-stop average speeds that did not fall far short of 55mph. Even with the heaviest trains, amounting to 350 tons behind the engine, they could be relied on to average rather more than 40mph, and for their size they were undoubtedly one of the most economical engines ever built. As renumbered by British Railways they became 32021-3/5-30, and with the exception of 2024, which was scrapped in 1944, the remainder lasted until 1950/52.

Chronologically, the next designer to exploit the 4-4-2 tank after Ivatt was G J Robinson of the Great Central. His first class consisted of 40 engines and were built between 1903/5. They worked the London suburban traffic until the advent of the 4-6-2 tank in 1911, and then migrated northwards. A second class of 12 engines appeared in 1907, identical with the first in all basic dimensions, but having a larger coal and water capacity, and therefore somewhat heavier. Like the Ivatt engines, they proved very suitable for cross-country and provincial suburban trains.

Subsequently, both classes were superheated, and they could be found all over the North Midlands from Hull to Liverpool and had a long working life. All entered British Railways stock as Nos. 67400-67451 with their LNER classification of C13 and C14, and were mostly withdrawn between 1955/1959, leaving one of each class in service at the beginning of 1960.

In 1905, the 4-4-2 tank really came to town when George Whale of the North Western, and G J Churchward of the Great Western, each adopted it for their London suburban services.

A further coincidence was that both types were derived from express passenger 4-4-0s. In the case of Whales' 'Precursor' tanks, the principal difference was that he reduced the

London, Tilbury & Southend Railway 4-4-2T works past Kentish Town on August 23, 1939, with a St Pancras to Barking service. The loco ended its days as No. 41974 at Skipton. *RM* ARCHIVE

LNER C16 class No. 67499 crossing the Tay Bridge from Dundee to Wormit with a local train in 1953. *RM* ARCHIVE

driving wheel diameter from 6ft 9in to 6ft 3in. They worked the London and Birmingham local services for many years, the London engines being displaced around 1932. Under the LMSR 1929 numbering scheme they were given Nos. 6780-6829, and the last one was withdrawn from service in 1940.

Churchward's 'County' tanks were, as their name implies, derived from the outside-cylinder 'County' class 4-4-0s. For a reason that is obscure, he retained the big 6ft 8½in driving wheels, although the engines were intended for suburban work. Combined with the very high running plate and relatively small boiler, the effect of the big wheels was emphasised, and the action of these engines when running bunker first was quite unforgettable. Throughout their comparatively short life they were mostly to be found on the services between Paddington and Didcot, their main shed being Old Oak Common.

They were numbered 2221-2250 and began to be withdrawn in 1930. During 1932/1933 most of their duties were taken over by 6100 class 2-6-2 tanks, and older readers may well remember that for a considerable time there was always a row of them lying derelict in the yard outside Old Oak Common shed. The last half-dozen of them was withdrawn from service in 1935, having outlived their 4-4-0 counterparts by rather more than a year.

The Great Western built one other 4-4-2 tank, a kind of miniature 'County' tank with 5ft 8in wheels, a smaller boiler, less grate area, and small 17in x 24in cylinders. This engine, No. 4600, was built at Swindon in 1914, and was evidently intended as the prototype for a standard class for branch-line and local service. For some reason that may have had to do with the outbreak of war, no further examples were built, and after an unusually ▶

short life, the prototype was cut up in 1925.

It is interesting to notice that until 1910, with the exception of a few brief essays by provincial companies, the use of the 4-4-2 tank was practically confined to London and the Home Counties. At about this time they could be found working into all the main line termini except those that were operated exclusively by the South Eastern & Chatham and the Great Eastern Railways. The position was somewhat altered in 1911 when the North British Railway introduced the type into Scotland. These engines were designed by W B Reid for secondary main-line passenger duties and suburban traffic in the Edinburgh and Glasgow areas.

The design was a very handsome one, with inside cylinders and 5ft 9in driving wheels. The first 30 engines, classified C15 by the LNER, used saturated steam, and were built by the Yorkshire Engine Company between 1911 and 1913. A later series, with superheaters and classified C16, was built between 1915 and 1921. Under the British Railways renumbering scheme the C15 class became 67452-81, and Class C16, 67482-502.

Although they never strayed far from the parent system, they were widely distributed, especially after 1930 when 2-6-2 tanks began to supersede them on the heavier duties. They then took over a wide variety of cross-country and branch-line services, but some could still be seen at work in the Edinburgh district during the 1940s. Although in no sense spectacular, they were sound runners and gave many years of useful service.

The scrapping of the C15 class commenced in 1952 and the C16s began to go in 1955. Both classes survived until 1961, but they did little work during their last years, spending most of the time in store, or on such humble duties as acting as stationary boilers.

While remarking that the NBR was the only Scottish railway to adopt the 4-4-2 tank, it is interesting to recall that the use of McIntosh designs in Belgium gave rise to two quite numerous classes of 4-4-2 tank that were developed from his 'Dunalastair' class 4-4-0s. Both of these classes survived on the SNCB until recent years, and it is very probable that some of the later class are still in service. The author saw two of them in a Dutch scrapyard only a few months ago.

Apart from the railways already mentioned, the only other lines to use the 4-4-2 tanks were the Midland & Great Northern Joint, the North Stafford, the Furness, and the Brecon & Merthyr. The latter only had one example, a converted 'Steamroller' which it purchased from the LSWR in 1914. This engine lasted just long enough to become GWR No 1391.

The MGN JR had three; they were derived from the earlier successful Beyer Peacock 'A' class 4-4-0 type, and are interesting as having been built at Melton Constable between 1904

The Midland & Great Northern Class A 4-4-2T (later LNER C17) No. 20 waits with a passenger train at Cromer Beach station in 1922. RM ARCHIVE

A classic Victorian design, LSWR 0415 class No. 30583 of Exmouth Junction shed, has come to a halt at Lyme Regis station with the 12.40pm from Axminster on May 11, 1958. This loco is preserved at the Bluebell Railway. BRIAN MORRISON

Beyer Peacock-built Wirral Railway No. 1 passes Bidston East Junction with the 3.16pm Birkenhead Park-West Kirby on April 20, 1919. The loco was absorbed into LMS stock and renumbered 6830, but scrapped in 1924. KEN NUNN NO. 2163

and 1909. They were taken into LNER stock on January 1, 1937, and classified C17. The first to be withdrawn was No. 020 in 1942, followed by Nos. 09 and 041 in 1944.

In 1911, the NSR introduced a handsome inside-cylinder design for its local services. This class consisted of six engines built at Stoke Works and was numbered 13, 14, 39, 45, 46 and 55. The LMSR renumbered them 2181-86 in order of building, but, like most NSR engines, their non-standard characteristics condemned them to a short life, and all were withdrawn by 1935.

The same remark applies to the six superheater tanks designed by Pettigrew for the Furness Railway in 1915. They were not unlike the NSR class in appearance, and deserved a better fate than to be written off after a working life of only 15 years. They were built to work the Coniston, Kendal, and Windermere branch lines, and also worked the local passenger service on the Cleator & Workington Railway. As built, they were numbered 38-43, and became Nos. 11080-85 on the LMSR. All were withdrawn between 1930 and 1932, and were largely superseded by 'Precursor' tanks.

It remains to deal briefly with subsequent developments on the LTSR, where in strange contrast to the brief encounters already noticed, the 4-4-2 tank still 'queened it' on an undisputed throne! Reference has been made earlier to the rebuilding of Nos. 37-48 from 1905 onwards, and that this enlarged version formed the basis of a third and final class – Nos. 37-48 (LMSR Nos. 2135-46), which were supplemented in 1909 by four new engines, Nos. 79-82 (LMSR Nos 2147-2150),

Former LNWR ''Precursor' tank loco No. 6811, designed by George Whale, heads the Penrith portion of the 'Lakes Express' away from Oxenholme in 1934. All 50 locos built between 1906/9 had been withdrawn by 1939. H GORDON TIDEY

of which No. 80 was the celebrated *Thundersley*. At this point the story of the Tilbury tanks might well have ended, as the next design was a class of eight rather unwieldy Baltic tanks, with a limited route availability.

Under the Midland regime no further construction was undertaken, but in 1923, when the need for new engines had become urgent, the LMSR decided (as was then its policy) to multiply the best available existing type, which in this case was the final version of the Tilbury's 4-4-2 tank. Altogether, between

1923 and 1930, a further 35 of this class was added to stock, bringing the total up to 51. These later engines were practically identical with the earlier ones and took the numbers 2110-2134 and 2151-2160. These were the last 4-4-2 tanks built for a British railway, and it is a most remarkable coincidence that they were put to work on the same line that had been the first to use them.

The withdrawal of this class was commenced in 1951 and the last to go was in 1960, and although they began to be superseded by the Stanier 2-6-4 tanks from about 1935 onwards, they remained very much in evidence on the Tilbury section until quite recently. None of them was ever superheated, and with their 6ft 6in wheels and modest dimensions it is a marvel that they did so well. One can only conclude that their performance owed a great deal to excellent maintenance, and the skill of drivers who knew their engines by long experience. It is a well-known fact that off the parent line they were cordially detested!

As to why a design dating from 1905 remained in sole charge of such exacting duties for so long, the most probable explanation is that the insularity of the Tilbury section caused the LMSR authorities to regard it as a system within a system, bound by its own traditions and able to manage well enough with the equipment it was used to. Such a policy could not last for ever, but at least it saved money at a time when it was needed elsewhere.

Whether or not this theory is the answer, the fact remains that the London, Tilbury & Southend made the 4-4-2 tank peculiarly its own, and few railways have ever been so closely identified with a single type of locomotive. ■

LT&S 4-4-2T No. 80 *Thundersley* is serviced at Shoeburyness shed after working the RCTS 'Southend Centenary' special on March 11, 1956. The tour started at Bishopsgate goods depot. TRACKS NORTH ARCHIVE

The vast size of Tinsley marshalling yard in June 1976 is seen behind EM1 class electric No. 76054 passing through the yard with a rake of empty coal wagons, while 'master and slave' shunter No. 13003 runs back to the reception sidings to collect more wagons to sort. RAIL PHOTOPRINTS

Hub of Sheffield

Tinsley marshalling yard, freight terminal and diesel depot are principal features of rationalisation scheme

CENTREPIECE of the rationalisation of railway facilities in the Sheffield area is the new freight marshalling yard at Tinsley, which was officially opened by Lord Beeching, formerly Chairman of British Railways Board, on October 29.

It is more than two miles long and nearly a quarter-of-a-mile wide – covering an area of 145 acres – contains nearly 60 miles of track, and can handle up to 4,000 wagons a day. Included in the £10million scheme is a large freight terminal at Grimesthorpe and a diesel locomotive maintenance depot, adjacent to the marshalling yard.

The yard, terminal and depot were the basic requirements of a plan by the Eastern Region to eliminate the many disadvantages inherent in the unplanned growth of railways in and around Sheffield. Choice of sites, and other features introduced into the rationalisation proposals, which were approved by the Minister of Transport four years ago, will be described in a further article.

Tinsley Marshalling Yard has been designed to deal primarily with traffic to and from the Sheffield industrial area. More than 70% will be of local origin or destination, and some 80% of this will be private-siding traffic: by its very nature, much is unsuitable for conveyance by 'freightliners', nor can it be received or forwarded in through trainloads.

The remaining traffic consists of wagons 'staged' through Tinsley between points which have no through services, or traffic which is unsuitable for existing through trains. The introduction of freightliners is likely to reduce the volume of such traffic passing through Tinsley Yard but, on the other hand, plans in hand for the re-routing of trans-Pennine traffic may well reverse this trend.

The yard and diesel maintenance depot together occupy an area of about 145 acres, 115 of which it was necessary to purchase from 12 owners. This area, north-east of the city, was virtually undeveloped, and acquisition did not involve disturbance of

From *The Railway Magazine*, December 1965

existing industrial, commercial or residential premises. Negotiations were, however, to some extent complicated by the necessity to provide replacement land for one of the vendors, who had developed plans for a foundry extension on part of the area required for the yard, and also by the fact that the proposed Sheffield-Leeds motorway would encroach on the area.

Parliamentary powers for the works and for the compulsory acquisition of the lands required (including the 'compensation' land) were obtained in the British Transport Commission Act, 1960.

While meeting operational needs in respect of access, the site chosen for the yard necessitated considerable earthworks before the layout could be started. In all, some 3.75 million tons of earth had to be moved.

The fact that traffic would arrive from and depart in all directions made it undesirable to provide separate up and down yards. A large double-direction yard was therefore decided on. The multiplicity of divisions required by the complex of private sidings in the area made necessary a number of sorting sidings greater than could be accommodated in a single layout. The additional sidings were therefore arranged in the form of a secondary yard, access to them being along a common feed road starting in the main yard switching area. Work started on the yard layout in August 1961.

There are 11 reception lines, with capacities of between 63 and 74 wagons each, together with a hump engine return line and a train engine line. The south-west arrival line and reception lines 6-11 are electrified on the 1500-V DC system as an extension of the existing Manchester-Sheffield electrification. This permits electric working

Examples of type 1, 3 and 4 diesels inside Tinsley's diesel maintenance shed. BRITISH RAIL

into and out of the yard, via Woodburn and Darnall Junctions, and thereby avoids the use of diesel locomotives between the yard and the electrified area, and the provision of traction-changing facilities.

In the main yard, there are 53 sidings in eight 'balloons'; their capacity varies from 53 to 77 wagons. Departures from sidings 16-48 are via the west departure lines, which are electrified.

Eastbound services from sidings 1-15 may be drawn back into the express freight and departure sidings before leaving in an easterly direction by a connection at the western end of the main yard, in order to avoid conflicting movements and possible

delay to hump shunting. The western ends of sidings 34-46 inclusive are wired for electric traction.

There are 25 secondary sorting sidings (Nos. 60-84), in four balloons; each has a capacity of 31 wagons. The sidings are used mainly for traffic for local destinations in the vicinity of Sheffield. As traffic is routed into the yard direct from the hump, it is thus subject to primary sorting, in the same way as traffic dealt with through the main yard.

There are five sidings in the express freight yard, wired for electric traction; each is capable of holding about 76 wagons. They are designed to accommodate through express freight trains requiring to detach and/or attach wagons, and also for eastbound departures from main yard sidings 1-15.

It was important that there should be access to the yard, from both directions, on both the former Great Central and the Midland lines. At the time the layout was planned, two connections only existed – that at Treeton, to the south-east, and at Brightside, to the south-west. Three new connections – towards Sheffield (south-west) and Mexborough (north-west) on the GC line, and towards Rotherham (north-east) on the Midland line – had, therefore, to be provided. The provision of these curves called for the acquisition of land from four owners.

The construction of the two curves at the western end of the yard involved the diversion of a length of the Sheffield & South Yorkshire Canal, the construction of a double-lift canal lock, and enlargement of a canal basin, and the building of two bridges (one of 70-ft span, the other of 164-ft span) over the canal.

One of the control tower staff discusses wagon movements with the arrivals yard. BRITISH RAIL

English Electric Type 3 No. D6806 and Brush Type 2 No. D5839 are just two of a variety of diesels that include Classes 08, 25, 31 and 47 outside Tinsley MPD on October 15, 1965. BRITISH RAIL

Dowty wagon speed control system

In a large hump marshalling yard, a wagon has to run between a quarter and a half of a mile from leaving the hump until it reaches the other wagons already in the sorting sidings. The more modern marshalling yards in this country have been equipped with two stages of retarders which brake the wagons by gripping the tyres in a vice-like action.

In the earlier installations of this type, the amount of braking applied was controlled by the retarder-operator, but more recently electronic equipment has been used to measure the weight of each wagon and its rolling resistance. This information is fed into a computer, which determines a suitable speed for the wagon and operates the retarder automatically to achieve the desired amount of braking.

This system has limitations, the principal one being that the computer has to predict how the wagon will run over the quarter-mile or more beyond the last retarder. Experience has shown that the rolling resistance of wagons is so variable that such predictions cannot be entirely reliable.

The Dowty system of wagon control, which is being used as a complete installation for the first time in the world at Tinsley, avoids the need for predicting the wagon's resistance by adopting a large

> "In the main yard, there are 53 sidings in eight 'balloons'; their capacity varies from 53 to 77 wagons."

number of small units, spaced out along the track. As the units are so close together – less than a wagon-wheelbase apart – no electronic equipment is required to vary the braking force. Instead, each unit contains a speed-sensing device which detects whether the wagon is going too quickly or too slowly compared with the designed speed, and actuates the appropriate response from the unit.

The unit consists of a small hydraulic ram in a cylinder, bolted vertically to the inside of the rail. The head of the ram normally stands above the rail and is pushed down by the flange of an approaching wheel (down stroke); it returns to the normal position as the wheel rolls away (up stroke). The incessant metallic clacks produced as the wagons pass over the apparatus are a distinctive sound of the yard.

The units are of two types. The simplest is the retarder, which has an effect only on a wagon which is exceeding the required speed, and is entirely self-contained. The other type of unit is the booster/retarder, which is capable of accelerating the slow wagon as well as retarding the fast wagon. For this dual action, it requires an external source of energy which is supplied from a high-pressure hydraulic pump and pipelines along the track. The fluid used is a light hydraulic oil. The units can be made for any

speed-setting but a small number of valves suffice for most conditions.

More than 20,000 of these various units are installed at Tinsley and it has been necessary to devise a means of testing them

From *The Railway Magazine*, December 1965

and identifying faulty units. Equipment for this purpose has been designed by the chief mechanical and electrical engineer and constructed under his control by a Doncaster firm.

The testing machine is in the form of a two-wheeled trolley, avoiding interference with the reading which the retarders might have on a second pair of wheels. A locomotive pulls the trolley over the units at controlled speeds just above or just below the operating speed of the unit, and the trolley equipment records whether the unit retards, boosts or fails to operate. A continuous tape record enables defective units to be identified at once, thus facilitating maintenance, which will normally be done on a unit replacement basis.

At Tinsley, the saving of a diesel shunting locomotive results from the installation of Dowty units (12ft/sec) all the way along the mechanical feed road from the main hump through the main yard to the secondary yard. The wagons pass over the secondary yard hump and are sorted into the appropriate sidings in accordance with the cut-card information transmitted to the main hump from the reception area.

Two control towers have been provided, one at the entrance to the main sorting sidings and one at the entrance to the secondary sorting sidings. The main yard control tower, west of the main hump, is

situated between the fourth and fifth balloons of the main sorting sidings. It is a four-storey building, comprising relay room, staff accommodation, signal engineering workshop and control room. The second yard control tower is a two-storey building – relay room and operating room – situated to the west of the secondary hump.

The administrative block is sited opposite the main yard hump summit, and accommodates the yard manager and his staff, together with accommodation for trainmen.

Three new power signalboxes have been built in the yard area, and all worked points are electro-pneumatically operated. These are Shepcote Lane, Tinsley Park and Tinsley Yard. Shepcote Lane controls all movement at the west end and also signals trains on the GC Rotherham line, between Darnall West and Woodburn Junctions and Tinsley East/West Junctions.

Tinsley Park box, situated at the western end of the main yard, controls movements in that area and at the eastern end of the express freight and departure sidings. Tinsley Yard box is situated at the western end of the reception lines and controls movements in the whole of the reception area up to Treeton Junction, including the junction of the north-east and south-east curves. The existing Treeton Junction signalbox controls the junctions of these curves with the ex-Midland

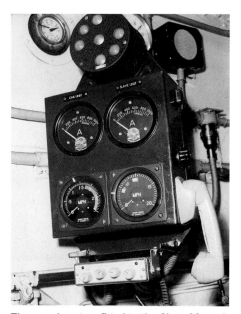

The speedometers fitted to the Class 13, and the cab control lights that repeat indications on ground signals. BRITISH RAIL

main lines.

A new signalbox – part power-operated, part mechanical – has also been built at Brightside Junction adjacent to the old box, to control the junction with the former Sheffield District Railway, and trains on this branch to Shepcote Lane Junction. The ex-Midland lines between Nunnery Main Line Junction and Wincobank station Junction are ▶

An overall view of Tinsley yard, with the control tower prominent. Since the yard closed in December 1984, the main part of the yard and the site of the MPD have been redeveloped. Through running lines remain, however, and there is a small freight terminal on site. TRACKS NORTH

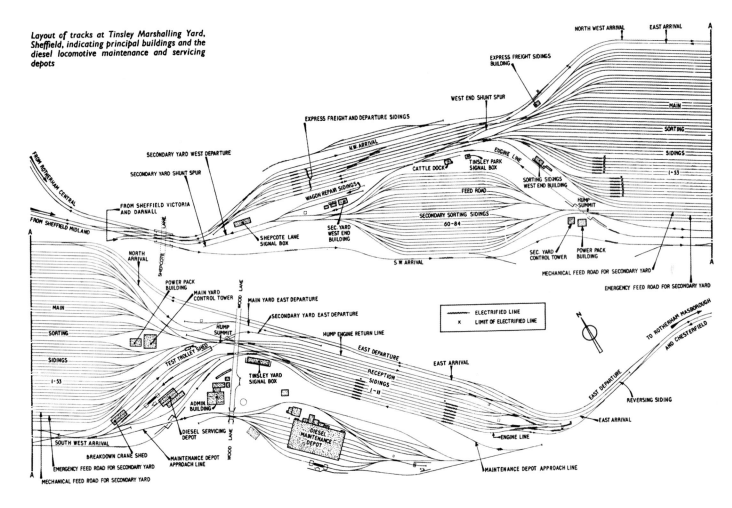

Layout of tracks at Tinsley Marshalling Yard, Sheffield, indicating principal buildings and the diesel locomotive maintenance and servicing depots

A diagram of the complex layout at Tinsley

also controlled from Brightside Junction.

An automatic telephone exchange serves the yard area for traffic and administrative purposes. The system also provides access to post-office lines, train control offices, local steelworks and Sheffield Midland station switchboard. Additional to the automatic system are special telephone circuits interconnecting the signalboxes in the yard area, and a regulating circuit connecting Aldwarke Junction with the yard boxes and main control tower.

Two-way loudspeaker circuits connect the main yard control tower and Tinsley Yard signalbox; and the signalbox, express freight

The booster and retarders that control a wagon's speed.

yard inspector, and main yard (west end) sidings. One-way amplified circuits are provided from the main control tower to the reception sidings and to the main yard (east end), and from Tinsley Park signalbox to the main yard (west end).

Radio-telephone equipment is provided from the main control tower and Tinsley Yard box to the 'humping' locomotives in the reception sidings. To facilitate fault-finding in the hydraulic system of the Dowty retarder installation, 'walkie-talkie' radio communication is provided to enable the maintenance fitters to keep in constant contact with the 'power-pack' cabins supplying the hydraulic power.

'Addo' data-transmission equipment has been installed to facilitate particulars of wagons arriving on the reception lines being accurately transmitted to the main control tower as quickly as possible. With a high degree of automation in the 'humping' process, accurate details of the make-up of trains in the reception area, which can be fed into the point-setting system, are essential.

On the arrival of a train on the reception line, the 'cutter' examines the wagons and records details in code on a cut-card. At the same time, the wagons are uncoupled according to route and destination. The cut

card shows the intended sorting siding into which the 'cut' will go, the number of wagons in each cut and the presence of a long wagon. This information is then sent by transmitting machine to the control tower. During transmission all details are printed in the same form as they appear on the cut-card and thus can be easily checked by the cutter.

The receiving instrument in the control tower also prints the information in the same form, and at the same time produces a punched tape for feeding into the point-setting control machine when the train is about to be shunted. This machine automatically sets the points for each cut in both the main and secondary sidings.

Special coding on the punched tape enables all the wagons to be counted and the total number of wagons in each siding is displayed on the indicators in the control tower. The main counter shows all the wagons, while a second counter records only those wagons which will later be re-sorted.

The yard has an allocation of three humping units, which provides one spare for maintenance. Each consists of two standard 350hp diesel-electric locomotives, permanently coupled and operated from one cab. They are modified to suit local conditions – such as train weights and

Master and slave No. D4502 (later 13002) propel a mixed rake of wagons over Tinsley's hump, before sorting into individual sidings.
TRACKS NORTH

gradients – and weighted with ballast in order to produce a 20-ton axle load. The units are fitted with cab-signalling apparatus, precision speedometers and two-way radio telephones.

The cab signals are displayed only when the units are between the east end of any of the reception sidings and the hump summit. The indications in the cab are controlled by signals transmitted through the rails from suitable points, governed by the condition of the track ahead. The indications in the cab, which do not necessarily repeat the fixed ground signals, enable the front of the train being propelled to proceed safely to a point within a few feet of a ground signal which is displaying a stop aspect, thus reducing to a minimum the time interval between the humping of consecutive trains.

The new marshalling yard at Tinsley is the concentration point for traffic originating and terminating within the area bounded by Penistone, Swinton and Mexborough to the north and Chesterfield to the south. The total volume of freight traffic originating within the Sheffield Division exceeds 24m tons per annum, the bulk of this emanating from the 150 private sidings located within this relatively small area. Sheffield is well placed in relation to the trunk routes which have been selected for development in the future,

and Tinsley Yard has convenient outlets to all these routes. The initial train plan does, in fact, anticipate the future freight train plan, so far as it is possible to do so at this stage.

Since July this year, under Stage I of the plan for the commissioning of the yard, when traffic was absorbed from the ex-Midland yards, through loads have been made up for Toton, Norton Junction, Washwood Heath, Healey Mills, Chaddesden, Leeds, Stanton Gate, Frodingham, Mottram, St Pancras, Gowhole, Leicester, Brent and Port Talbot. Additional outlets to Hunslet, Nottingham, Carlisle, York and Glasgow have been provided by through freight services calling at Tinsley.

With the start of the winter timetable, in October, traffic was absorbed from the former GC yards and through services provided to Lincoln, New England, Hull, Birkenhead, Liverpool Brunswick, Colwick, Doncaster, Whitemoor, King's Cross, Ferme Park and Worksop.

It was expected that at this stage the yard would be working near to the planned capacity of 4,000 wagons a day but, in the light of experience under actual working conditions, consideration will be given to transferring some of the remaining work from Masborough sorting sidings to Tinsley,

and to the extent to which work can be absorbed from farther afield. There are now about 130 trains into and out of the yard daily.

Diesel locomotive maintenance and servicing facilities

Tinsley Diesel Locomotive Maintenance Depot (code 41A) was completed in January 1964, but, because of restricted access, only daily servicing was undertaken up to April 1964, when all maintenance work was transferred from Darnall. When the changeover to diesel traction in the Sheffield Division is complete, the depot will maintain about 190 main line (mostly for freight duties) and 80 shunting locomotives. It will then cater for the maintenance of all diesel locomotives in the division, other than those allocated to and maintained at Wath.

The new shed is of the double-ended type, with a central administrative, amenities and workshop block. There are six tracks at each end of the shed, each providing accommodation for two main line locomotives, giving a total of 24 berths. The design permits of work on the locomotives being carried out simultaneously at three levels.

The equipment includes overhead cranes ▶

Almost new, D4502 stands by the maintenance shed. BRITISH RAIL

on selected roads, and bulk storage and dispensing facilities for lubricating and fuel oils. A locomotive washing plant is provided.

A servicing shed is situated to the south-west of the main hump. It contains two two-berth through lines, with facilities for refuelling, lubricating, examining and sanding locomotives, together with ancillary workshop, stores and office accommodation. A locomotive washing plant is provided at this shed also. The breakdown crane is stabled nearby.

Servicing depots also are located at Wath, Shirebrook and Barrow Hill.

Sheffield Freight Terminal, constructed on land already owned by the board (it was the site of Grimesthorpe motive power depot), is designed to play a major role in the British Railways concept of a National Sundries Plan.

The Sheffield terminal has been designed to cater for all forwarded and received small consignments in the entire Sheffield division, including Sheffield, Barnsley, Rotherham and Chesterfield. Traffic for depots outside Sheffield, previously moved by rail to and from Sheffield, will be conveyed direct by road motor vehicles based on the new terminal.

It also acts as a residual tranship depot for sundries traffic for which through wagons cannot be made, and deals with warehouse and wagon-load traffic formerly accommodated at Bridgehouses, Wicker, Queens Road and Wharf Street, thus enabling those depots to be closed.

The goods shed – 920ft long and covering an area of about 25,000sq yd – operates in two sections, for received and forwarded

"There are about 130 trains in and out of the yard daily"

sundries. Capacity exists for dealing with more than 600 tons of sundries traffic each day.

Discharge is manual from wagon to trolleys, which are hauled in 'trains' along a raised deck to the delivery front, where there are berths for 90 road vehicles. Forwarded sundries are loaded to stand wagons by perambulation, under cover, using internal movement vehicles.

Alongside the sundries shed is a warehouse, 960ft long and with 15,000sq yd of floor space, all at wagon floor level, with a

stacking height of 20ft and with virtually no load limit on the floor. Handling and stacking equipment, with racking as necessary, is provided to meet customers' requirements.

There is accommodation in the yard for 200 wagons in position for loading or unloading, and the equipment includes end- and side-loading docks, mobile cranes (fitted with magnets for steel items) and a 35-ton *Goliath* crane. There is standage for 56 wagons beneath the *Goliath* crane.

Siding accommodation is available within the shed for full-load traffic requiring to be dealt with under cover.

A workshop is provided for servicing and running repairs to cartage vehicles, trailers and all mechanical-handling equipment. It also deals with repairs to outdoor machinery. This building, like the goods shed and warehouse, is of portal frame construction.

Offices and staff accommodation have been provided in a separate building at the Upwell Street entrance to the terminal.

A small number of the existing depots have been retained for specific purposes, including freightliner traffic, coal and timber. The depots at Barnsley, Rotherham and Chesterfield continue to deal with wagon-load traffic.■

Visible from the station platform was Bournemouth depot, and in this view on September 24, 1966, on shed are 'West Country' No. 34052 *Lord Dowding*, BR 4MT No. 80138 and Ivatt 2MT No. 41320.

B1 No. 61050 looks forlorn and carries the departmental number 30 as it sits at the back of Barrow Hill shed on February 15, 1968, latterly used for carriage heating.

Steam on shed

Trainspotters visited steam sheds in their thousands, often in search of that elusive 'cop' or rare loco. Remember scenes like this?

Left: Destined for preservation, Neville Hill, Leeds, provides a temporary home for the ex-LNER trio of K4 No. 3442 *The Great Marquess*, K1 No. 62005 and N7 No. 69621.
All pictures: TRACKS NORTH COLLECTION

Above: The scrapman is about to deal another blow to BR Standard 2MT 2-6-2T No. 84028 as it becomes 63tons 5cwt of scrap at the Central Wagon Co, Ince, Wigan, on March 28, 1966, after less than nine years in traffic. JOHN CLARKE

Right: 'Grange' No. 6868 *Penrhos Grange* meets its end at Friswells yard, Banbury on February 26, 1966. N E PREEDY

Steam for scrap

THE 1960s saw thousands of steam locomotives sent for scrap by British Railways. It was a move that was seen by many enthusiasts as premature, made all the worse as British Railways pushed forwards with its modernisation plan to introduce diesel and electric traction, while other railways in the world pressed on for many more years with steam. A number of the locomotives, particularly the BR Standard Class 9F 2-10-0s, had a little more than five years or so mainline use, and in reality, had a couple of decades of life in them, but there was to be no reprieve. At that time, the preservation movement was still in its early stages, and British Railway selected particular locomotives for museum display, so many classes of loco that should have been saved for the nation, sadly never were. More than a dozen scrapyards in various parts of the country were used to cut up these giants of steam, giving them an ignominious end. Our brief tribute is a poignant reminder of some of the examples of what was lost. ■

Right: The first cut with the oxy-acetylene torch is made on Prairie 51XX No. 4155 at Bird's Long Marston scrapyard on February 2, 1966.
N E PREEDY

From *The Railway Magazine*

Hacked into two pieces, 'Merchant Navy' No. 35023 *Holland-Afrika Line* meets its end in Cashmore's Newport scrapyard on April 10, 1968, while behind No 35008 *Orient Line* awaits a similar fate. J A IMBUSH

Above: Close up of the cutter's torch working on 'Black Five' No. 45108 being scrapped on March 23, 1966, at Central Wagon Co, Wigan. JOHN CLARKE

Right: BR Standard 5MT No. 73037 awaits its fate at Cashmore's yard, Newport in August 1968, while 'Warship' No. D604 *Cossack* lies in pieces. C D GIBBONS

Notes and NEWS

The last steam tram engines

DURING the 1880s and early 1890s, steam traction was in use on quite a number of tramway systems in these islands, especially in the Midlands, though there are even more isolated examples of steam tramways in most parts of the country.

Municipal authorities and tramway companies were still shy of electricity, and the steam locomotive was accepted for a time, albeit somewhat reluctantly, as a mechanical substitute for horse traction. Nevertheless, steam tramways as a whole were not an unqualified success; they involved the use of cumbersome and uneconomical apparatus, they were slow, noisy, ugly and dirty. In certain cases, indeed, the horses were reinstated.

By 1905 electric traction had made a pretty clean sweep, and at the present time, in Great Britain, the steam tramway locomotive is completely dead as an active agent in passenger transport, if one excepts such instances as those working on the Glynn Valley Tramway in Wales, which is actually a rural light railway serving an agricultural district. Since October 10, this line has operated only one train daily from Chirk to Glynceiriog and Lack.

The Wantage Tramway possessed, until recently, two steam tram locomotives of the traditional boxed-in type with all-over roofs. One of these, designed by James Matthews of Bristol in 1879, is illustrated. The photograph was taken in the coal yard at Wantage in March, 1929, when the locomotive and two of its attendant cars were standing derelict on a piece of isolated track. This example was described in *The Railway Magazine* for September, 1928, on page 188, but the main details of this and the other may be recapitulated. The Matthews engine was a side-tank design with four coupled wheels 2ft 4in in diameter, cylinders 6in by 104in,

A Matthews patent steam tram at Wantage in March 1929. C HAMILTON-ELLIS

and had a working pressure of 120psi. The boiler was of the ordinary loco. type, with a pair of Salter safety valves on the dome.

The article on the Wantage Tramway, which was written by T R Perkins and F Merton Atkins, continued as follows: "Much of its past history is obscure, but it is possible that Fox, Walker & Company were the builders, although the writers have no proof of this. According to a magazine published in 1881 a Matthews patent tram locomotive was tried on the Liverpool tram-ways: if this statement is correct and if only one was built it would appear to be the same engine that was put to work at Wantage in 1885". The other tram locomotive at Wantage, which was broken up about 1920, was built by Henry Hughes & Company (afterwards the Brush Electrical Engineering Company) of Loughborough in 1876. This was of the saddle-tank variety with 2ft 6in coupled wheels and cylinders 7in by 12in. During the latter part of the 19th century Hughes' locomotives were used extensively on various tramways, both at home and abroad.

But the last steam tram locomotive to belong to a British town corporation is still in

existence at Rawtenstall, in Lancashire, and recently made a journey under its own steam. It originally belonged to the Rossendale Valley Tramways Company, which was incorporated in 1888. In 1908, the Rossendale Valley system consisted of six miles of 4ft gauge track, worked by 12 locomotives and a like number of tramcars; steam traction having been in use from the first. In the year in question, the Rossendale Valley lines were taken over by the Rawtenstall Corporation, which body electrified it, the electric cars running for the first time on May 15, 1909.

The Corporation kept one of the old locomotives, an ordinary four-wheeled closed-in tram locomotive with a condenser mounted on the roof, and when, on April 7, 1932, motor omnibuses in their turn superseded the electric trams, the surviving steam locomotive headed a procession composed of the successive modes of transport through the streets of Rawtenstall. Thus, the old engine lasted to "celebrate" the passing of its own usurpers. Efforts are being made by the Omnibus Society to have the engine preserved.

From the January 1933 issue

The twenty-four hour clock

THE adoption of the 24-hour system for railway timetables has frequently been urged on the grounds that it would obviate the confusion between a.m. and p.m.

It is used on the Continent because international journeys, and night travel, are involved, and, for the same reasons, in the timetables of Continental services issued by British Railways.

On the other hand, quite apart from public opposition to a departure from an old-established practice (which probably would be considerable), it is doubtful whether the introduction of the 24-hour system for internal services in Great Britain would justify the high cost of the typographical alterations to timetables.

The change proved expensive in France before the First World War, when printing costs were relatively low.

The railways of the USA, South Africa, and Australia use the 12-hour system, although in South Africa a vertical line designates p.m. times, as it did on the former LMSR.

From the December 1958 issue

68   From *The Railway Magazine*

The McIntosh locomotives of the Caledonian Railway

The graceful lines of 3P 4-4-0 'Dunalistair IV' class No. 150 are captured with a four-coach train at Rockcliffe, just north of Carlisle on the West Coast Main Line. This engine became LMS No.14359 and survived until 1938. *RM* ARCHIVE

By ALEX K BOWMAN

I N view of the retirement of Mr John Farquharson McIntosh, MVO, from the position of locomotive, carriage and wagon superintendent of the Caledonian Railway, which he has held since February 1895, this article is peculiarly apposite.

It is not too much to claim that Mr McIntosh's influence upon modern locomotive design has been far-reaching.

To him is generally attributed the initiation of the cult of the big boiler, and the earlier 'Dunalastairs' were largely responsible for the high standard of locomotive performance and traffic working which has for so long been characteristic of the Caledonian Railway. It is true that No. 721 and her sister engines would not now rank as anything exceptional in respect of boiler and general dimensions, but when first introduced 'Dunalastair I' represented a considerable advance.

Mr McIntosh has also the unique distinction of having influenced the locomotive practice of a foreign country.

Ever since five engines of his 'Dunalastair II' design were built by Messrs Neilson, Reid

and Co, Springburn, Glasgow (now The North British Locomotive Co Ltd) to the order of the Belgian State Railways, the older methods of construction previously in vogue in Belgium have been almost entirely discontinued; and although M Flamme and his colleagues have produced their own designs in course of

John Farquharson McIntosh.

development, Mr McIntosh's influence can still be observed.

It was in 1896 that No. 721 *Dunalastair* – since provided with the suffix 'I' to distinguish it from its larger successor, No. 766 – was constructed at the St Rollox Works of the Caledonian Railway, the series being completed by Nos. 722 to 735.

The engines which ran over Beattock summit had at all times been classed among the smartest, but the 'Dunalastairs' at once established themselves in a position far ahead of the best of earlier years.

Their success was assured from the first, and ever since, the course of locomotive construction, not only on the Caledonian, but also on other lines, has been set definitely in the direction of large boiler dimensions.

The heating surface of the first 'Dunalastairs' totals 1,403sq ft-218sq ft, greater than that of the most famous of the 1895 'racers':

Mr John Lambie's No. 17 class had at one time been the most important and most powerful engines on the line. The following ▶

comparison between No. 17 and No. 721 is of interest:

During the great coal strike of 1912, No. 724 and a few others were adapted to the use of oil fuel. It cannot be said that these were actually in regular service, but should such conditions again arise, they will no doubt be ready to take over any work which may be allotted to them.

Simultaneously with the 'Dunalastairs', two other classes of engines were turned out from St Rollox – No. 25 class of side tank engines, and the No. 747 series of goods locomotives. The former were of the 0-4-4 T type, and are now largely employed on local services in the Glasgow district, while the latter are 0-6-0s with 5ft coupled wheels and a heating surface of about 1,200sq ft. The varied duties performed by the latter speak eloquently of their qualities. They work all over the system, particularly, however, in the haulage of heavy mineral and goods trains in the Glasgow and Motherwell districts. A number of them are permanently employed on passenger trains out of Glasgow Central, these being fitted with Westinghouse brakes and painted the usual Caledonian blue.

The work done by the 721 series was so remarkable that an enlarged design was almost immediately taken in hand, and in 1897 the second class of the name was introduced. Of these, No. 766 – for a long period this engine was known as *Dunalaslair II* and No. 780 as *Breadalbane* — is representative. In passing, it is perhaps worthy of note, that the naming of Caledonian locomotives appears to have gone out of fashion. Among others, Nos. 723 and 724, once named respectively *Victoria* and *Jubilee*, have been divested of their significant titles.

The coupled wheels of the 766 class were identical with those of their predecessors, but the cylinders were enlarged to 19in diameter, and the heating surface to 1,500sq ft, while the working pressure was increased to 175lbs per sq in. The tractive force is 16,840lbs, and the weight in working order (94 tons) was considerably augmented, as compared with that of No. 721, by the fact that the tenders of the 766 series were very much enlarged and, for the first time in Scotland, were carried on two four-wheeled bogies. They have capacity for 4,125 gallons of water, together with a fuel space of five tons.

The arrangement of the springs on these tenders was new. Instead of springing each axle separately, a method similar to that on the leading bogie of the engine was adopted. A large inverted laminated spring, situated between the axle-boxes of each bogie, was used in place of two ordinary ones.

All engines so fitted are likely to remain unaltered, but in 1910 the separate springing of each axle was reverted to on all new engines. In the construction of each engine are

Built in 1902, McIntosh Class 55 4P 4-6-0 No. 14607 simmers at Stirling in the early 1920s. By 1937 the loco had been scrapped. P RANSOME-WALLIS

In plain livery, 'Dunalistair I' No. 731 is seen at Lanark in the spring of 1922. Note the bent running plate. The loco was scrapped in 1931. *RM* ARCHIVE

With its stove pipe chimney, Caledonian 0-4-4T 439 class No. 15197 sits at Ayr in the early 1920s. TRACKS NORTH COLLECTION

An example of McIntosh's 29 & 782 class is 3F No. 56325 heading down the Motherwell-Hamilton Branch with a load of furnace ashes from Ravenscraig to be dumped on September 14, 1962. NORMAN POLLOCK.

embodied many of the minor details which go to make up the striking individuality of the Caledonian locomotive – the conventional whistle, for example, is absent, and in its place is a deep-sounding horn, dominant over all others in a joint station.

Again, the non-acceptance by the Caledonian of the usual standard code of headlights has led to the placing of two brackets, one on each side, near the top of, and outside, the cab. The lamps are placed on these, and show, generally, one white and one green light from the front, and one white and one red from behind.

The utility of this practice is readily seen. The additional height brings them earlier into the line of vision, and — a more practical result – they can be manipulated by the fireman without his leaving the cab. Then, so far as internal design is concerned, Mr McIntosh's spark-arrestor and steam reversing gear call for special notice. By the former the live sparks that may be sucked through the boiler tubes strike against the arrestor and are precipitated into a pit at the bottom of the smokebox. In the steam reversing gear the usual hand lever and notch-plate have been retained, so as to accord with ordinary methods.

While the 721 class are now mostly employed in the Glasgow and Edinburgh districts, with an occasional run north to Crieff or Perth, the 766 series are still widely used on

'Dunalastair II' 4-4-0 No. 766 leaving Edinburgh Princes Street Station with the 10.55 Glasgow express on September 20, 1910. LCGB/KEN NUNN

main line work all over the system. Their performance is consistent and remarkably fine, and, in common with the 900 class – the third 'Dunalastair' series, next to be considered – they excel not only on the long non-stop runs, as between Carlisle and Perth, but also on the short, fast point-to-point runs for which the Caledonian is well known – such as the 33min (summer) booking from Perth to Forfar, and the

37min booking from Perth to Stirling. The class numbers inclusively 766 to 780.

The years 1898 and 1899 witnessed the introduction of the 900 class, the engines of which, with their 4ft 9½in boiler diameter, mark still a further advance in size and power. The cylinders and coupled wheels remained the same as in the 1897 engines, but the grate area became 23sq ft, the heating surface 1,540sq ft, and the working pressure 180lbs per sq in. The tenders are substantially similar to those of the 766 series, but the weight overall and in working order is 96.7 tons.

These locomotives have great capabilities for hard running with heavy trams. They rank among the most efficient locomotives in the country, possessing, as they do, qualities which frequently enable them to get there ahead of larger and more powerful classes which, in theory, should make the better time. They number inclusively 887 to 902, and until 1906 the brass plate of the last of the series bore a higher number than that of any other locomotive in Scotland, save those of a few engines on the duplicate list, which are distinguished by having 1,000 added to the original figures.

Members of the 900 class are naturally to be found on every section of the main line. Their work on the Carlisle road, which involves the climbing of the 1,014 ft to Beattock summit, is particularly gratifying. One night last summer, when the writer had occasion to travel south by the 10.45pm ex-Glasgow Central, No. 895 ran to Carlisle in just over the two hours, including a stop of almost five minutes at Carstairs Junction, whence the load was 310 tons. This is the finest run on this section which has hitherto come under notice, and it is to be regretted that the darkness of the night prevented detail timing.

THE BELGIAN DUNALISTAIRS

IN 1897, a McIntosh 'Dunalistair' 4-4-0 was exhibited at an exhibition in Brussels.

The performance of the loco with its speedy performance, free running and economic coal consumption greatly impressed Belgian State Railways and over a 10-year period, they ordered a total of 720 Dunalistairs – more than were ever built to work in Scotland.

The first batch of five locos to the 'Dunalistair II' design were built by Neilson & Co of Glasgow, virtually identical to the Scottish locos. They even had Caledonian blue paint. An order for a further 90 followed that were built in Belgium and known as Type 17. After this came a further order for 140 locos, but with larger cylinders, and these were built by St Leonard and designated Type 18, although the three locos with superheaters became Type 19s.

A final batch batch of 'Dunalistairs' was built in 1907, and these superheated locos were Type 18bis, later to become Type 20.

Of all the 'Dunalistairs' built in Belgium, just one survives, No. 18051 that was

built in 1905, and is on display in a lilac livery at the railway museum in Treignes, the southern terminus of Le Chemin de fer à vapeur des Trois Vallées. CHRIS MILNER

There is one run, however, which, so far as Scottish locomotive performance is concerned, stands out as almost a record. This was made by driver Ranochan with No. 902 and about 150 tons on February 6, 1906, between Glasgow Central and Dundee, a distance of 88 miles 64 chains, involving three distinct climbs of 327ft (Cumbernauld), 133ft (Plean), and 422ft (Blackford) respectively, and a slack to 10mph through Perth.

Leaving the Central station at 1.20pm, a stop was made at Coatbridge (11m 13ch) from 1.35.30 till 1.36.1; Stirling (34m 52ch) was passed at 2 exactly, and thence the initial five miles of the Dunblane bank were covered in 5min – this is partly at 1-in-73. The summit (50m 55ch) was reached at 2.17, and the remaining 17 miles to Perth (falling to an altitude of 28ft at Hilton Junction) occupied only 13min. The level road to Dundee (21m 10ch) accounted for 20min, and No. 902 brought the special to rest in Dundee station at 2.50, after a very brilliant run of 90min.

In the aggregate, the largest individual class of tender engines on the Caledonian is the No. 282 series of goods locomotives, their numbers appearing no less than 132 times between 282 – the first – and 878 – the last – of the series. These are handsome engines of the 0-6-0 type, with 5ft wheels, $18\frac{1}{2}$in x 26in cylinders, a total heating surface of 1,403.23sq ft, and working pressure 160lbs per sq in.

They are utilised, in the main, for goods traffic, but a large number of them are employed in mineral working in the coal and iron districts of Lanarkshire, while Nos. 812 to 828 are engaged on the Clyde coast passenger trains between Glasgow and Wemyss Bay, a section which includes some heavy gradients near Greenock. In the season they are frequently called upon to manage loads of from 300 to 350 tons, and make excellent times, the fastest net booking for the 31 miles being 49min. The tenders have capacity for 3,000 gallons of water and 41 tons of coal; total weight in working order is 83 tons 10cwt and tractive force 17,790lbs.

A considerable number of passenger (0-4-4T) and goods (0-6-0T) engines were turned out from St Rollox during 1897, 1898, and 1899. The former have 5ft 9in coupled wheels, and the latter 4ft 6in; the cylinders are 18in x 26in. Several are fitted with condensing apparatus for working over the Glasgow Underground lines, and these are painted black.

In 1901 and 1902, Mr McIntosh re-built 11 of Mr Drummond's No. 60 class – Nos. 60 to 70. These he practically converted into 'Dunalastairs' of the first series, but the working pressure was increased to 175lbs, and each was fitted with through-pipe and ejector for vacuum-brake working, in addition to the usual Westinghouse fittings standard on the

Caledonian 903 class 4-6-0 No. 907 was the locomotive involved in the Quintenshill crash on May 22, 1915, and was subsequentally withdrawn. The crash reamains the UK's worst in the term of loss of life. *RM* ARCHIVE

2P 0-4-4T 439 class No. 55233 runs round its train at Ballachulish after working the morning train from Connel Ferry on September 1, 1961. M S WELCH

Built in August 1900 as No. 849, later BR No. 57587, the loco was withdrawn on the 62nd anniversary of its construction, and is seen at Perth in 1957. TRACKS NORTH COLLECTION

Caledonian.

1901 was a year of considerable activity in the locomotive construction department of the Caledonian. Besides the re-building of Mr Drummond's engines, a new 0-8-0 series of mineral locomotives was introduced – the No. 600 class (Nos. 600 to 607), the first eight-coupled engines in Scotland.

The spacing of the wheels is peculiar. The chief dimensions are: cylinders 21in x 26in; coupled wheels 4ft 6in diameter; heating surface 2,108sq ft; grate area 23sq ft; working

pressure 165lbs per sq in; weight in working order (including tender with 3,570 gallons of water and 4½ tons of coal) 971 tons; and tractive force of 26,276lbs.

The type was introduced to meet the demands of the then newly introduced high-capacity mineral wagons, and these engines have proved themselves capable of taking, on the main line, 60 fully loaded vehicles and 20-ton brakevan. So lengthy, indeed, are many of the trains behind the 600 series that the question often is to find siding accommodation in which to place them. The principal mineral trains are nearly all run within a radius of 30 miles of Motherwell, but there are exceptions which go to Dundee, Perth, Edinburgh, etc.

In 1902, the first five of the new 'Oban' bogies were constructed – 'new' to distinguish them from the 'old' engines of the same name built by Mr G Brittan prior to 1880. These were Nos. 55 to 59, and were the first 4-6-0 engines on the Caledonian Railway.

In several respects they are of uncommon interest. The six-coupled wheels are only 5ft in diameter, which is peculiarly small for engines destined to engage in express passenger work. They are primarily intended, of course, for the Oban road, with its stiff gradients and mountain curves; but at such times as they have been given a wider field for their activities they have compared most favourably with all other types in service. They constitute the first British instance – possibly the first instance in the world – of the association in the 4-6-0 type of six-coupled wheels with inside cylinders only, the leading coupled wheels being directly driven. The principal dimensions are given separately in tabular form together with those of other engines referred to on page 74.

Further engines of this class – Nos. 51 to 54 – were built in 1905.

The immediate success of the 'Oban bogies' led to the construction in the following year of the two great locomotives No. 49 and No. 50 *Sir James Thompson*, for the Carlisle road.

These did remarkable work for a long period, and in 1911 were partially rebuilt and fitted with Schmidt superheating apparatus, the working pressure being then reduced from 200lbs to 175lbs, and with this appendage they continue to maintain the high standard of efficiency which they established in their earlier years.

On account of their third pair of coupled wheels, adhesion is 15 tons greater than that of the largest of the Caledonian 4-4-0 engines, and this was such a telling factor in the climbing of the Beattock bank in unfavourable weather that surprise was frequently expressed during the years intervening between their introduction and that of the 903 series of 1906. As a result Mr McIntosh refrained from building supplementary locomotives of the same type with which to augment the tractive power on the Carlisle road.

One reason for their non-appearance certainly was that prior to 1906 there were no turntables on the Caledonian large enough to accommodate engines of this class, so that when No. 49 or No. 50 reached Carlisle, engine and tender required to be uncoupled, turned individually, and thereafter recoupled, before it was possible to commence another run to the north. At Glasgow the conditions were similar, but the men at the running sheds were often enough relieved of the uncoupling

One of only two preserved McIntosh locomotives is 812 class 0-6-0 No. 828, heading south from Bridgnorth for Kidderminster on October 4, 2011. ROBIN STEWART-SMITH

business through the big engines being sent to work a local train from the Central round the Cathcart Circle Railway, tender first. The result was that when they arrived back in the terminus their position was reversed and correct for the journey south.

It was in 1903, also, that a new type of goods and mineral tank engine was introduced – the useful series 492-497. These are of the 0-8-0 class, with 19in x 26in cylinders, 4ft 6in coupled wheels, 1,189sq ft of heating surface, 19½sq ft of grate area, and 175lbs per sq in working pressure. Their adhesion and tractive force (62 tons 16cwt and 22,813lbs respectively) are each the second largest in Scotland; they work at

Motherwell, Hamilton, and Dundee, and as banking pilots.

In 1904 came the first of the No. 140 series of 4-4-0 engines – Nos. 140 to 144. These were succeeded by Nos. 145 to 150 in 1906, and are handsome locomotives with 19in x 26in cylinders and 6ft 6in coupled wheels. The total beating surface is 1,615sq ft, and the working pressure 180lbs per sq in. In running order the weight of the engine is 54 tons 7cwt 2qrs, and of the tender 53 tons, while the tractive force is 17,320lbs.

The 'Dunalastair IV' class, as the above are sometimes called, are a hard-working and highly efficient series of engines. Their best work is done with the postal expresses, ▶

LMS "Crab" No. 42739 on a northbound goods passes Caledonian 3F No. 57572 shunting the yard at Kilmaurs in North Ayrshire on April 29, 1963. DEREK CROSS

especially with the 8.30pm ex-Euston, which, north of Carlisle, runs under the appellation 'Caledonian TPO Night Down'. Leaving Carlisle at 2.54am, the Glasgow and Edinburgh coaches are dropped at Carstairs at 4.14, while the main train continues on the north road. At Stirling, it makes a halt from 5.10 to 5.12, and, having attached passenger coaches from Glasgow Central, commences its run over the Dunblane bank to Perth, arriving in the General station at 5.53. Five minutes later it steams out on the only non-stop run of the day between Perth and Aberdeen, reaching the granite city at 7.35. The 2,401 miles are thus covered at an average speed of 51.3mph – creditable work for everyday conditions over such a road, especially as this is inclusive of stops.

One of the most interesting points in connection with the history of modern locomotive practice is Mr McIntosh's refusal to adopt the principle of the Atlantic locomotive, and thereafter work it out to suit his especial requirements. During the closing months of 1905 it was under consideration at St Rollox whether or not it would be advisable to build a few 4-4-2 engines for exclusive use on the Perth and Aberdeen road, which would appear to offer considerable scope for this type; but if the project ever took definite shape, it fell through, for Mr McIntosh could never reconcile himself to a principle which demanded the addition of 10 to 18 tons to the running weight of an engine, while the adhesion could not be appreciably increased.

More power was required, however, and therefore, the turntable difficulty having been eliminated, Mr McIntosh again turned to the 4-6-0 type to help him out, the trains having grown about 40% heavier on the introduction of the new 'Grampian' passenger stock. The outcome was three new classes, all of them 4-6-0s.

The No. 903 'Cardean' class are well adapted for working over the difficult roads of the Caledonian. No. 903 itself has, for a long period, regularly worked south with the 2pm dining car express ex-Glasgow Central, returning with the 8.13pm ex-Carlisle – adhering strictly to time in all weathers with loads which occasionally exceed 400 tons. No. 907, similarly, usually works the 10am up from Glasgow Central, and the other engines of the series have their standard duties, this being a policy in considerable favour on the Caledonian Railway. Some of the class also work on the Aberdeen road.

As in the case of the 903 class, the piston valves of the 908 series are situated above the cylinders, but while all the 'Cardean' engines are now fitted with Schmidt superheaters, the principle has not yet been applied to any of the 5ft 9in locomotives, of which No. 909 *Sir James King*, and No. 911 *Barochan*, are members. The reason may be that the 908

Leading Dimensions of Caledonian Locomotives.

Designed by Mr. J. F. McIntosh.

R—Rebuilt. A—As originally built. B—As rebuilt and fitted with Schmidt Superheaters. C—Built with Schmidt Superheater. D—Built with Robinson Superheater.

Number of Locomotive Initiating Class	721	25	747	766	897	282	97	169	787	60 R	600	55
Type	4-4-0	0-4-4 T	0-6-0	4-4-0	4-4-0	0-6-0	0-4-4T	0-4-4T	0-6-0T	4-4-0	0-8-0	4-6-0
Cylinders (in.)	18¼x26	18 × 26	18 × 26	19 × 26	19 × 26	18½x26	18 × 26	17 × 24	18 × 26	18 × 26	21 × 26	19 × 26
Coupled wheels	6′ 6″	5′ 9″	5′ 0″	6′ 6″	6′ 6″	5′ 0″	5′ 9″	4′ 6″	4′ 6″	6′ 0″	4′ 6″	5′ 0″
Leading or bogie wheels	3′ 6″	3′ 2″	—	3′ 6″	3′ 6″	—	3′ 2″	2′ 6″	—	3′ 6″	—	3′ 6″
Steam pressure (lbs. per sq. in.)	160	150	150	175	180	160	150	150	156	160	165	175
Heating surface, tubes (sq. ft.)	1284·5	984·6	1056·8	1381	1402	1284·5	894·6	975	975	1284·5	1970	1705
,, ,, firebox (sq. ft.)	118·7	111·16	112·4	119	138	118·7	111·16	111	111	118·7	138	105
,, ,, superheater (sq. ft.)	—	—	—	—	—	—	—	—	—	—	—	—
,, ,, total (sq. ft.)	1403·2	1095·76	1169·2	1500	1540	1403·2	1095·7	1086	1086	1403·2	2108	1810
Grate area (sq. ft.)	20·6	17	19·5	20·6	23	20·6	17	17	17	20·6	23	20·6
Adhesion weight (tons)	31¼	32½	40¼	32¾	34¾	45¾	33½	32	47¾	31	—	42¼
Total weight, engine (tons)	47	53¾	40¼	49	51¾	45¾	55¾	51¼	47¾	46	60½	57½
Weight, engine and tender (tons)	86¼	—	75¼	94	96¾	83½	—	—	—	86	97¼	94¾

Number of Locomotive Initiating Class	49 A	49 B	492	140	903 A	903 B	908	918	139 C	120 D	30 C	34 C
Type	4-6-0	4-6-0	0-8-0T	4-4-0	4-6-0	4-6-0	4-6-0	4-6-0	4-4-0	4-4-0	0-6-0	2-6-0
Cylinders (in.)	21 × 26	20¾ × 26	19 × 26	19 × 26	20 × 26	20¼x26	19 × 26	19 × 26	20¼x26	20 × 26	19½x26	19½x26
Coupled wheels	6′ 6″	6′ 6″	4′ 6″	6′ 6″	6′ 6″	6′ 6″	5′ 9″	5′ 0″	6′ 6″	6′ 6″	5′ 0″	5′ 0″
Leading or bogie wheels	3′ 6″	3′ 6″	—	3′ 6″	3′ 6″	3′ 6″	3′ 6″	3′ 6″	3′ 6″	3′ 6″	—	3′ 6″
Steam pressure (lbs. per sq. in.)	200	175	175	180	200	175	180	175	165	170	160	160
Heating surface, tubes (sq. ft.)	2178	1509·3	1076·3	1470	111·75	1666	1895	1716	1220	1220	1071·3	1071·3
,, ,, firebox (sq. ft.)	145	145	112·7	145	148·25	148·25	128	128	145	145	118·8	118·8
,, ,, superheater (sq. ft.)	—	515·7	—	—	—	515·75	—	—	330	295	266·9	266·9
,, ,, total (sq. ft.)	2523	2170	1189	1615	2260	2330	2023	1844	1695	1666	1457	1457
Grate area (sq. ft.)	26	26	19·5	21	26	26	21	21	21	21	20·6	20·6
Adhesion weight (tons)	53½	54½	62¾	35¾	54½	55¾	49	46	38	38	51¼	46
Total weight, engine (tons)	70	71½	62¾	54½	73	74¼	64	60½	59	59	51¼	54¼
Weight, engine and tender (tons)	125	126½	—	107½	130	131¼	102	98½	115	115	89¼	91½

A summary of McIntosh locomotives.

series are largely employed on the short runs of the Clyde coast services.

No 917 of this class is fitted with an American cab. A further series have, however, been constructed recently, intended mainly for express goods traffic, and these are fitted with Robinson superheaters, piston valves, closed-in cabs, and other improvements.

As regards the 918 series, these were constructed for fast, long-distance goods work, and have dual-brake fittings. The cylinders are as large as is possible to retain the direct Stephenson link motion with valve chest between them, and, in common with all other Caledonian 4-6-0 types, the engines are driven off the leading axle.

The safety-valves are of the double description now standard on the Caledonian, and have four valves, each 4in in diameter, and with independent springs. Apparatus is provided for sanding both the driving and the trailing wheels, which is particularly useful in any necessary shunting work. The principal services on which they run are between Carlisle, on the one hand, and Glasgow, Edinburgh, Greenock, Perth, Dundee, and Aberdeen, on the other. The longest journeys which they make unaided (leaving out of

2P No. 55209 arrives at Aberfeldy on May 24, 1957, with the 10.28am from Ballinluig with a single carriage that had worked through from Perth on the 9.25am to Blair Atholl.
J SPENCER-GILKS

account banking assistance to Beattock summit, or from Buchanan Street to the top of the incline out of Glasgow) are from Carlisle to Dundee (172 miles); Edinburgh to Aberdeen (159 miles); and Glasgow to Aberdeen (153 miles).

In 1906 and 1907, a large series of 0-4-4 tank engines was introduced. These have 5ft 9in coupled wheels, and are doing excellent work on the local services in the Glasgow and Edinburgh districts, as well as on express work between Perth and Dundee, Crieff, etc.

In the summer of 1910 a superheater locomotive – the first in Scotland – was placed in regular service on the main line between Carlisle and Perth. This was No. 139, and already a large class has grown up round it – Nos. 117 to 122, 132 to 135, and 43 to 48 – a few of these having the Robinson apparatus and the others the Schmidt design.

To make any extended remarks relating to superheating on the Caledonian is hardly necessary. Suffice it to say that the practice has realised notable results. In external design the main differences between the 140 and the 117 series (superheaters) consist in the forward extension of the smokebox, the steam cylinder for the superheater damper, the forced lubrication apparatus, and the separate springing of the axle-boxes on the tenders of the latter class.

In the superheater engines piston-valves are used, and their position above the cylinders rendered the employment of a rocking-shaft imperative. The mechanical lubrication is worked from the motion, and has eight feeds running to the cylinders and valves. The superheater damper in the smokebox is controlled by a small cylinder and piston which receive steam on the opening of the regulator, and is so adjusted that it closes automatically when steam is shut off. The boiler pressure is 165lbs as

compared with the 180lbs of the non-superheater engines. At a pressure of 160lbs, the temperature of saturated steam is about 363°F, and to this is added 280° of superheat. Thus the temperature at which the steam enters the cylinders is from 640° to 670°F, it having been found that in practice only inconsiderable economies result when less than 200° of superheat is added to the saturation temperature, which, of course, varies in accordance with the boiler pressure. Mr McIntosh states that owing to the decreased working pressure a very gratifying saving in the wear and tear of the boiler is being effected.

In 1912 four new 0-6-0 locomotives, forming a substantial supplement to the 282 series of goods engines, were turned out from St Rollox, and these, together with a series of the 2-6-0 type – built a few months ago, and the first of their kind in Scotland – will be an important factor in the long-distance goods working of the company, for which duty they are primarily intended, although Nos. 30 and 31 are at present taking charge of local passenger trains in the Glasgow district.

The 0-6-0 engines number inclusively 30 to 33, and the 'Moguls' 34 to 38 and, apart from the addition of the leading pony truck and consequent alterations in adhesion and wheelbase on the latter, they are substantially similar. The super-heater is of the Schmidt pattern, as are also the piston-valves, the position of which has again rendered necessary the use of the rocking shaft.

Recently, superheaters of the Robinson pattern have been fitted to a few engines of the 766, 902 and other classes, in addition to the superheater equipments previously referred to.

In conclusion, it will be seen that Mr McIntosh will leave behind him a record of things achieved which will long be remembered in the annals of locomotive practice and enterprise. The years during

which he has been superintendent at St Rollox have been years of striking advance in the mechanical side of railway engineering in Great Britain. He has always seen to it that the Caledonian retained its position in the forefront, and has displayed wonderful discrimination in his choice of labour-saving and fuel-economising devices. He has succeeded, too, in not only maintaining but also in adding to the gracefulness of design which has always been characteristic of Caledonian construction, and his retirement will mean the loss of one who has served his own and future generations faithfully and well.

The up-to-date methods of the locomotive department will long be associated with his name; it is satisfactory to know that his opportunity came at a time when a strong man was needed to supply haulage power for the traffic increases which marked the concluding years of the 19th century. At the present time the daily average of locomotives in active service numbers about 1,050, the aggregate tractive force of which is about 15,000,000lbs, while the miles run per annum total 30 million.

In the coming struggle for supremacy between electricity and internal combustion on the one hand, and steam on the other, the steam engine may, after a lapse of time, begin to give place to other means of long-distance traction. But, whatever may be the issue, the McIntosh locomotives will always be remembered as among the most successful engines in service, and one feels justified in saying that it will be many years before such splendid machines will be called upon to take a secondary place.

Mr McIntosh joined the then Scottish North Eastern Railway at Arbroath in 1862, and after duly qualifying in the mechanical as well as in the locomotive running departments, was appointed locomotive inspector of the northern section of the Caledonian Railway in 1876. Six years later he was made district locomotive foreman at Aberdeen, from which he was subsequently promoted to Carstairs Junction, and eventually was put in charge of the company's most important engine shed at Polmadie.

After remaining there for five years he was appointed chief inspector of the running department in 1891, and took up his present duties as locomotive, carriage and wagon superintendent in February, 1895.
Mr McIntosh was president of the Association of Locomotive Engineers in 1911.

In October of the same year, His Majesty King George V honoured Mr McIntosh by creating him a Member of the Royal Victorian Order, and on the occasion of the last royal train journey a few months ago Mr McIntosh, in obedience to a 'command', attended at the Royal Saloon, where His Majesty in hearty fashion wished him goodbye. ∎

Crompton versatility

First introduced in 1960 for the Southern Region of British Railway, a total of 98 locos were built. Their versatility meant they were found all over the SR, and in later days as far north as Crewe. Twenty six examples have been preserved, but here are varied workings of the class in their prime.

Top right: The pairing of Nos. 33026 *Seafire* and 33030 work past Crediton on January 29, 1993, with a heavy ballast train from Dartmoor quarry.
ALL PICTURES: TRACKS NORTH COLLECTION

Right: Push-pull fitted Class 33 No. 33118 eases along Weymouth Quay on June 14, 1974, with an oil train to provide fuel for the ferries to the Channel Islands.

Below: On October 27, 1983, "Slim Jim" Class 33/2 No. 33204 was used to move a nuclear waste flask from Winfrith to Eastleigh and is seen at Dorchester South.

Above: Regulars on Cardiff-Crewe services, No. 33007 passes Sutton Bridge Jct, Shrewsbury, with a southbound service on October 6, 1984.

Left: Rolling into Weymouth, prior to electrification, hauling a 8-TC set that forms an express from Waterloo is No. 33110 on June 20, 1987.

Below: On May 27, 1985, No. 33029 was employed on the Channel Islands Boat Train, formed of the Orient Express Pullman stock, and passes Dorchester South.

Over Stainmore Summit

An express to Newcastle, double-headed by BR Standard Class 3 2-6-0 No. 77001 and Ivatt 4MT No. 43126, crosses the magnificent Belah Viaduct in August 1961. COLOUR RAIL/T B OWEN (BRE606)

By KEN HOOLE

January 20, 1962, saw the end of a two-year fight to keep open the line between Barnard Castle, Kirkby Stephen, and Penrith, with which was associated the line from Kirkby Stephen to Tebay.

It was early in 1959 that rumours began to circulate regarding the forthcoming closure of these routes, and on December 9, 1959, the North Eastern Area Transport Users'

Consultative Committee announced its proposals, which were:

■ **Lines to be closed and lifted**
From Tees Valley Junction (one mile west of Barnard Castle) to Merrygill (one mile east of Kirkby Stephen); from Kirkby Stephen to

Tebay; and from Appleby East to Clifton Moor.

■ **Lines to be retained for freight traffic**
From Merrygill to Appleby East; and from Eden Valley Jct to Clifton Moor.

This envisaged the withdrawal of passenger facilities from the stations at Lartington, Bowes, Barras, Kirkby Stephen East, Warcop, Appleby East, and Clifton Moor, and the closure of the goods depots at Bowes, Ravenstonedale and Temple Sowerby. Restricted goods facilities were to be provided at Kirkby Stephen East, Warcop, Appleby East, and Clifton Moor.

On February 24, 1960, a joint meeting of the North Eastern and North Western Area Transport Users' Consultative Committees was held at Carlisle to hear the 51 objectors to the proposals of the British Transport Commission, headed by three MPs, three county councils, three borough councils, four urban councils, five rural councils, and eight parish councils. Also objecting were organisations such as the Youth Hostel Association and the Cyclists' Touring Club; industrial concerns, such as Dorman Long; chambers of trade; and numerous individuals.

It was announced at the meeting that the closure would give an estimated saving of £103,274 a year, together with an additional £257,000 for recovered material, and that a capital works expenditure of £45,000-£50,000 at Kirkby Stephen would be avoided.

A map of the Stainmore route across the north Pennines.

The outcome was a decision to re-route the freight traffic via Newcastle and Carlisle, and an exhortation to increase passenger receipts by attracting more tourist traffic.

The Central Transport Users' Consultative Committee refused to accept the decision, and returned it to the joint North Eastern and North Western Committee with the instruction that when they were satisfied that the diverted freight traffic was being handled satisfactorily the line should be closed.

Freight traffic started running via Newcastle and Carlisle on July 4, 1960, and the joint committee next met at Newcastle on December 9 of that year to consider the results, but it was decided to postpone the decision for another month. At this meeting it was stated that closure would result in a saving of £36,000 a year, or £30,000 if the line was singled throughout – figures vastly different from the original statement.

The next meeting took place at Leeds on January 16, 1961, when the majority of the North Eastern members voted to keep the line open, and the majority of the North Western members voted to close it: however, the total voting was 10 for closure and six against. Because of the split between the area committees, the Central Committee once again refused the decision and also refused to submit the matter to the Minister of Transport, but referred it back, with the result that on June 8, 1961, the North Eastern Committee announced that it had agreed to the closure.

A month later the Central Committee announced that it had confirmed the closure, and it only remained for the Minister of Transport to give his approval, which he did on December 7, 1961.

The North Eastern and London Midland Regions of British Railways moved quickly, and only 12 days later they announced that the last trains would run on January 20, 1962. Normally, the last passenger train would have been the 8.30pm diesel from Penrith to Darlington, but the Railway Correspondence & Travel Society had arranged for a special steam-hauled train, conveying enthusiasts and others on that day, and this was actually the last train conveying passengers to run between Penrith, Kirkby Stephen and Barnard Castle.

So ended what had been a fascinating line which passed through some beautiful countryside, ranging from the wild bleak moors of Stainmore to the lush green fields of the Eden Valley. In its wake the closure leaves a large area of the North of England bereft of a train service, and there is now no cross-country route between the Newcastle-Carlisle line in the north and the Leeds-Skipton-Morecambe line in the south.

The line over Stainmore was built to carry coal and coke from east to west, and iron ore in the opposite direction.

Much is made of this in the early

Last-day picture of the sign alongside the railway at Stainmore Summit, between Barnard Castle and Kirkby Stephen PHOTO: P J LYNCH

references to the route, and its passenger potentialities are not mentioned – no doubt because of the sparsely populated area through which the line passed. In looking at the closed section we must also take into account the lines radiating from Barnard Castle to Bishop Auckland and Darlington, which remain open.

The latter was the first line to reach Barnard Castle (on July 8, 1856), and it was in the following year that the South Durham & Lancashire Union Railway was formed, with the object of building a line from Bishop Auckland to Barnard Castle and on to Tebay, over the Pennines separating Yorkshire and Westmorland.

The engineer appointed to supervise the construction of the line and to design the numerous viaducts was Thomas Bouch,

whose brother William was locomotive superintendent of the Stockton & Darlington Railway.

Thomas was later the designer of the ill-fated Tay Bridge, for which he received a knighthood on June 27, 1879, six months and a day before the bridge collapsed.

The Act for the construction of the Lancashire Union line encountered practically no opposition, and the Royal Assent was granted on July 13, 1857. However, it was necessary to change the route slightly between Bishop Auckland and Barnard Castle to avoid passing through the game preserves of the Duke of Cleveland. Unless it was diverted, he insisted on a tunnel where it passed through his land, but he must have been friendly to the railway as he cut the first sod at Kirkby ▶

BR Class 3MT No. 77002 leads a classmate through Barras on August 12, 1961. COLOUR RAIL

Stephen on August 25, only six weeks after the line was authorised.

Work on the 35-mile stretch between Barnard Castle and Tebay was carried on rapidly and uneventfully – in spite of the difficult terrain – and this section was opened throughout for mineral traffic on July 4, 1861. The formal opening took place on August 7, 1861, and the line was fully opened to the public on the following day.

The remaining section – between Barnard Castle and Bishop Auckland – was not opened to passenger traffic until August 1, 1863, and in the intervening period all traffic between Bishop Auckland and the west had to be worked via Shildon and Darlington. Near Bishop Auckland, between Spring Gardens Jct and Fieldon Jct, the new line used a portion of the Stockton & Darlington Haggerleases branch, which was opened in 1830, and which still exists as the Butterknowle freight branch. From Fieldon Junction, a new section was built to join the Stockton & Darlington main line, just south of Bishop Auckland station.

In the meantime, the Eden Valley Railway had been built from Kirkby Stephen to a junction with the Lancaster & Carlisle Railway at Clifton, four miles south of Penrith. The first sod of this line was cut at Appleby on August 4, 1858, and it was opened for mineral traffic on April 8, 1862, and for passenger traffic on June 9.

The connection at Clifton was unsuitable for through-running and on August 1, 1863, a more convenient connection with the Lancaster & Carlisle was given at Clifton Jct (now known as Eden Valley Jct), thus allowing trains to run through from the Eden Valley line direct into Penrith. When through-running to Penrith was first considered it was decided to build a separate line running parallel to the Lancaster & Carlisle, but this idea was dropped when running powers were obtained.

The Lancashire Union and the Eden Valley lines were worked by the Stockton & Darlington Railway from the outset, and that company took them over on June 30, 1862, only to be swallowed by the North Eastern Railway on July 13, 1863.

The cost of building the railways had been: South Durham & Lancashire Union, £666,879 3s 9d; Eden Valley, £204,803 0s 8d; and Eden Valley extension, £15,906 3s 3d.

The whole of the Lancashire Union line was passed by the inspecting officer on his first visit – Barnard Castle to Tebay in July, 1861, and Barnard Castle to Bishop Auckland in July, 1863.

During construction of the line, the local inhabitants complained of the behaviour of the navvies and the Chief Constable of Westmorland and Cumberland agreed to provide a constable to curb their activities, provided his wages were paid by the railway company. Actually, he suggested that four constables would be necessary to cover the whole of the line, but the railway company would only pay for one. His wages were £1 1s a week, plus 1s 6d a month boot allowance, and 1s a month for oil (for his lamp?). The navvies received 3s 1d-3s 4d a day and masons 5s a day.

All the lines enumerated were still in use at the time of closure in January, although the section between Kirkby Stephen and Tebay had lost its passenger service nine years earlier.

One section which had disappeared was the isolated NER line running from Eamont Bridge Junction on the LNWR main line, south of Penrith, to Redhills Junction on the Cockermouth, Keswick & Penrith line. This line was built to enable mineral trains to reach the CKPR without reversal at Penrith, and was opened in 1866. It was 1 mile 3 chains long, and fell into disuse after the First World War. The 1932 working timetable gives the timings for one Kirkby Stephen to Cockermouth freight train, which ran only if required. The line was finally closed on June 5, 1937.

Although the first station at Barnard Castle was opened in 1856, it was not suitably placed to allow the railway to be extended to Kirkby Stephen. Consequently, the Lancashire Union line had to strike off half a mile short of the original station, and it was at this junction that the present station was built.

The 1856 station was left at the end of the spur and became the goods station. The portico was purchased by the Saltburn Improvement Company and re-erected in the Valley Gardens at Saltburn as a memorial to Prince Albert. Northern newspapers have recently carried paragraphs stating that the structure is dangerous and may be demolished.

Apart from its natural beauty, the outstanding features of the Lancashire Union line were the graceful viaducts of Thomas Bouch, notably the all-metal structures of Belah and Deepdale, the stone-pillared Tees Viaduct, and the stone Smardale Viaduct. The last-named, 553ft long and 90ft high, stands between Kirkby Stephen and Tebay, while the other three are all between Barnard Castle and

The deep snow drifts at Barras station looking west on February 19, 1947. BR (NER)

BR Standard 4MT No. 76048 leaving Barras with the 2.55pm Penrith-Darlington on June 25, 1956. F HEBRON

The last passenger train over Stainmore Summit – the Railway Correspondence & Travel Society special on January 20, 1962, arriving at Ravenstonedale, double-headed by 2-6-0s Nos. 77003 and 76049. COLOUR RAIL/DAVID A LAWRENCE

Kirkby Stephen.

Tees Viaduct is 732ft long and 132ft high; Belah Viaduct is 1,040ft long and 196ft high; and Deepdale Viaduct is 740ft long and 161ft high. Because of its exposed position and the height reached at Stainmore Summit (1,370ft above sea-level) the weather has always been a great adversary during the winter months, and many times the line has been blocked by snow for days, and sometimes weeks. The winter of 1947 was one of the worst ever experienced.

Over the years little alteration to the stations has taken place. Ravenstonedale was named Newbiggin until 1877, and Clifton Moor was plain Clifton until 1927. Appleby became Appleby East (to distinguish it from the former LMSR station on the Settle & Carlisle line) in 1952, and Kirkby Stephen also had 'East' tacked on for the same reason at about that time. However, it did not appear in the North Eastern Region time-table as Kirkby Stephen East until 1959.

The passenger service between Kirkby Stephen and Tebay was withdrawn from December 1, 1952, and from that date Smardale and Gaisgill stations were closed completely, but Ravenstonedale remained open for freight traffic until January 22, 1962.

On the Eden Valley line, Musgrave was closed completely on November 3, 1952, and Kirkby Thore on December 7, 1953. Temple Sowerby was closed to passengers on December 7, 1953, and for freight from January 22, 1962. Cliburn was closed completely on September 17, 1956.

Between Barnard Castle and Kirkby Stephen, Barras was converted to an unstaffed halt (and closed to freight) from December 1, 1952, and Lartington similarly from February 2, 1953. Both these stations remained as unstaffed halts until the closure of the line.

Of the remaining stations which handled passenger and freight traffic to the end, Bowes was closed completely from January 22; Kirkby Stephen East, Warcop and Appleby East were closed to passengers and to freight in less than full wagon loads; and Clifton Moor was closed to passengers and converted to an unstaffed goods depot.

The first timetable (for September 1861) showed trains from Darlington (North Road) at 7am and 1pm, arriving at Tebay at 9.15am and 3.15pm, respectively. In the opposite direction, departures from Tebay were at 10.15am and 4pm, arriving at Darlington at 12.45pm and 6.20 p.m. Ninety-one years later, when the Tebay service was withdrawn, there were still only two trains in each direction, and only one of these bettered the fastest 1861 time.

During the whole of its existence the line has struggled for passenger traffic, and even at the turn of the century, long before the advent of the motor bus and private car, one or two of the smaller stations were having difficulty in making ends meet. For instance, between 1897 and 1907, Smardale showed yearly takings varying between £91 and £166, but the yearly expenditure was never less than £189.

Apart from the normal passenger service, other interesting trains have used the line, and the summer Saturdays-only trains between the North East coast and Blackpool are well known.

Another odd service which lasted until the end was the fortnightly train conveying County Durham miners to and from their convalescent home at Ulverston; in the 1930s this turn was worked by the six-cylinder Sentinel railcar North Briton. An interesting through-coach working was that between Newcastle and Barrow (Ramsden Dock), which was attached to the 10.32am train from Darlington. Also of interest was the NER working over the LNWR from Tebay to Kendal, which necessitated a reversal at Oxenholme.

Finally, brief mention must be made of the service between Appleby (Midland) and Penrith, introduced in 1880 at the request of the Midland Railway, which wished to compete with the LNWR. Three trains in each direction were provided, and originally the Midland paid 2s a train mile, but in 1882 this was reduced to 1s 6d, and abolished completely in 1886. The service ceased in 1893. ▶

When opened, the lines from Barnard Castle to Tebay and Kirkby Stephen to Penrith were single, but sufficient land was purchased to enable a double line to be constructed, if required.

On the Lancashire Union all but three of the viaducts were built to take double track – the exceptions, all between Belah and Kirkby Stephen, had new viaducts built alongside when this section of the line was doubled around the turn of the century. Bowes to Stainmore Summit was doubled in 1867; Barnard Castle to Bowes in 1873; and the summit to Barras in 1874.

Eventually, double track extended from Barnard Castle to Kirkby Stephen West Jct; from Sandy Bank (one mile east of Ravenstonedale) to Tebay; and on the Eden Valley, from Appleby Station to Appleby Jct, and Clifton Moor to Eden Valley Jct. The single-line section from Kirkby Stephen to Sandy Bank was later extended to Ravenstonedale so that Sandy Bank signalbox could be abolished.

To serve the line, locomotive sheds were opened at Kirkby Stephen and Tebay in 1861, each holding two engines. That at Kirkby Stephen was enlarged to hold four engines in 1865, and in the following year more space was required as there were six engines stationed there. Consequently, in 1867, almost £2,000 was spent on further extensions to accommodate an unspecified number of engines.

Apart from slight alterations and repairs, little else seems to have been done to the shed, which was closed on November 20, 1961. Under the British Railways' scheme it was allocated the code 51H, but on transfer to the London Midland Region in 1958 it was changed to 12D.

The original shed at Tebay did not last long, as in 1866 expenditure of £41,972 was authorised for the building of a new shed, and this four-road structure remained open until October 31, 1902, in spite of a petition to the directors presented by the staff in an attempt to keep the shed open. The building has now disappeared, but the water tank and traces of the pits still remain.

Barnard Castle shed was authorised in 1864 and extended in 1875. This two-road shed, situated immediately east of the level crossing, was closed in 1937, and has since disappeared.

North Eastern engines also shared the shed at Penrith with the LNWR engines which worked on the Keswick line, but this practice ceased in 1937. However, steam locomotives from the Kirkby Stephen direction regularly turned and took water at the shed until the diesel railcars were introduced on the Stainmore line on January 6, 1958.

Extensive records have survived of the locomotives used on the Stainmore line, and

With its tender water filler cap open, Ivatt Class 4MT No. 43040 potters around the derelict Kirkby Stpehen East station on April 23, 1965, with a rake of mineral wagons.
COLOUR RAIL/T B OWEN

Left: A new BR Metro-Cammell DMU waits in Barras station with the 10.52am Darlington-Penrith on October 14, 1961. HUGH BALLANTYNE

Below: Ivatt 2MT No. 46470 leaves Barnard Castle with the Darlington portion of a train from Blackpool on August 30, 1960.
J MARSHALL

the BTC archives at York include a report by William Bouch (dated December 31, 1858), regarding the provision of engine power for the South Durham & Lancashire Union Railway.

Before he wrote his report, Bouch went to Devon where he travelled on the footplate of the 4-4-0 tank engines owned by the South Devon Railway, and he was most impressed with their riding qualities. He also visited the

North London Railway to sample its 4-4-0 tank engines.

On his return to Shildon, Bouch discussed the matter of leading bogies with Mr Weallens of Robert Stephenson & Company, who also recommended bogies, and it was decided that, initially, two 4-4-0 engines should be ordered.

These engines differed little from the rough specifications drawn up by Bouch. They had

16in x 24in cylinders (instead of the envisaged 17in x 24in), the total heating surface was 1,048sq ft (against the proposed 1,150sq ft), and the tenders carried 1,500 gallons of water (against the 1,000 gallons originally suggested). The engines were fitted with large double-window cabs, but these were later removed, and subsequent engines were turned out new with the typical abbreviated Stockton & Darlington cab of the period.

In addition, various 2-4-0 locomotives built in the 1850s were used on the line, such as No. 71 *Hackworth*, No. 98 *Pierremont*, and No. 116 *Lartington*. On the mineral trains, 0-6-0 engines from various makers were used, such as No. 149 *Fox*, by R & W Hawthorn; No. 155 *Saturn*, by Gilkes Wilson; No. 184 *Lark*, by Robert Stephenson & Company; No. 190 *Summer*, built at Shildon; and No. 175 *Contractor*, the first locomotive built at North Road Works, Darlington.

Exactly three weeks after the opening of the line, an excursion was run from Darlington to Windermere, with return fares of 7s 6d first class and 4s second class. Some 175 passengers took advantage of the trip. On the return journey, the train was derailed 2.1 miles west of Bowes, and the engine and coaches ran down an embankment into a field. The driver died later from his injuries, and a number of passengers were injured. Claims for compensation ranged from £300 to £3 5s, but no-one got what they had claimed! The claimant of the £300 settled for £150, that for £150 settled for £50, and the lowest (for £3 5s) settled for £3.

Ivatt 4MT No. 43073 works hard up the 1-in-60 bank between Bleatfield and Stainmore Summit with the 11.05am Blackpool to South Shields on August 2, 1958. ROBERT LESLIE

In 1889, the new Worsdell two-cylinder compound 0-6-2 tank engines began to take over from the SDR 0-6-0s, but after 13 years service these, in turn, gave way to the 0-8-0 engines of classes T and T1.

The 0-8-0s continued working between West Auckland and Tebay for 10 or 12 years, until restrictions were imposed which kept them to the short stretch between Kirkby Stephen and Tebay, where one or two remained until about 1943.

Two class Q6 engines were sent to Kirkby Stephen for similar duties in 1955, but after only a few weeks they were both derailed whilst double-heading a train from Tebay and were immediately replaced by smaller engines.

During the Second World War – and the years immediately following – mineral traffic was worked by 0-6-0 engines of classes J21, J24, and J25, and it was not until 1955 that Ivatt Class 4 2-6-0 engines began to appear. These were later joined by the similar locomotives to BR design.

On the passenger side, the SDR 4-4-0 engines were rebuilt as 2-4-0s, and this wheel arrangement remained faithful to the line for many years, with engines of classes 901 and 1463.

After another spell of 4-4-0-working by former NER and GNR engines, the 2-4-0 type reappeared in 1935, when a number of GER Class E4 engines were transferred to the line.

After five years, these engines were transferred away, and then began a spell of regular working by the Class J21 0-6-0s, which reigned supreme until replaced by Ivatt Class 2 2-6-0 engines from 1951.

These in turn succumbed to the BR Class 3 2-6-2 tank engines Nos. 82026-9 in 1954/5, and these locomotives worked the passenger service until the diesel trains took over in January, 1958. ∎

My thanks are due to the keeper of records at the BTC archives, York, for the facilities for carrying out some research into the history of the line.

Shabby looking Ivatt Class 4 2-6-0 No. 43056 pilots BR Class 4MT No. 76050 on the climb to Stainmore on August 12, 1961. COLOUR RAIL/T B OWEN

The Inter City Years

BR's final InterCity livery first appeared on the APT in 1978. The stylish colour scheme was gradually extended to locomotives and carriages, with just a few small livery modifications over the years - a scheme that lasted well into Privatisation in the 1990s. A selection of workings are reprised

Above: Swansea was once part of the InterCity network, which is where No. 47805 arrives with a cross-country duty from Birmingham.

Right: Rare use of an InterCity loco on a freight diagram, as No. 37416 passes Lostwithiel on June 25, 1993, with china clay hoppers.

Below: Working down from Shap towards Tebay on June 25, 1995, is Class 86 No. 86216 with a cross-country working from Glasgow to Penzance.

From *The Railway Magazine*

Above: Class 87 No. 87002 *Royal Sovereign* passes Rugby on June 16, 1997, with a Euston to Birmingham express.

Left: A very clean Class 91 No. 91011 arrives at Leeds from King's Cross with the 'blunt' end first on May 24, 1995.

Below: Route availability meant that Class 37s were used on the 'Royal Scotsman' for many years and on May 28, 1990, No. 37402 climbs from Inverkeithing to North Queensferry, the gorse in full bloom.
ALL PICTURES: TRACKSNORTH COLLECTION

A three-engined Westland 'Wessex' monoplane used on Cardiff-Torquay-Plymouth air services from April 1933 by the GWR.

Inauguration of GWR air services

IN our May issue we illustrated on page 340 the aeroplane used at the opening of the Great Western Railway's pioneer air service between Cardiff, Torquay and Plymouth on April 12.

The route followed by the GWR air line extends from the Cardiff airport to Roborough aerodrome, Plymouth, the one intermediate stop being made at Haldon aerodrome (for Teignmouth and Torquay). A Westland 'Wessex' machine maintains the service and has been supplied by Imperial Airways Limited, Imperial Airways pilots being employed on the route.

The machine is finished in the standard Great Western Railway chocolate & cream colours externally. The passenger cabin seats six persons. Two services a day (including Sundays) are being run, but this will be modified with the impending extension to Birmingham.

From the June 1933 issue

Railway relics destroyed

IN a letter to *The Times*, published on November 21, Mr Henry Maxwell drew attention to the fact that "three irreplaceable items (of railway rolling stock) already scheduled for preservation – namely the restored London, Tilbury & Southend Railway coach, the Wisbech & Upwell Tramway car, and the former Great Eastern Railway tram locomotive", had been destroyed at Stratford Works. It is officially stated that the two passenger vehicles were destroyed in error, but the tram locomotive was not scheduled for preservation. Mr Maxwell was even more disturbed "to find out that many other valuable pieces of rolling stock are deteriorating through exposure and neglect, in spite of all the assurances which have been given from time to time that they would be properly preserved".

He added it was already seven years since the British Transport Commission announced its intention of forming a proper transport museum, and nothing has been done and much is in danger of being lost.

From the January 1958 issue

Photography in Wartime

THE many enquiries we continue to receive from readers all over Great Britain indicate that there is still considerable misunderstanding about the position of private photography during wartime.

Generally, there is no ban upon the carrying of cameras in public places by persons other than enemy aliens, who require a permit for this purpose, and it is not forbidden to photograph views or objects except those expressly-prohibited items specified in the Control of Photography Orders (Nos 1 and 2) 1939.

The restrictions imposed by the No 1 Order, which were announced on September 11, were summarised by Mr Charles E Lee in the first of his articles entitled Railways and the War, which was published on page 320 of *The Railway Magazine* for November last. A permit must be obtained before a person, either professional or amateur, may take a photograph (including a cinematograph film), or sketch, plan, or make any other representation, of any lengthy list of objects, mainly of direct military import. These include "assembly of persons for transport or evacuation, or transport vehicles used for evacuation; roads or railways exclusively connected with roads of defence". The photographic restrictions also apply to any object damaged by enemy action or as a result of any steps taken to repel enemy action.

Early in the war the British railway companies notified holders of photographic permits that it was no longer possible to grant facilities for taking photographs on railway premises, and holders of then-current permits were asked to return them. There is no prohibition of taking railway scenes other than those including troop trains or similar objects of military importance. The railway companies naturally possess the ordinary rights of property owners to prevent their premises being used by photographers (whether fare-paying passengers or otherwise), and in all cases of doubt, members of the railway staffs normally tend to err on the side of caution.

So far as concerns Government restrictions, the list of prohibited objects is extensive, and all persons, before taking photographs of any kind, are advised to study the orders. They are obtainable from His Majesty's Stationery Office, or through any bookseller, price 1d each net. The principal order (No 1) which gives the list of prohibited objects is SR & O 1939 No 1125; order No 2 (SR &O 1939 No 1710), relates to photographs from aircraft only. It should be borne in mind that all photographs exported to certain foreign countries are liable to censorship.

In wartime, photographs of prohibited objects may be taken only by those who can show good reasons why they should be permitted to do so. Accordingly, photographers, whether professional or amateur, who for some good reason desire to take a photograph of a prohibited object, should apply for permission to the competent military authority in the command in which the object is situated. The granting of permits is entirely at the discretion of the competent military authority which will require all applicants to establish their bona fides and, if he decides to grant a permit, will impose such conditions as he thinks necessary for security. The address of the competent military authority for the purposes of the orders can be obtained from any police station.

This advice does not apply to photographers who are engaged in work specially authorised by the Ministry of Information, Admiralty, War Office, Air Ministry, or the police, for approved purposes.

From the May 1940 issue

The Palace Gates to North Woolwich line

Thompson L1 2-6-4T No. 67716 sits at a tired looking Palace Gates station on October 6, 1962, about to depart for North Woolwich.
COLOUR RAIL/ M ALLEN

By JEFFREY MORSS

MODERNISATION on the Eastern Region of British Railways has resulted in the changeover to electric traction of practically all the Great Eastern and London, Tilbury & Southend Lines in the London area.

An outstanding exception, however, is the Palace Gates to North Woolwich line, which cuts diagonally across the district from north-west to south-east, and tunnels under the main line at Stratford. But recent official announcements by British Railways indicate that change is imminent and the coming closure of Palace Gates, Noel Park & Wood Green and West Green stations will shortly end the 76-year-old connection between Palace Gates and North Woolwich.

The first part to be built was from Stratford to the River Lea at Barking Road, Canning Town, a single-track line of 2½ miles for the use of coal traffic only. It was opened by the Eastern Counties & Thames Junction Railway on April 29, 1846. In extension of this, the North Woolwich Railway

> "Fares were revised in 1868 and all three classes of carriage were provided."

was authorised in July 1845, and on June 14, 1847, was completed to North Woolwich, using a route along the riverside. The line from Stratford to Barking Road had also been doubled and a pier built opposite North Woolwich station. Ferry steamers provided a service to the south bank, and a service down river was also operated by arrangement with the Gravesend Steam Packet Company.

The Eastern Counties & Thames Junction in August 1846, and the North Woolwich Railway in 1847, were acquired by the Eastern Counties Railway. A spur was opened at Stratford on June 14, 1847, enabling trains to work through to Shoreditch (renamed Bishopsgate in the previous year).

The ferry service down river became so popular that a platform and booking office was reserved at Bishopsgate for Woolwich line trains. In June 1848, a short branch for goods only was opened from Canning Town across Bow Creek to Blackwall, to serve pepper warehouses rented by the Eastern Counties Railway from the East India Dock Company.

The line between Stratford and Hackney Wick (later known as Victoria Park) was constructed by the Eastern Counties Railway. This connected the North Woolwich line with the North London Railway and was opened for goods on August 15, 1854. On October 16, 1854, the low-level platforms at Stratford were brought into use and a passenger service to and from Stratford Bridge was worked by the North London Railway, the trains calling at Stratford Low Level. The North London continued this service until 1866 when the Great Eastern took over. The two companies then worked the passenger service alternate years from November 1. This arrangement operated until October 31, 1874, which was the last day the North London operated the service.

Stratford Bridge station was renamed Stratford Market on November 1, 1880. The Victoria Park trains were extended to and from Canning Town on October 1, 1895, where an additional line and platform had been provided for them.

An Act passed on July 7, 1856, authorised the construction of two spurs from the London, Tilbury & Southend Railway to the Woolwich line, but only the southern loop from Upper Abbey Junction was ever built. This was opened on March 31, 1858.

The Northern & Eastern Railway opened a line from a junction at Stratford, to Broxbourne, as early as September 15, 1840. This had been built to a gauge of 5ft, but during September and October 1844, it was altered to the standard gauge of 4ft 8½in. In the same year the Northern & Eastern Railway was leased to the Eastern Counties.

On July 21, 1868, the Tottenham & Hampstead Junction Railway was opened from a junction on the Cambridge main line, now known as Tottenham North Junction. A few years later the Great Eastern Railway, successor to the Eastern Counties, opened a spur from the South Junction to the West Junction at Tottenham. A line from Bethnal Green to Stoke Newington and Lower Edmonton had been built by the GER in 1872, and a branch from this at Seven Sisters was opened to Green Lanes on January 1, 1878, and extended to Palace Gates on October 7 of the same year. On January 1, 1880, a spur connecting South Tottenham (Tottenham & Hampstead Junction Railway) with the Enfield and Palace Gates branches was brought into use, thereby enabling a through service to be

GER N7/3 No. 69664 rolls into Severn Sisters in July 1959 with an Enfield train.
COLOUR RAIL/ C HOGG

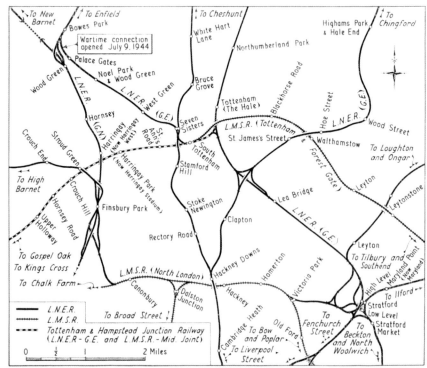
Map showing the route of the Palace Gates-North Woolwich line to Stratford Low Level Station

Restarting a North Woolwich train from Stratford Low Level on February 14, 1961 is N7/3 No. 69725. COLOUR RAIL/TONY COOKE

From *The Railway Magazine*, September 1962

established between Palace Gates and the Stratford line; this service later ran to North Woolwich.

The North Woolwich branch has been diverted twice, first in the early 1850s, and again in 1880. An Act of 1850 authorised the Victoria Dock Company to construct a dock about half a mile east of Bow Creek on the land north of the Woolwich line. The entrance to the dock from the River Thames cut across the railway, and, to avoid interrupting traffic, a new line was built from Thames Wharf Junction around the north side of the dock to Silvertown, where it rejoined the original line. The cost was met by the dock company. The Victoria Dock was opened on November 26, 1855, and a station built on the new line at Custom House was brought into use on December 1, 1855. Owing to local development, stations were also opened at Tidal Basin in 1858 and Silvertown on June 19, 1863. The old line, locally known as the Silvertown Tramway, has not been removed (excepting the swing bridge over the entrance to Victoria Dock), and now serves factories built alongside the river.

Originally, the North Woolwich trains were composed only of first- and second-class carriages, but the fares were lower than on most other lines. The fares were revised in 1868 and all three classes of carriage were provided.

An Act passed in 1875 authorised the construction of the Albert Dock, which was

An RM Routemaster, also heading to North Woolwich, paces N7/3 No. 69692 on the final approach to the Thamesside terminus on June 24, 1961. COLOUR RAIL/M ALLEN

eventually opened in 1880, and had its own entrance from the Thames as well as a cut through from Victoria Dock. This Act also gave powers to the dock company to build a substitute line for the Great Eastern, which formed a tunnel under the link between the two docks.

The original high-level line still remains and is the property of the Port of London Authority, which is responsible for its maintenance. This authority absorbed all the dock companies in 1909.

A swing bridge, to carry both railway and road over the waterway between the two docks, was constructed at Connaught Road. If, for any reason, the tunnel becomes impassable, traffic may work free of charge over the original line until the use of the tunnel is again possible.

A branch from Custom House to Beckton was opened on March 18, 1874, but a

"The southern part of the line handles the most freight traffic."

service for workmen had been provided for the previous 12 months. The line was authorised by an Act of 1871, and was built by the Beckton Gasworks owners, who leased it to GER. On August 3, 1880, another branch was opened, from Custom House to Gallions. This was owned by the Albert Dock Company, but from 1896 the GER took over the working. Although the GER ferry service between North and South Woolwich was withdrawn on October 1, 1908, the pier on the north bank remains to this day, and is used by pleasure vessels to Southend, Margate, and other places.

Over the years, many interesting services have been operated on the North Woolwich branch, including those to Woolwich from Victoria Park, Liverpool Street, Fenchurch Street, Palace Gates, and Stratford Low Level. The branch has also served trains from Stratford Market and Fenchurch Street to Beckton, as well as trains to Gallions, and those that terminated at Canning Town. The Fenchurch Street to Woolwich trains ran either via Stratford, using independent tracks between Bow Junction and Stratford Western Junction, or to Gas Factory Junction, then on Tilbury metals to Upper Abbey Mills Junction.

An interesting but short-lived service was that from Fenchurch Street to Palace Gates, which was begun on January 1, 1880. This was withdrawn and in place thereof trains ran through between Blackwall and Palace Gates from September 1, 1880, but this service lasted only until the end of February 1881. A service between North Woolwich and Palace Gates commenced on June 1, 1887, and this still operates. ▶

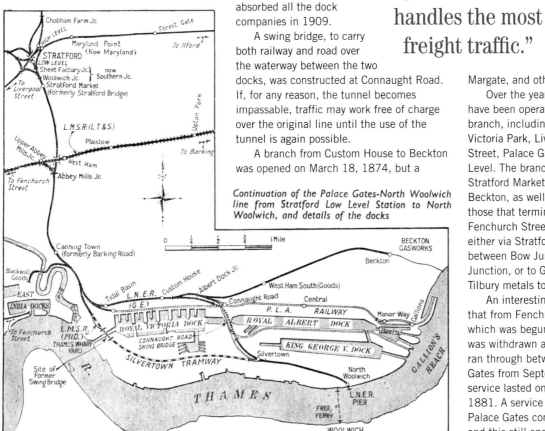

Continuation of the Palace Gates-North Woolwich line from Stratford Low Level Station to North Woolwich, and details of the docks

Palace Gates was served by trains to Liverpool Street as well as those to Woolwich. In the early years of the present century, six trains ran between Liverpool Street and Palace Gates in the peak hours between 6 and 8pm. In later years, a shuttle service was provided by a push-and-pull set between Palace Gates and Seven Sisters during the day. This connected with trains from Liverpool Street. It was withdrawn on and from July 6, 1942, and two of the sets were transferred to the Great Northern line. This service was reinstated in 1948 but finally withdrawn on and from January 15, 1951.

In 1930, the LNER (successor to the GER) built a connection between Palace Gates and Bounds Green (GN), so that Great Eastern coaching stock could be worked through to the carriage washing plant there. This connection was rearranged for through working in 1944 and a regular service of goods trains commenced to run via Palace Gates on July 9, 1944.

Towards the end of the last century some 0-4-4 tanks of Bromley's 'E10' class had their chimneys shortened to enable them to work on the North Woolwich line. The low

Above: Easing away from Silvertown is N7/5 No. 69640 on October 14. 1961. The Regent petrol sign and blue police box add extra interest. COLOUR RAIL **Right: N7/3 69681 smokes into Custom House with a North Woolwich local. Note the GER bracket signal, and serried gas lamps.** COLOUR RAIL/T B OWEN

bridge that necessitated this was later rebuilt. In the 1890s, 'R24' 0-6-0 tanks replaced the 0-4-4 tanks on the Liverpool Street-Palace Gates service, as on some other lines.

Rolling stock from elsewhere often finds itself on the North Woolwich line. By reason of many curves, particularly between Seven Sisters and Stratford, no great speed is possible, so wear and tear is kept to a minimum. Even remaining steam-hauled trains are formed of stock displaced from other lines, following electrification. Some of these coaches still display lettering of their former haunts such as Liverpool Street and Hertford, or Clacton and Walton, and are of LNER type, used in four-coach sets giving second-class accommodation only. Semaphore signals, mostly of the upper quadrant variety, are still used here, although replaced on other GE suburban lines.

The North Woolwich end of the branch suffered severely during the war, and for a time trains from North Woolwich terminated

The outside of Palace Gates station, which closed to passengers on January 7, 1963.

With a myriad of dock cranes in the background, L1 2-6-4T No. 67715 gets away from North Woolwich with a four-coach train. COLOUR RAIL

at Custom House. Tidal Basin station was badly damaged; it was closed on August 15, 1943, and not reopened. Custom House Station still bears scars of enemy action.

Many of the services disappeared after the outbreak of war. Trains to Gallions ran for the last time on September 7, 1940, and the passenger service to Beckton was withdrawn a few months afterwards. Stratford Market station was closed on May 6, 1957. Through workings from other lines were withdrawn from November 21, 1960, when the Chingford and Enfield lines were electrified, and the service was revised.

This 12½-mile line now has 37 trains to North Woolwich, six starting at Palace Gates, and the others commencing at Stratford Low Level, excepting the 8.28am from Stratford, which now starts from Cheshunt at 7.54am. This began with the introduction of Rolls-Royce three-car diesel units, towards the end of last year. In the up direction there are 38 trains, nine running to Palace Gates the rest terminating at Stratford Low Level. A Saturday service is operated, but the Sunday service was withdrawn on and from March 23, 1947. At present 'N7' 0-6-2 tanks and 'L1' 2-6-4 tanks work the remaining steam trains.

The southern part of the line handles the most freight traffic, with marshalling yards at Silvertown and Thames Wharf. The PLA has a sorting yard at Custom House. Freight

Easing to a halt at Severn Sisters station is L1 class 2-6-4T No. 67705 on March 19, 1960. COLOUR RAIL/ L W ROWE

services are run between Temple Mills and the Docks, with through services from the London Midland Region, including those from Acton and Camden. These run via Victoria Park or via South Tottenham. Freight trains from the Tilbury line and from Temple Mills to the Great Northern line pass over the Palace Gates branch.

Boat trains, too, often run from Liverpool Street via Stratford and Custom House to the docks in connection with various sailings. For

instance, an eight-coach special ran from Liverpool Street on February 27, 1962, to King George V Dock for Union Castle Line *ss Rhodesia Castle*. On the next day a first-class special of four coaches ran to the Royal Albert Dock in connection with the Ellerman Lines *ss City of Durban*. For supplying these and other interesting facts, thanks are due to the kindly assistance of Mr D Cook, Public Relations Officer, British Railways, Eastern Region, at Liverpool Street. ∎

Working hard, LMS 3F No. 3738 heads an up mixed goods near Berkswell in the early 1930s. W VAUGHAN-JENKINS

End of a Great class

The 0-6-0 locomotives of the Midland Railway

No example remains in service of the once-numerous Fowler 0-6-0s of the Midland Railway.
With their extinction, one of the most ubiquitous classes ever to run in this country
ceased to exist, apart from a single engine scheduled for preservation.

NO less than 772 Fowler 0-6-0 locomotives were built by the Midland Railway and its successor – the LMSR – between 1911 and 1941.

The full story, however, goes back farther – very much farther – than that, for these engines are the direct descendants of the even more numerous class of general-purpose freight and mixed-traffic locomotives originally introduced by Mr S W Johnson soon after the start of his long reign as chief mechanical engineer of the Midland Railway in 1873.

In 1875, now more than 90 years ago, there appeared the first of a long line of standard 0-6-0 freight engines with single frames (in contrast to those of Johnson's predecessor William Kirtley, who had built

By H C CASSERLEY

several-hundred 'double-framers', but that is another story).

Moreover, this design was produced initially in quite large numbers – 'straight off the drawing board' as the saying is nowadays – most unusual for those times; along with the DX class of the London & North Western Railway, in particular, it was among the first examples of mass standardisation so common of recent years.

Johnson took the plunge by ordering a total of 140 engines straight away, from four different outside builders of already established wide reputation – 30 from Kitson, another 30 from Dubs, 50 from Beyer

Peacock, and another 30 from Neilson. Whether by chance or otherwise, it is worthy of note that no less than 23 of the Neilson engines were still at work as late as 1956, 80 years after construction, which seems to indicate that these must have been exceptionally well built. Many of the others could also boast equal longevity, however.

The original Johnson engines had 4ft 11in driving wheels, but in 1877 he increased the diameter to 5ft 3in for the next batch of 110 locomotives, reverting to 4ft 11in, again, for another 60 examples, after which 5ft 3in became standard for all future construction.

This dimension was adhered to not only for the remainder of his superintendency, but perpetuated by his successor R M Deeley and,

From *The Railway Magazine*, January 1967

again, by Sir Henry Fowler in his final enlarged version of 1911.

Naturally, over the period of years, sundry modifications of other dimensions were embodied, but generally they incorporated three broad stages for successive enlargement of the boiler, the original type of which eventually became known as Class 2, the enlargement introduced by Deeley in 1903 as Class 3 and finally Fowler's ultimate development in 1911 as Class 4 – the Class 4 'goods' which we have known during the last decade. Initially, there were two of these engines only, Nos. 3835 and 3836: it was not until 1917 that construction was proceeded with on a large scale.

The later history of the Johnson engines themselves is an involved and complicated one, which would need a volume in itself to record in detail, and only the briefest summary can be given here.

All of the engines built up to 1902 – totalling 865 examples – appeared with Johnson's distinctive type of boiler with brass safety valves and spring-balance safety valve on the dome. The Deeley engines, on the other hand, which appeared in 1903, had his larger boiler with Ramsbottom safety valves over the firebox – he later rebuilt a large number of the original Johnson engines (mostly the more recently built ones) to this pattern.

Later, the Belpaire firebox was introduced, at first confined to the larger Class 3 examples but, in 1917, Fowler began applying a smaller Class 2 Belpaire boiler to many of the un-rebuilt engines, chiefly to the very earliest 130, none of which was ever converted to Class 3.

All that can be recorded here is that many rebuildings took place from 1904 onwards by conversions from Class 2 to 3 (in some cases '3' rebuilds subsequently reverting to Class 2), complicated in later years by the provision of

LMS 2F No. 58236 stands at Horninglow, near Burton-on-Trent, on August 28, 1954. R M CASSERLEY

The cab number on the side of the Johnson 0-6-0 at Highbridge on May 30, 1925, looks temporary and shows 69, particularly as the 0-6-0s were numbered 62-66 and 72-76, and No. 69 was a 4-4-0. H C CASERLEY

Belpaire fireboxes, both of '2' and '3' variety.

All the survivors of Class 3, from about 1925 onwards, acquired Belpaires, but a few Class 2s – one as recently as 1959 – retained Johnson boilers to the end.

Apart from these numerous rebuildings and interchange of boilers, there were few other departures from standard, though three Class 3 engines – Nos. 3326, 3333 and 3387 – were, in 1906, provided with 6ft 0in-diameter driving wheels to make them suitable for faster passenger work, but they reverted to the standard 5ft 3in between 1918 and 1924.

Although the class as a whole was designed mainly for freight duties, nearly all of the 5ft 3in engines, and latterly some of the 4ft 11in ones, were fitted with vacuum brakes and often used on excursion traffic and holiday specials, but were mainly ousted by Fowler's Class 4 engines on those duties in later years.

The Class 3s worked almost the whole of the passenger service on the Stratford-upon-Avon & Midland Junction Railway in its declining years, until this finally ceased in 1952. Both Johnson and Fowler engines remained throughout their lives as typical 'maids of all work' locomotives, of which this country has had numerous examples, usually of the 0-6-0 wheel arrangement. The Midland was the largest user of the type and had some 1,500 in service at the time of the Grouping, far more than any other railway.

Kettering coaling stage is where LMS 2F No. 23011 sits on July 7, 1948, soon before renumbering to 58183. H C CASSERLEY

One of the Johnson 0-6-0s built for the Midland & Great Northern Railway, No. 061, near Melton Constable on March 13, 1939. H C CASSERLEY

LMS 4F No. 43902 passing Stainforth Sidings on the Settle & Carlisle line with a down freight on June 20, 1959.
R H SHORT

Only two of the Johnson engines received superheaters – Nos. 3792 and 3806 in 1923 – but, for some reason, they were later removed. All of the Class 4s were, however, superheated from the start.

It is convenient at this point to tabulate briefly a list of all engines built. The numbers quoted are those which they acquired after the 1907 renumbering scheme or as subsequently built by the MR and LMSR. In addition to these, both Johnson and Fowler designs were built for the associated Midland & Great Northern Joint and Somerset & Dorset Joint Railways, for which the parent Midland Railway Company was responsible. These were as follows:

The whole of the 935 Midland Johnson/Deeley engines survived at the LMSR Grouping, and initial withdrawals did not take place until 1925; Nos. 3198 and 3694, cut up in August of that year, appear to have been the first, followed by No. 2952, then 3033/4, 3053/9, 3106, 3179, 3272, 3303, 3390, 3495, 3557 and 3563, in September.

Withdrawals thereafter were fairly steady, but comparatively slow, with virtually none during the war period, with the result that 205 of the smaller Class 2 engines and 398 Class 3s, including nine Somerset & Dorset, were still running at Nationalisation.

British Railways, thereupon, decided that at last the two classes, hitherto hopelessly interwoven, should be sorted out. The Class 3s were renumbered by the addition of 40000 to their numbers, in common with most other LMSR engines, but the Class 2s were entirely renumbered into a new block – 58114-58310 (eight being scrapped before the scheme was drawn up).

Many of the survivors continued to perform useful work for a number of years: in 1956, for instance, there were still more than 100 Class 2s and 300 Class 3s in service, and it was not until the general reduction on a large scale began in the 1960s that their numbers were really greatly reduced. After that their rapid demise was inevitable, but even so three of the Class 2s – Nos. 58143, 58148 and 58182 (old 22955, 22967, 23010) – lasted until 1964, with a working life of 88 years.

Oddly enough and very appropriately, their last duties were on the old Leicester & Swannington line, genesis of the Midland Railway, and only quite recently closed to all traffic. It was a great pity that one of these veterans could not have been spared for preservation – I suggest far more worthy of such distinction than many other classes which have recently been accorded such honour. The last of the Class 3s also lingered on until 1964, these being Nos. 43620, 43637 and 43669.

The engines of the SDJR were incorporated into LMSR stock in 1930 and renumbered accordingly, the surviving Class 2 engines, some with Johnson boilers and others rebuilt with Ramsbottom safety valves, becoming 2880-2890, while Nos. 62-66 and 72-76 – all of which had been rebuilt to Class 3 Belpaire – took the first numbers in the Midland list above 3190 which were vacant due to the scrapping of the original engines, becoming 3194, 3198, 3201/4, 3211/6/8, 3228, 3248 and 3260.

The Class 4 engines 57-61 followed on the then-existing LMSR series as 4557-4561. The MGNJR engines, of which Nos. 62, 68, 69 and 71 had acquired Class 3 Belpaire boilers with extended smokeboxes, continued under independent status until 1937, when they were taken into the LNER stock. Most of them duly appeared in the unusual guise of a Johnson engine in LNER colours as Nos. 058-073.

The LNER livery did not, however, seem to settle very happily on the Johnson outline, and being non-standard with LNER practice it is perhaps not surprising that Stratford did not even consider them worthy of continued assistance with the war effort, and all had gone by 1944.

In 1934, Nos. 2900-2984 had 20000 added to their numbers to make way for Horwich and Stanier 2-6-0s. The same thing happened with 3000-3018, in 1947, on the appearance of the new Ivatt 2-6-0s and when this class eventually reached No. 43137, in 1952, the 0-6-0 of that number, then the only survivor of that group, became No. 43750. A batch of 28 engines built for the Somerset & Dorset Joint Railway had 4ft 6in driving wheels.

From *The Railway Magazine*, January 1967

Final development of the Midland 0-6-0 locomotives was in the shape of the super-heated Class 4 variety, now, in their turn, on the verge of extinction.

It may be fairly claimed that the whole of the 1,761 engines constructed over a period of 65 years stem from Johnson's original design of 1875, with successive enlargements but retaining all the basic elements. As such, they constitute by far the most numerous class this country has ever seen.

The only possible parallel might be the endless succession of Great Western 0-6-0 saddle tanks, of which nearly 2,400 were built between 1860 and 1956, but including so

With its Midland Railway crest prominent, 3F No. 3834 sits on an unknown shed in 1920.
RM ARCHIVE

Clearly no urgency for the locos: LMS 4F Nos. 44263, 44276, 43999, 44277, 44211 and 43893 sit at Skipton on June 9, 1962 still carrying snowploughs. J G BLEARS.

many considerable varieties that they cannot, by any reasonable stretch of imagination, be considered as one homogenous family in the same way that the 'Midlands' can.

The varieties of 'standard' pannier tanks introduced from 1929 onwards might well be regarded as of one general class in the same way as the Johnson-Fowler 0-6-0s, but even so

they only total some 1,250 engines, far short of the MR figure.

Other numerous classes which might be recalled include the 842 standard 'Black Fives' of the LMSR, and in earlier years the 943 Ramsbottom DX engines of the LNWR, built between 1858 and 1874.

The Class 4 engines had a wide range of

duties over a large area, having regularly worked at some time or another to such extremeties as Bournemouth, Shoeburyness, Swansea and over the whole of the LMS system as far north as Inverness, where a few were stationed for a time in the late 1920s. I have never heard of one penetrating the Far North Road of the Highland, although they might well have done so.

They were used a good deal on passenger trains, especially on excursion work and summer specials. The five Somerset & Dorset engines, together with other subsequent LMSR-built importations, could be regarded as exclusively passenger engines, as they were rarely seen on anything else – as recently as May, 1964, I came across Nos. 44422 and 44560 in the Poole area, on what must have been the last regular passenger workings of the type, or indeed of any 0-6-0s in the country.

An interesting booklet published by the Railway Correspondence & Travel Society, of a report compiled from a massive observation exercise of train workings on a Saturday in the summer of 1956 over the whole of the former Midland system, reveals that no less than 112 Class 4 goods were engaged on passenger duties on that day, many of them naturally on seasonal holiday trains of the type which has been so drastically reduced under the Beeching regime.

All the Class 4s were still running in 1948, and had 40000 added to their numbers under Nationalisation. The first engine to be scrapped

LMS 4F No. 4314 heads a goods train at Druimachdar Summit on the Highland Main Line on May 15, 1928. H C CASSERLEY

was No. 43862, in 1954, and a very early casualty was the original 43835, of 1911, which went in 1955. Withdrawals proceeded thereafter at a gradually increasing tempo, and after 1961 no further general repairs were undertaken, with the result that the class as a whole has been gradually run down until but few survivors remain, and most of these in unserviceable condition.

The last Midland-built engine in traffic was No. 43953, withdrawn late in 1965. The final two representatives of the class – Nos. 44311 and 44525 – were withdrawn week-ending October 8, 1966; they were latterly used as shunters in Crewe Works.

Preservation hope

The only hope for a permanent memorial to this great class now lies in the original LMSR-built engine (No. 4027), which was one of those scheduled under the official preservation plan.

As this has been whittled down, however, the position regarding this particular locomotive seems in some doubt and its future is not, so far as it can be ascertained, assured. It is to be hoped that the worst will not happen – although only second best from the point of view of the original Johnson design it is at least as representative of the class, as a whole, as the Hawksworth tank No. 9400, preserved at Swindon, can be said to be of the Great Western panniers.

The memory of S W Johnson is, of course, fortunately kept in mind by the preservation of an example of what was perhaps his finest achievement, the lovely single-wheelers, although at the present time well hidden from public gaze, and in a slightly more indirect way by his famous compounds, but in its rebuilt Deeley version.

As regards his earlier more mundane designs, there are still, fortunately, in existence a few of his 0-6-0 tank engines, tank counterparts of the more numerous tender engines just described, and there is a scheme in hand for preservation of one of them. If it is no longer possible to keep one of the tender engines, let us hope that the project for the tank will achieve its object and, together with the Fowler 0-6-0, still secure for posterity an important representative link in the chain of locomotive development in this country that these engines so rightly deserve.

The Midland was probably not one of the most generally popular of the old railways, in fact it might even have only just got into the 'top ten'.

Devotees of other railways are sometimes prone to belittle the efforts of Johnson and his successors, but in this particular case the fact that the engines were built in such large numbers over such a lengthy period and, moreover, that so many of them lived to a ripe old age, must be conclusive evidence of the soundness of the design. ∎

LMS 4F No. 43940 inside Swindon roundhouse on September 20, 1964. BRIAN STEPHENSON

Nos.			C.M.E.	Wheel dia.		Dates	Totals
				ft.	in.		
2900-3019	...	...	Johnson	4	11	1875-1876	120
3020-3129	...	...	,,	5	3	1877-1884	110
3130-3189	...	...	,,	4	11	1885-1888	60
3190-3764	...	...	,,	5	3	1888-1902	575
3765-3834	...	...	Deeley	5	3	1903-1908	70
3835-4026	...	...	Fowler	5	3	1911-1922	192
4027-4556	...	...	,,	5	3	1924-1928	530
4562-4606	...	...	,,	5	3	1937-1940	45
S.D.J.R. 25-28, 33-44, 46-51, 56-61	...		Johnson	4	6	1878-1890	28
S.D.J.R. 62-66	...		,,	5	3	1896	5
S.D.J.R. 72-76	...		,,	5	3	1902	5
S.D.J.R. 57-61	...		Fowler	5	3	1922	5
M.G.N.J.R. 58-73	...		Johnson	5	3	1896-1899	16
							1,761

Summary of locos built for the Midland and LMS.

A double-headed pairing of LMS 4F Nos. 3542 and 3856 head a down freight near Hendon on May 10, 1927. H C CASSERLEY

Railways at Night

There's something special about railways at night, when stations and locos take on a different ambience. More than 20 years ago, many night operations were postal, parcels or newspaper trains, but that became traffic lost. Here's a reminder of not only how grand stations looked under artificial light, but the trains that served them too.

Right: 'Deltic' No. 55009 *Royal Highland Fusilier* stands at York one evening in September 1980 with a Newcastle to Leeds service. ALL PICTURES: TRACKS NORTH COLLECTION

Below: Bristol Temple Meads is the location where double-headed Class 50 Nos. 50042 *Triumph* and 50034 *Furious* stand with a Plymouth-Paddington working in January 1988.

Above: 'Peak' No. 45105 and its rake of BG vans are loaded with parcels at St Pancras on September 17, 1984, before heading to Derby.

Above left: Class 86 No. 86214 *Sanspareil* sits at Crewe with the down West Coast Postal on June 3, 1982.

Left: A Newcastle to Liverpool Provincial Railways evening service is loaded with mail at Manchester Victoria in February 1989, with No. 47434 *Pride in Huddersfield* at the head.

Below: 'Peak' No. 45146 has just arrived at Derby on April 4, 1984, with a three-carriage parcels train from Birmingham, one carriage about to be removed by a Class 08 shunter.

'Terrier' A1X class 0-6-0T No. 32655 approaches Tenterden with the last BR passenger service train from Robertsbridge to Headcorn on January 4, 1954. *RM* ARCHIVE

Kent & East Sussex Railway closure

THE Southern Region of British Railways has announced that passenger services on the former Kent & East Sussex Light Railway will be withdrawn as from January 4, 1954.

As there are no Sunday services, the last trains will run on Saturday, January 2.

The 13½ miles from Robertsbridge to Tenterden Town will remain open for freight traffic, but the remainder of the line, the eight miles from Tenterden to Headcorn, will be closed completely.

The stations and halts affected are Salehurst Halt, Junction Road Halt, Bodiam, Northiam, Wittersham Road, Rolvenden, Tenterden Town, Tenterden (St Michaels), High Halden Road, Biddenden, and Frittenden Road. Authorised under the Light Railways Act of 1896 as the Rother Valley Railway, the 12 miles from Robertsbridge to Rolvenden (then known as Tenterden) were opened on April 2, 1900.

The railway was extended to Tenterden Town in 1903, and to Headcorn in 1905.

The name of the undertaking was changed to the Kent & East Sussex Railway in 1904.

From the December 1953 issue

Decline of the rail motor

AT the end of 1922 the total of steam rail motors owned by British railways was only 115. Thirteen years earlier the total was 185.

This decrease, which year by year becomes more marked in the number of rail motors, shows that such combinations are not altogether successful. Yet, theoretically, a self-contained unit for railway working is ideal for branches and sections where traffic is light, and also for providing frequent services.

The chief drawback to the success of the rail motor is that when the engine requires repair or attention the whole car is put out of service. This defect has in a measure been met by making the locomotive detachable from the passenger car, but the separation of the two parts is not a simple matter that can be performed in a short time.

The weight of the combination and the need for absolute rigidity of the whole require the connections between the units to be of a strong and substantial character.

Duplicate engine portions must be available if the passenger unit is to be kept in traffic, and the parts of both units that are connected must be standardised to enable exchanges to be made.

The 115 steam rail motors existing at the end of 1922 were owned as follows: GW 65, L & NW, 25; North Staffordshire, 3; and Knott End and Nidd Valley, 1 each.

Of these, the GW only had 36 available for use and but 23 in actual service, the figures for the late L & NWR being 15 and 11, respectively. The five railways only had 37 in actual use.

From the March 1924 issue

Freight trains on a tramway

IN order to provide facilities for the handling of rail traffic in the Cleveleys area, previously dealt with at Thornton, two miles distant, a siding from the Blackpool Corporation tramway line was laid in at Thornton Gate in 1927, and a connection established with the LMSR at Fleetwood. The tramway, over which the wagons are worked, is a double track of standard gauge, ballasted with stone.

An electric locomotive is provided by the corporation, capable of hauling 150 tons, and weighing 10 tons; it was built by Dick Kerr, of Preston, in 1927. Coal is the chief commodity carried.

The siding at Thornton Gate has two tracks, each running alongside a roadway, and is equipped with wagon and dray weighbridges; it can accommodate about 45 wagons.

Daily, just after midday, a shunt is made by the LMSR at the Fleetwood siding, and the electric engine leaves Thornton Gate with the empty trucks to make the exchange for loaded wagons brought in by the railway company's pilot.

To reach the siding at Fleetwood, a branch leaves the tramway at Copse Road, just outside Fleetwood Town, and passes through a stores yard (owned by the corporation), joining the LMSR after completing a semi-circle.

Five tracks are provided on the corporation side for shunting purposes.

The time taken on the journey between the two sidings varies from 10 to 20 minutes, according to the load.

Speed has to be reduced for the crossing of two main roads.

Although a familiar sight to residents in the area, visitors display considerable curiosity when they see a goods train proceeding along the tramway ahead of their tramcar. (F W)

From the June 1934 issue

The Great Eastern 1500s

Holden-designed B12/5 No. 61530 rolls into Cambridge on June 13, 1959, with a train from King's Lynn. In 1959, just eight of the class survived. COLOUR RAIL

IT is, perhaps, remarkable that the last representatives of two once-numerous types of British mainline locomotives are Eastern Region stock, and that both designs originated at Stratford Works. However, whereas the sole-surviving 2-4-0s (James Holden, 1891) have remained largely unaltered, the last 4-6-0s with inside cylinders (S D Holden, 1911) are, because of rebuilding, hard to recognise as former Great Eastern Railway engines. The larger of these two classes has been given somewhat secondary duties in comparative old age, but still has many admirers.

Although the 4-6-0 with inside cylinders was common enough at one time, some of the pre-Grouping railways never built one: designers were said to be hesitant (or very definite) about a layout which involved the leading axle of a set of three taking the drive, not to mention the problem of fitting inside the frames a valve motion robust enough for a powerful locomotive. The obvious – and what became the classic – form of 4-6-0 has outside cylinders driving the centre pair of coupled wheels, and this design was introduced to Great Britain by David Jones on the Highland Railway in 1894.

It was another eminent Scottish designer, John McIntosh, of the Caledonian, who took the bold step of trying inside drive on a "10-wheeler" (as 4-6-0s were once commonly called). His No. 55, of 1902, although

By R S McNAUGHT

earmarked for the heavy gradients of the Callander & Oban line, was completely successful, and did not merit early criticisms that strain might be caused by leading axle drive. The class was added to, and McIntosh proceeded to design much larger and more truly express engines with the same arrangement, which soon was used on more than one English system as well.

"They proved to be a masterly instance of getting vast power in comparatively short bursts"

The Great Eastern was late in adopting the design, and it was even then largely dictated by the track and certain bridges being unable to take a large and heavy 4-4-0 which was planned to augment the 'Claud Hamilton' class. The latter had set high standards of express work for more than a decade, but as time went on a select few, specially maintained, were alone able to keep to schedule with increasingly heavy

'Hook Continental' and 'Cromer' expresses. So, on the last day of 1911, there issued from Stratford the pioneer 4-6-0 – GER No. 1500 – which underwent lengthy trials before being allocated to Parkeston to take over certain of the 'Continental' trains; it was joined there by Nos. 1501-1504 as they were completed.

It may be recalled that this was in accordance with the time-honoured GER custom of shedding practically all its main line engines 'in the country': they normally worked up to London and back once or several times a day, and those kept at Stratford overnight were mostly visitors. The unusual arrangement had the advantage of minimising light engine workings between Liverpool Street and Stratford on already very congested tracks.

The next six of the new class – Nos. 1505-1510 – were allotted to the 'Cromer' expresses, including the 'Norfolk Coast Express'. They differed slightly in appearance from the initial batch by having the ornate brass beading of their coupled wheel splashers extended to the side panelling of their large cabs, which necessitated a much smaller numberplate than standard, placed lower down.

It was one of this series – No. 1506 – which acquired the melancholy distinction of being one of the shortest-lived locomotives in British railway history, not even excepting the GER Decapod tank of 1902, Paget's ▶

experimental 2-6-2 on the Midland (1908), and the LMSR high-pressure *Fury* (1929). After only a trifle more than 12 weeks' service, this fine new 4-6-0 collided with a light engine at Colchester on July 12, 1913, and was damaged beyond repair. Strangely enough, the light engine involved was No. 471, one of the 'Intermediate' 2-4-0s, already mentioned as the last British representatives of this wheel arrangement, and, contrary to what one would expect, it suffered comparatively little damage, and was soon back in service.

The old custom on some lines of not using again the number of an ill-fated engine, but leaving it permanently blank as a kind of memorial, was adopted, and what would now presumably have been British Railways No. 61506 is non-existent. However, a new engine – No. 1535, and similar in all respects – was built in 1915 to replace the Colchester casualty, and incorporated its repaired boiler. The 1500 class, with variations, ultimately totalled 80.

To those who admired the early 20th century school of lineament as seen in the 'Clauds', and were not unduly put out by the remark of a certain Royal Academician (in a letter to *The Times*) that the Stratford blend of blue and "too much scarlet" was "garish and juvenile", the Holden 4-6-0s were the last word in magnificence. There were some, it is true, who preferred the unusual light grey with white lining which was a spasmodic GER alternative, but an opinion shared by many is that it was undoubtedly in the apple green, with polished brass and touches of vivid red, of early LNER days, that the class looked best: they would, perhaps, have made a still finer impression if coupled to tenders of Great Central or North Eastern style, instead of their own necessarily short- and high-sided ones. In the final survivors, painted black with a niggardly allowance of old-time Crewe lining-out, there is little to please the artists, and the livery only accentuates the portly look of the round-top boilers and top-heavy front ends surmounted by ugly Doncaster-style chimneys.

Practical critics, who saw beyond details of livery and trimmings, regarded the 1500s as elongated 4-4-0s, the additional pair of coupled wheels appearing to carry little more than the footplate. Perhaps, they thought, the ample firebox would make up for an unduly short boiler, following contemporary Derby practice. Some apprehension was expressed at the packing of two cylinders so large as 20in x 28in between the frames, it being remembered that the Great Western had decided that inside cranks of 14in throw could not easily be made strong enough after they had been tried on some 2-6-0 goods engines, later well known as the 'Aberdares'.

Other practical critics, whose opinions

B12/3 No. 61555 passes Trumpington, south of Cambridge, with the 5.50pm Sundays only stopping train to King's Cross on May 12, 1957. J A COILEY

Climbing Brentwood bank on April 21, 1951, is No. 61579, leading the 12.50pm Liverpool Street to Ipswich train. R W BEATON

were on solid foundations, were the footplate crews. They did not take well to an enormous cab which belied its commodious appearance by so much room being taken up by the trailing wheel coverings, and meant their standing in a narrow alcove with no escape from scorched legs when the firebox door was open.

Moreover, the firemen found that coal had to be carried about a yard further from the tender than on their well-liked 'Clauds', and it is probably this drawback that led to the nickname of "Hikers", although some historians assert that it emanated from the rucksack-like appearance of the boiler-top tanks of the feedwater heating apparatus that was later fitted to certain of the class. The firemen on the Great North of Scotland

section, to which a number of 1500s were transferred early in LNER days, got over the fuel difficulty by having especially long shovels made for the job in order to reduce their 'hiking' to a minimum.

In service, the new Holden type was immediately successful, and coped with ease with a speeded-up Great Eastern timetable which included much heavier restaurant car expresses. They proved to be a masterly instance of getting vast power in comparatively short bursts out of a unit with severe weight restrictions, but they also showed surprising ability for long-distance journeys, when, for instance, a special Ipswich link worked right over the Pennines daily into Manchester with cross-country boat trains, and made a good job of it.

Their gleaming brasswork and polished chimney tops carried a cheerful glint into the murky North West, and local enthusiasts of the day, whose acquaintance with Stratford engines was confined to irregular goods workings, went specially to Manchester Central to admire the "Big Swedies" (all GER engines were "Swedies" off their own metals). Some wondered to what extent speed fell off up the long gradients, and more than one footplate crew agreed that time had to be won back by very fast sprints down the other side. But this is anticipating the early Grouping era.

Stratford Works added to the class steadily until the latter part of the First World War; No. 1540 appeared in 1917. Then, in 1920, another 30 were ordered – 10 from Stratford and 20 from Beardmore's Naval Construction Works at Dalmuir, near Glasgow. The latter was changing over from building warships to railway work, including engine repairs. I was associated with the firm when the contract was in progress, and watched several of the Great Eastern engines undergoing erection and steaming tests in the immediate company of some of the 90 'Prince of Wales' 4-6-0s then being constructed for the London & North Western Railway, and also a batch of powerful 2-8-0s for an Indian railway. The two somewhat different conceptions of inside-cylinder "10-wheelers" made an interesting comparison, and the smaller and more closely-set wheels of the Crewe pattern led the workmen to speak of them as "the goods engines", although it is probably safe to say they were destined to attain higher speeds than were the Holdens. Perhaps it was because frames and all other components for the 'Princes' were much the less robust of the two, and it may be significant that the Great Eastern locomotives have long outlived a much more numerous class. The Beardmore batch of 1500s left for the south painted grey, and I do

With an ACFI feedwater heater, B12 No 8568 approaches Manningtree with an up Lowestoft to Liverpool Street slow train in the summer of 1938. G R GRIGS

not think that Stratford blue intervened before they were repainted in LNER green.

Following the merging of the owning company into the London & North Eastern Railway in 1923, the 1500s became Class B12, (sub-divided at intervals up to B12/4 as

"Their gleaming brasswork and polished chimney tops carried a cheerful glint into the murky North West"

rebuilding was undertaken). Their coal consumption figures were impressive, but not favourably so, when seen alongside certain other top-link engines in the greatly enlarged family, and the three-cylinder 'Sandringham' design was brought out (from other Scottish

builders) to supplant them. However, much improved coal figures were obtained by rebuilding No. 8516 with Lentz poppet valves, and other modifications.

So satisfactory was the rebuild, that a batch of 10 duplicates was constructed by Beyer, Peacock & Co Ltd. They were distinguishable at once by a simple raised running plate, like that of the Great Central 'City' and 'Improved Director' classes, instead of the ornate slotted pattern, reminiscent of Crewe compounds, which was a legacy from the 'Claud Hamiltons'. They also carried plain cast-iron chimneys, set back on extended smokeboxes. Some of the original engines were also Lentz-fitted, but gradually there was a reversion from this system of valve gear. Another general modification to the class, in keeping with the times, was the replacement of Ramsbottom safety valves housed in a rectangular casing by a pair of Ross "Pop" type.

By 1932, most sections of the old Great Eastern system had been made available to heavier locomotives, and Nigel Gresley rebuilt a 1500 almost out of recognition with a 5ft 6in boiler and round-top firebox in place of the original Belpaire one. It also had long lap valves as a result of their revolutionary effect on his modified Pacifics. This increased the weight from 64 to 69 tons, but the modified front end made for smarter work, and the coal consumption figures improved. As the backplate was now two feet nearer to the tender, the fireman's task was considerably eased. Ultimately, 54 of the class were similarly treated, the outward effect being a sudden development of elegant debutantes into portly and self-satisfied matrons.

It was found necessary to retain a group with the original layout and reduced axle loading for use on the GNSR lines, where they were chosen to augment, although not entirely supplant, the traditionally modest-sized 4-4-0s used for all kinds of work. Although the Scottish drivers, in unguarded moments, ▶

Working hard up Belstead bank in 1938 is B12 No. 8575 with the 11.50am Ipswich to Liverpool Street train. G R GRIGS

Epitaph for an Engineman

THOSE who collect curious epitaphs may like to have this one, noted by a reader while browsing among the tombstones in the churchyard of Corwen, Merionethshire.

Owen Owen. Engine Driver.
Died 1872. Aged 29 years.
His last drive is over, death has put on the break (*sic*)
His soul has been signalled its long journey to take.
When death sounds the whistle the steam of life falls,
And his mortal day shunted 'till the last trumpet calls.

From *The Manchester Guardian*

Well away from its intended area of operation, B12 No. 61552, one of several allocated to Aberdeen Kittybrewster shed, stands at Banchory on the line from Ballater with an up Aberdeen train on July 7, 1951. G H ROBIN

agreed that they had never had such power and 'sweet runners' on their line, their enthusiasm was a muted one: it was the notion of second-hand engines being sent north that rankled – that and the firing snag which the special long shovels only partly overcame. With the instinctive Scots' affection for all machinery, however, they polished and burnished the fittings up to their customary standard, and got some first-class work out of the "Hikers". Yet another variation of the class as a whole was the reboilering of nine of the Scottish migrants with round-top fireboxes of the original dimensions. This produced the B12/4 sub-class, the appearance of which made one realise how modest the primary design was for a 4-6-0; these nine engines quickly gained a high reputation for steaming and speed.

In England, the Gresley rebuilds were excellent express engines, until it was evident

that the main frames were over-strained by strenuous driving – not the first instance of a natural tendency in engines rebuilt with larger boilers than originally fitted. They then became odd-job men, and were to be seen heading trains that an old J15 0-6-0 could easily have worked, but their excellent weight distribution and clearances still enabled them to operate almost anywhere, and these advantages made them an obvious choice for semi-permanent attachment to hospital trains during the Second World War.

In this capacity, they worked through to places far from the LNER, and railway enthusiasts serving abroad would ponder over letters from home mentioning that a Great Eastern engine had been noted at Plymouth or Southampton. The most unlikely place where one was reported on hospital trains was the Leominster-Kington branch, in Herefordshire, where nothing more than Great Western 0-4-2

or pannier tanks normally worked. This tendency of Stratford engines to wander was of long standing, and a correspondent recently reminded me that one of the pioneer batch of the 1500s turned up at Preston with a train of prisoners of war in 1915; its blue livery and throbbing air-brake compressor started a local rumour that the Caledonian *Cardean* had crossed the Border again.

As recently as May 8, 1955, No. 61554 was used to haul a railway enthusiasts' special from Nottingham to Crewe by a devious route of historic interest, and actually penetrated the former London & North Western Railway's works. This, it was suggested, was delayed retribution for 'Princes', and other Crewe engines, besmirching with their smoke the fair atmosphere of Cambridge.

A regular express service the B12s have operated for several years is the daily through one between Birmingham, Leicester, and the East Coast via the Midland & Great Northern joint line. They formerly ran through from Yarmouth to Leicester and back, but that regular penetration of the Midlands ceased when the winter timetables of 1955/6 included a stop at Spalding, previously bypassed, and consequent reversal of the train. Engines are now changed at the latter point, and Class 4 Moguls work the train to Leicester. The GER engine returns to Yarmouth with the reverse evening working.

The day cannot be long delayed when the 1500s become extinct, and admirers of them, even in their final portliness and BR black livery, will hear no more their measured exhaust note, or delight in the neat sweep of old-fashioned side rods unencumbered and festooned with clanking outside valve gear ■

An early 1920s picture of B12 No. 1503 piloting an unidentified Claud Hamilton 4-4-0 near Chadwell Heath. *RM* ARCHIVE

LNWR 'Precedent' No. 364 *Henry Pease* pilots Claughton No. 2097 on an Aberdeen to Euston Express at Carlisle circa 1920. RM ARCHIVE

'Precedent' London and North Western four-couple Locomotives

By REGINALD H COE

THE 2-4-0 two-cylinder Simple locomotive has always been a great favourite on British railways, and few, if any, of the leading lines in this country hesitated to build large numbers of them.

It is not hard to account for this popularity if one remembers that when the 2-4-0 type was introduced, the chief and virtually only type of passenger engine existent, was the single-wheeler. Now, while these engines were, for their time, first-class locomotives, they had two great defects.

Even in those far-off days, loads were continually on the increase, and gradually getting beyond the capacity of the small single-wheeler. Then there was the vexed question of 'slipping' – always a prominent feature of the locomotive without coupled wheels. Therefore, when the 2-4-0 type was brought into being, it rapidly became a favourite on nearly all British lines. But on no railway, perhaps, did it attain such success as on the London and North Western, and it is noteworthy that it has maintained its popularity down to the present time. The 2-4-0 locomotives on this system have had an interesting history, and their career has

been one of the most creditable in the history of locomotives.

As is usual with most new types of engine, they were built because they were badly needed. At the time when they first made their appearance, the chief type of

engine were the 'Problem' single-wheelers, which although doing valuable work for the North Western, were beginning to get outclassed in the heavy traffic, especially on the Crewe to Holyhead line – it is reported, on some of the very rough days, they were almost brought to a standstill by the great gales, which swept across that part of the country.

'Precedent' No. 419 *Zillah*, in a photograph taken in 1890. RM ARCHIVE

Seeing this, Mr John Ramsbottom (who was then chief mechanical engineer of the line, and also the designer of the 'Problem' locomotives just referred to), turned his attention to designing an engine that would be better adapted for the heavier traffic, and in May 1863, turned out the first coupled passenger engine on the line. This locomotive, bearing the name of *Samson*, excited a great deal of comment in the railway world at the time. Its dimensions were as follows: Driving wheels, 6ft in diameter; weight in working order (without tender), 26 tons 2cwt

Mr Ramsbottom continued building these engines in batches of ten, until January 1866, when 50 had appeared. These bore the following numbers and names:

'Precedent' No. 2005 *Lynx* pilots 'Prince of Wales' class No. 5894, which has arrived at London Euston with the up 'Irish Mail' in August 1924. A S W MACE

Initial batch 1896-1866

No.	Name	No.	Name
35	Talisman	746	Castor
36	Shalaba	748	Waterloo
81	Greystoke*	752	Glowworm
124	Marquis Douro	757	Banshee
234	Firefly	758	Hardman
401	Zeno	763	Voilet
404	Zopyrus	764	Shap
418	Zygia*	793	Marten
419	Zillah*	794	Woodlark
609	The Earl of Chester	795	Falstaff
628	Tartarus	814	Henrietta
632	Ostrich*	817	Constance
633	Samson	819	Puck
634	Ellesmere	821	Diomed*
642	Bee	824	Adelaide
724	Eden*	828	Tubal*
731	Axteth	829	Turk*
732	Hecta	830	Trent*
733	Chimera	832	Sanspareil*
735	Charon	885	Vampire
737	Memnon	901	Hero
737	Roberts	902	Onyx*
738	Terrice*	934	North Star
739	Sutherland	935	Planet*
742	Spitfire		

* All marked thus are now scrapped.

He then started building a similar type of engine, only having larger driving wheels and dimensions. When Mr Webb ascended to the 'throne' at Crewe, in 1871, he continued for some years to build engines of both types, until 1875, when he brought out his own 'Precedent' type.

The locomotives built between 1866 and 1879, of the old type, are as follows : ▶

Small type

No.	Name
90	Luck of Edenhall
209	Petrel
263	Pheasant*
285	Phalaris*
414	Prospero*
424	Sirius
434	St Patrick
444	Typhoon*
445	Ixion*
446	Siren*
468	Wildfire
469	St George*
479	Mastodon
485	Euxine
486	Skiddaw
487	John O' Groats
604	Narcissus
631	Hotspur
635	Zantiel*
636	Eclipse*
773	Centaur
852	Kestral*
995	Medea
1045	Whitworth
1162	Saddleback
1163	John O'Gaunt
1164	Odin*
1166	Wyre
1168	Cuckoo
2150	Atlas*
2151	Baltic*
2152	Sybil
2153	Isis
2154	Loadstone
2155	Liver*
2156	Sphinx
2157	Unicorn
2158	Sister Dora
2159	Shark*

An unidentified LNWR 2-4-0 'Precedent' class on an up passenger service passes Harrow & Wealdstone in early 1923. *RM* ARCHIVE

From *The Railway Magazine*, September 1912

Large type

No.	Name
271	Minotaur
275	Vulcan*
276	Pluto
295	Penmaenmawr*
304	Hector
308	Booth
379	Sedgwick
380	Quernmore
381	Patterdale
382	Buckingham
393	Brougham*
394	Eamont
395	Scotia
396	Tennyson
403	Isabella
480	Duchess of Lancaster
512	Lazonby
514	Lawrence
517	Marathon
787	Clarendon
789	Breadalbane
790	Hardwicke
919	Nasmyth
941	Blenkinsop
942	Shah of Persia
945	Humphrey Davy
974	Richard Cobden
1020	Wordsworth*
1105	Hercules
1132	North Western*
1141	S R Graves*
1170	General
1173	The Auditor
1211	John Ramsbottom
1212	Pioneer
1213	The Queen
1214	Prince Albert
1215	Albion*
1216	Premier
1217	Florence
1218	Phaeton*
1219	Lightning*
1220	Belted Will
1480	Newton
1481	The Duke of Edinboro'
1482	Herschel*
1483	Newcomen*
1484	Telford
1485	Smeaton
1486	Dalton
1487	Faraday*
1488	Murdock
1489	Brindley*
1513	Shakespeare*
1514	Scott
1515	Milton
1516	Byron*
1517	Princess Helena
1518	Countess
1519	Duchess
1520	Franklin
1521	Gladstone
1522	Pitt
1523	Marlborough*
1524	Wolfe*
1525	Abercrombie
1526	Drake*
1527	Raleigh
1528	Frobisher
1529	Cook
1530	Columbus
1531	Cromwell
1532	Hampden*
1666	Ariadne
1667	Corunna

'Precedent' No. 324 and a Claughton 4-6-0 head an up express over Bushey troughs in the early 1920s. H GORDON TIDEY

'Large Precedent' No. 1518 Countess pilots Claughton No. 110 Lady Godiva through Tebay troughs with an express from Manchester and Liverpool to Glasgow in September 1923.
O S NOCK

No.	Name		No.	Name
1668	Dagmar		1681	Minerva
1669	Ilion		1682	Novelty
1670	Ganyrnede*		1683	Sisyphus*
1671	Shamrock*		1684	Speke
1672	Talavera		1685	Gladiator
1673	Lucknow		1744	Magdala
1674	Delhi		1745	John Bright
1675	Vimera		1746	Bevere
1676	The Nile*		1747	John Mayall*
1677	Badajos		1748	Britannia
1678	Airey		1749	Hibernia
1679	Benson			
1680	Livingstone			

* All marked thus are now scrapped.

The 'Precedent' lot were the best of all, and a large number were turned out between the years 1874 and 1882.

Their numbers and names were as follows:

Improved 'Precedents'

No.	Name
193	Rocket
253	President Garfield
254	President Lincoln*
256	President Washington
257	Duke of Albany
260	Duke of Connaught
262	Wheatstone
264	Buckland*
265	Thomas Carlyle
364	Henry Pease
477	Caractacus
478	Commodore
482	Pegasus
506	Sir Alexander Cockburn
619	Mabel
696	Director
749	Mercury
857	Prince Leopold
858	Sir Salar Jung
860	Merrie Carlisle
861	Amazon
862	Balmoral
863	Meteor*
864	Pilot
866	Courier
867	Disraeli
868	Condor*
869	Llewellyn
870	Fairbairn
885	Envoy
871	Proserpina
872	Wizard
883	Phantom
890	Sir Hardman Earle
955	Charles Dickens
1183	Plynlimmon*
1187	Chandos
1189	Stewart
1193	Joshua Radcliffe
1194	Miranda
2001	Henry Crossfield
2002	Madge
2003	Alecto*
2004	Witch
2005	Lynx
2006	Princess
2175	Precedent
2176	Robert Benson
2177	Edward Tootal*
2178	Pluck
2179	Patience
2180	Perseverance
2181	Buffalo*
2182	Giraffe
2183	Antelope
2184	Reynard
2185	Alma
2186	Lowther
2187	Penrith Beacon
2188	Chillington*
2189	Avon
2190	Princess Beatrice
2191	Snowdon
2192	Caradoc
2193	Salopian
2194	Cambrian

* All marked thus are now scrapped.

'Improved Precedent' No. 1668 *Dagmar* pilots a 'Precursor' through Willesden Junction station with an up express to London Euston in 1920. J MACARTNEY ROBBIN

These engines had 6ft 6in driving wheels and cylinders 17in by 24in, and their total weight, with tender, was 57¾ tons. So successful were they, that about the 'nineties' all the earlier 2-4-0 locomotives were rebuilt, with the 'Precedent' as a pattern, and they are, therefore, now generally known as the 'Precedent' class.

It is amazing when one considers the work they have done during the 40 odd years they have been running. They have had their share of the fastest and heaviest main line trains, the most noted expresses and the crack trains of the line. They have hauled goods and mineral trains, suburban trains, excursion 'specials', and have often been seen shunting. Surely they were veritable mixed-traffic engines.

It would be hard to say which was the most noted 'Precedent' built. Perhaps, if any one of the class could lay claim to that distinction, it would be the *Charles Dickens*, No. 955, which for 20 years, ran daily between Euston and Manchester.

In 1907 this engine had run more than 2,000,000 miles since it was built in 1882. On one occasion, in the summer of 1902,

while running an heavy morning non-stop train from Manchester to London, it covered the 116½ miles from Lichfield to Euston in just under two hours, travelling at an average rate of nearly 60mph. This engine is now preserved at Crewe, and it is to be hoped that it will not ultimately come to the scrapheap like so many of its contemporaries are doing.

Hardwicke, No. 790, was another locomotive that gained great popularity. This engine was built in 1873, and won renown by running the race train between Crewe and Carlisle in 1895. The train started from Euston on August 22, in that year, and from Crewe, *Hardwicke* hauled the train on to Carlisle at an average speed of 62.2mph. It is a singular fact that three years previously the same locomotive fell from a viaduct into the street below. It was on May 27, 1892, to be precise, when a North Western train, pulled by *Hardwicke* was approaching Birmingham, when it was run into by a Midland Railway train, through a fault of the signalman. The engine of the North Western train was pushed over the viaduct into the street, where it lay for some time, arousing

LNWR 'Jubilee' No. 1923 *Agamemnon* is piloted by 'Improved Precedent' No. 2185 *Alma* past Bushey troughs in 1902. *RM* ARCHIVE

From *The Railway Magazine*, September 1912

considerable interest in the town. *Hardwicke* is now stationed at Chester, still performing some very useful work.

Another famous 'Precedent' was *Zygia*, No. 418, which was in the terrible Chelford accident of 1894, when 14 persons were killed. *Shark*, No. 2159, and *Vulcan*, No. 275, both met with accidents on the Preston curve. *Vulcan* ran in the race of 1888, from Crewe to Carlisle. *Caliban* was one of the first to be built by Mr F W Webb, and was originally named *Cyclops*. These four engines have now been scrapped.

Several of the 'Precedents' changed their name soon after their birth. In addition to *Caliban*, *Sister Dora* was originally named *Serpent*, *Tennyson* first came out as *Dunrobin*, while *Princess Beatrice* first bore the name *Beatrice*. Special mention should also be made of *Eamont*, No. 394, which was in the races of 1895.

The general work of the 'Precedents' has always been of the finest. As far back as 1884, the late Mr Charles Rous-Marten recorded some brilliant performances of these engines. In that year he travelled behind *Sir Hardman Earle*, No. 890, when it covered the distance of 77 miles between Rugby and Willesden in 73min.

In the same year, Mr Rous-Marten recorded *Commodore*, No. 478, as covering the 37½ miles from Shap Summit to Lancaster in 35¾min, attaining a speed of 74mph down the bank.

The 'Precedents' have always been great favourites on the Carlisle section, where, ever since they came out, they have been running in large numbers; and it is on this line that they have achieved some of their best performances. In August 1895, a most praiseworthy run from Crewe to Carlisle was made by *The Queen*, No. 1213, with an old single-wheeler (*Prince Alfred*) as pilot.

Courier, *Mercury*, *Odin*, and many others, also made highly meritorious runs on that section. They are now used to assist the 'Experiments' (4-6-0), a work which they carry out most satisfactorily. In the south their work has also been very fine. Until a few years back they were often to be seen on the London and Birmingham expresses, but of later years have been somewhat outclassed for that traffic. The last famous run between those two points was made by *John Ramsbottom*, No. 1211, on one of the crack two-hour trains. The train was the 2.45pm, ex-Birmingham, and with a fairly heavy load, it reached London two minutes early, although having left a minute late.

The writer once travelled behind *Princess Helena*, No. 1517, when it made an even better performance, but it was on that occasion assisted by another 'Precedent'. A second good run by a North Western locomotive was that of *Lightning*, No. 1219,

'Precedent' No. 790 *Hardwicke* and LNER A3 4472 *Flying Scotsman* make an odd combination as they head out of Giggleswick with the S&C Centenary train on May 1, 1975. DAVID EATWELL

assisted by a single-wheeled locomotive (*Victoria*).

The 'Precedents' have also, during their day, made good pilots, and the assistance which they gave to the old compounds was invaluable. It was a 'Precedent' – *Snowdon*, No. 2191 – that piloted *Superb* (4-4-0 compound) when it made its fine run from Rugby to Euston, in 1902, covering the distance in 87min 18sec, or nearly five minutes under scheduled time. The old three-cylinder compound, *Oceanic*, once, when piloted by the 'Precedent' *Alma*, No. 2185, made a good journey from Euston to Crewe, covering the 158 miles in 185min.

Coming to more modern times, we find that they still do some good piloting work. In February of last year, *Abercrombie*, No. 1525, piloted a 'Precursor' on a Euston-Birmingham train, when a very fast journey was made, with a huge load.

In the preceding month, *Bevere*, No. 1746, ably assisted an 'Experiment' with a heavy train from London to Crewe. They

still make some good performances with excursions, and in the summer of 1909, *Isis*, No. 2153, brought a tremendous load from Blackpool to Birmingham in fine style, the journey on the last stretch, from Crewe, being equal to the express work of some of the most modern locomotives.

They are also very extensively used, nowadays, on local stopping trains, for which they are found very useful.

To turn to their last sphere of work, they still manage heavy goods trains most admirably. A few months ago the writer saw *The Earl of Chester*, No. 609, pulling a large number of loaded good and mineral wagons at a fair speed. They are often to be seen performing shunting work in the various shunting yards on the system.

They are now being gradually withdrawn from service, and replaced by more modern engines. Nevertheless, it will be some years yet before they have all finally disappeared. They have had a remarkable career, and been one of the finest examples of early British locomotives ever built. ∎

National Coal Board Hudswell Clarke 0-4-0ST No. 1893 of 1961 shunts in the yard at Barrow Main Colliery, Worsbrough, Barnsley, on September 8, 1969. The colliery closed in 1991. PETER A HOGARTH

NCB Austerity 0-6-0ST *Respite*, with a Giesl ejector, shunts wagons alongside a steam crane on PW Work at Astley Green Colliery, just west of Manchester, on May 14, 1969. The loco survived into preservation and is now based at the Ribble Steam Railway, Preston.

Peckett 0-6-0ST No. 8 (works No.1971 of 1939) shunts spoil wagons from the washery for tipping at Pegswood Colliery, near Morpeth, on

Above: NCB Barclay 0-4-0ST No. 885 of 1900 and Hunslet 0-6-0ST No. 2880 of 1943 haul loaded wagons from Polkemmet Colliery, West Lothian, to the BR exchange sidings on September 1, 1969. J G GLOVER

Above: The winter light of February 17, 1969, catches RSH 0-6-0ST No. 6 (7603 of 1949) at Derwenthaugh Coke works, near Blaydon, shunting hoppers, while another saddle tank waits in the distance.
V C K ALLEN

Left: A trio of 0-4-0 crane tanks lined up at lunchtime in the Doxford Shipyard, Sunderland on May 16, 1966, including RSH-built *Roker* and *Southwick* (left and centre). Both these locos have been preserved.
RM ARCHIVE

An early 1900s photo of an LBSCR 4-4-0 heading a Victoria-Brighton Pullman service past Tooting Common. *RM* ARCHIVE

By Pullman to Brighton

By CHARLES E LEE

PULLMAN cars have been a feature of the train services to Brighton for 83 years, but in early days they were by no means an unqualified success, mainly because the open saloon was in contrast to the British love of seclusion.

Nevertheless, the London, Brighton & South Coast Railway was unwavering in its faith, and the popularity of the Pullman increased with the early years of a new century. This culminated exactly 50 years ago in the inauguration of the famous all-Pullman train 'The Southern Belle', claimed to be the most luxurious train in the world, and the golden jubilee of that event is an opportune time to recall something of the story of the Pullman on the Brighton service.

A Pullman car first ran on the London-Brighton service on November 1, 1875. This was the 28-ton 'parlor' car *Jupiter*, built in the USA and assembled in 1875 at Derby by the Pullman Palace Car Company, a branch of the American organisation formed in 1867 by George Mortimer Pullman. This car was attached to a train of six new first-class coaches which left Victoria at 10.45am and ran non-stop to Brighton in 70 minutes, a timing on the London-Brighton service which had been established as early as April 1858. The Pullman supplementary charge was 1s 6d over the first-class express fare. Later, the two cars *Alexandra* and *Albert Edward*, built in 1877, were added to the Brighton service.

The first all-Pullman train to run on the LBSCR was introduced in 1881, very largely on the initiative of Mr J P Knight, the railway company's general manager from 1870 to 1886, who is credited with a considerable share in the design of the vehicles. This train also was assembled by the Pullman Palace Car Company at its Derby shops. It consisted of four Pullman day cars, named respectively *Maud*, *Victoria*, *Beatrice*, and *Louise*. Although

"The first all-Pullman train to run on the LBSCR was introduced in 1881."

described as a new train, the vehicles do not appear to have been new, but were probably refurbished and partly rebuilt for the service. Thus, the *Louise* was built in August 1876, and the *Victoria* in 1877. The *Maud* would seem to have been the *Ceres* of 1877, redecorated and renamed.

The *Beatrice* appears to have been a product of 1881, but was used experimentally between Victoria and Brighton in October of that year as the first railway carriage to be

lighted by electricity. This was 11 months before a similar experiment in the USA. As a result, the new train was electrically lighted throughout using Swan's and Edison's incandescent lamps in series with 80 Faure accumulators in the guard's compartment at each end of the train. The accumulators were charged every evening at Victoria. The train was heated by Baker heaters, then in general use on all American trains. The heat was kept uniform throughout, at about 58 deg, by a continuous circulation of hot water in pipes distributed through the train and regulated by the attendant.

Each car was 58ft 5in in overall length, making the total of the train 233ft 8in. The height of each car, from the top of the rail to the centre of the roof, was 13ft 2in, and the width at the eaves outside 8ft 11in. The car *Maud* consisted of three compartments, the largest of which was for smoking and accommodated 26 in 22 fixed seats and four chairs; next to this was a compartment holding six, intended for passengers' servants; beyond was the guard's and luggage compartment. The parlour and restaurant car *Victoria* contained 28 seats and a bar counter from which light refreshments were served. A newspaper stand and letterbox also were provided. In this car were electrical discs and a bell indicating in which part of the train the attendant was required. A barometer, thermometer, and clock also were provided. The drawing-room car

Beatrice had 21 revolving chair seats; this was the ladies' car, intended to be used by ladies travelling alone or accompanied by gentlemen. This car contained a ladies' boudoir and dressing-zoom. The parlour car *Louise* was arranged similarly to the *Maud*, but was a non-smoker. The capacity of the train was thus 113 passengers.

As with all Pullman cars before 1908, the vehicles were of the clerestory type. They had open end balconies, with wooden platforms covering the connections between the cars giving a gangway communication throughout the train.

The livery was a deep umber, with black and gold lining. The train was fitted with the Stroudley and Rusbridge electric communication between train staff and driver. The train was claimed as the most luxurious of its kind in Europe, and the cost was said to be about £12,000. Before being placed in service, the train was exhibited at St Pancras (en route from Derby) where it was inspected by a representative of *The Times*, which published a detailed description on November 19.

On December 1, 1881, a special inaugural trip was made to Brighton via Dorking, Horsham, and Shoreham, and back by the direct route. The train was hauled by William Stroudley's 'G' class 2-2-2 No. 329 *Stephenson*, with 6ft 6in driving wheels, built at the Brighton works in that year. On December 5, 1881, as 'The Pullman Limited Express', the train was placed in regular service. On weekdays it left Victoria at 10am and 3.50pm, returning from Brighton at 1.20pm and 5.45pm. The company's timetable had this note: "On and from Monday, December 5, this train will consist of Pullman cars only".

The Sunday train ran first on December 11. It left Victoria at 12.30pm and returned from Brighton at 9.30pm and also consisted

LBSCR 'Atlantic' No 422, immaculately presented, heads the 'Southern Belle' past Tooting Common. *RM* ARCHIVE

only of Pullman cars. The 10am (80min) called at Clapham Jct and Preston Park; the 3.50pm (75min) was non-stop; the 1.20pm up train (80min) called at East Croydon and Grosvenor Road; and the 5.45pm up was relatively the fastest, as, with stops at East Croydon, Clapham Jct, and Grosvenor Road, it took 77min. At this period, all trains to Victoria stopped at Grosvenor Road for ticket collecting, and, with very few exceptions, down trains stopped at Preston Park for the same purpose.

In an appreciative account of the train, *The Times* said "the experiment is one deserving of a sympathetic response by the travelling public for it exhibits for the first time in this country a mode of travelling in which every want of the passenger is anticipated and by which the art of travelling will be shorn of every unnecessary inconvenience".

Nevertheless, the all-Pullman train was poorly patronised, and in less than two months

the Sunday train was withdrawn. The weekly service was continued, but, from December 1, 1882, ordinary first-class compartment coaches from the railway company's stock were attached, and the train ceased to be all-Pullman. The name 'Pullman Limited Express' remained in the timetable until 1887, when the words 'Fast Train' were substituted for 'Express'.

In 1882 a British company called the Pullman Co Ltd was formed, but under American control.

A new three-car Pullman train with vestibulated connections (a recent invention and an advance on the open balcony connections of the 1881 train) was built in 1888 in the USA by the Pullman Palace Car Company and assembled at the LBSCR carriage works at Brighton. The three vehicles were the 27-seat *Princess*, a parlour car, with 19 revolving chairs and eight sofa seats; the *Prince*, a 26-seat buffet car, with 17 revolving chairs and nine sofa seats; and the 40-seat smoker *Albert Victor*, with 30 fixed seats and 10 wicker chairs. Each car was 58ft long and the train was lighted by electricity, but the current was generated by the motion of the train.

A trial trip was made on December 10, 1888, and on the following day the train was put into general service. It took the place of cars used on the existing Victoria-Brighton 'Pullman Limited Fast Train', and on Sundays it was substituted for the 'Pullman Drawing Room Car Train' which left Victoria at 10.45am and returned from Brighton at 8.40pm. No improvement was made in the timing. First-class compartment coaches were always attached to the new train and sometimes additional Pullman cars. By 1895, the Sunday train frequently consisted of no fewer than seven Pullman cars, with six or seven first-class compartment coaches. The time allowed ▶

LBSCR Class J2 4-6-2T No 326 *Bessborough* heads a Brighton-bound Pullman train south near Croydon. It was the last of the class when scrapped in 1951. *RM* ARCHIVE

from Victoria to Brighton on Sundays, with stops at Clapham Jct and East Croydon, was 80min.

A new train of three Pullman cars, each 62ft long, was introduced on November 4, 1895. The vehicles were a 26-seat parlour car *Her Majesty*, a 26-seat buffet car *Duchess of York*, and a 36-seat smoking car *Princess of Wales*. They were American built, and were assembled at the LBSCR Brighton works. Both oil-gas and electric lighting were provided. The train ran on weekdays from Victoria to Brighton at 10.50am and 3.50pm, and from Brighton at 1.20pm and 5.45pm. On Sundays there was a single journey each way, at 10.45am from Victoria and 8.40pm from Brighton.

On Sunday, October 2, 1898, a train consisting exclusively of Pullman cars was once again put on, and, in contrast to 1881, was well patronised. The new train left Victoria at 11am and returned from Brighton at 9pm. It ran only on Sundays, and not at all during July, August, and September, by reason of the difficulty in securing a clear road in the holiday months.

During June, the train left Brighton an hour later. Like its predecessor, it was at first called 'The Pullman Limited Express'. Early in 1899, the title 'Brighton Limited' began to be used, but not to the exclusion of the earlier one, which was retained until 1908, when the train was superseded. From the outset, this train was the first to be timed to run from Victoria to Brighton in an hour, and to do the same on the return journey. Its first run was made with five Pullman cars and two baggage cars; there was seating accommodation for 150 passengers. On the following Sunday, an extra Pullman car was attached, and later the normal number of cars was seven.

On December 21, 1902, the train, hauled by R J Billinton's 4-4-0 locomotive No. 70 *Holyrood*, built by Sharp, Stewart & Company

LBSCR B2X class 4-4-0 No 201, designed by Billington, leads the 'Southern Belle' to Brighton. Taken in the early 1920s, the loco was scrapped in 1930. *RM* ARCHIVE

in September 1901, made a record by reaching Brighton in 54min from Victoria. The average speed was 54mph, and that between East Croydon and Brighton more than 62mph.

On Sunday, July 26, 1903, the same engine with a special train of three cars and two brakevans (about 130 tons behind the tender) made two very fast runs to demonstrate the capabilities of steam at a period when the possibility of a 50-min schedule between Victoria and Brighton by a proposed competitive electric railway was being discussed.

The down trip from Victoria to Brighton (50 miles 73 ch), was run in 48min 41sec start to stop, at an average speed of 63.4mph. The maximum of 90mph was attained near Horley. The return trip took 50min 21sec, an average of 60.8mph, and the maximum was 85mph. The timings were recorded by Charles

Rous-Marten in *The Railway Magazine* of September, 1903 (p208).

In 1906, the livery of the Pullman cars was changed from all umber to the now familiar cream for the upper panels and umber below, lined out in gold. Sixpenny Pullman car supplementary fares were introduced on April 1, 1908, available to first-class passengers travelling distances up to 26 miles. The charge of 1s for distances over 26 miles remained unchanged.

A fundamental change in the British Pullman organisation took place in 1907, when Mr Davison (later Lord) Dalziel acquired control from the American interests. The use of the American spelling parlor was discontinued, and even 'parlour' began to give place to 'drawing room'. Of greater consequence was the fact that all subsequent rolling stock has been British built. Until 1908, all the Pullmans running in Great Britain had been built in the USA, and only assembled in this country.

On August 29, 1908, it was announced that a new seven-car Pullman train de luxe, 'the most luxurious train in the world', was being built at the Lancaster works of the Metropolitan Amalgamated Railway Carriage & Wagon Co Ltd for daily service between Victoria and Brighton. A month later, it became known that the train would be named the 'Southern Belle', which caused *The Railway Gazette* to comment on "the growing appreciation of the fact that a named train is an advertising asset". The time for the venture was opportune. Victoria station had been completely rebuilt, and the final section opened on July 1, 1908. The main line had been widened as far as Three Bridges, and Brighton traffic was on the increase.

The original make-up of the train had composite parlour cars with guard's

LBSCR 'L' class 4-6-4T No. 332 awaits the right away at London Victoria with the 'Southern Belle'. *RM* ARCHIVE

From *The Railway Magazine*, November 1958

BR's 5-Bel Pullman set No. 3051 passes Preston Park with a down 'Brighton Belle' service on June 23, 1968. COLOUR RAIL

compartments at each end, the *Alberta* and the *Verona*. Each accommodated 30 passengers. There were four 33-seat parlour cars, the *Bessborough* (named after the Earl of Bessborough, Chairman of the LBSCR), the *Cleopatra*, the *Belgravia*, and the *Princess Helen*. In the middle of the train was the buffet car *Grosvenor*, with seating accommodation for 25. The total capacity was thus 217.

The cars were comfortable and luxuriously equipped, with distinctive and varied panelling, but with avoidance of unnecessary projections of mouldings and cornices. The vehicles had elliptical roofs, and were the first Pullmans to be so built; all previous cars had had the clerestory roof. Each car was 63ft 10in long, 8ft 8in wide, 13ft 6in from rail to roof top, and ran on six-wheel bogies.

An inaugural trip was made on Saturday,

October 31, and the train was placed in public service on Sunday, November 1, 1908. As the 'Sunday Pullman Limited' had been restored on October 4, after its customary summer suspension, the date November 2 has sometimes been given wrongly for the 'Southern Belle'. In fact, on the Sunday that the 'Southern Belle' made its first run in public service, the demand for seats was so great that a relief Pullman train had to be run, and this also was filled. From the outset, 'The Southern Belle' left Victoria at 11am on weekdays and Sundays, and returned from Brighton at 5.45pm on weekdays and 9pm on Sundays. The Sunday workings superseded those of the 'Sunday Pullman Limited'.

In 1910, the daily service was doubled, weekday workings at 3.10pm from Victoria and 12.20pm from Brighton being added. On Sundays, the departures from Victoria became 11am and 6.30pm, and from Brighton 5pm and 9.30pm. The quadrupling of the main London-Brighton line to the north end of Balcombe tunnel was completed by the opening of the widened section from Three Bridges to that point on May 22, 1910.

Until June 1915, the 'Southern Belle' was an all-Pullman exclusively first-class train, but from that month third-class passengers were conveyed in an ordinary compartment bogie attached to the rear of the train. From Sunday, September 12, 1915, third-class Pullmans were provided for the first time; they seated 56 and the supplement was 9d. They were ▶

The sumptious interior of a Pullman car as used on the Brighton line.

'Brighton Belle' EMU No. 3052 leaves Brighton with the afternoon service to Victoria in March 1968. WWW.RAILPHOTOPRINTS.CO.UK / JOHN A M VAUGHAN

attached to many trains, and were included in the regular formation of the 'Southern Belle' on weekdays only. The first-class cars had always been known by names, but the third class bore numbers only. The early ones were converted from old American-built first-class cars. The first three to enter third-class service were No. 1 (*Jupiter* of 1875), No. 3 (*Alexandra* of 1877), and No. 4 (*Albert Edward* of 1877). On October 7, 1915, a new company called the Pullman Car Co Ltd was incorporated to take over from Lord Dalziel, as from September 30, 1915, the rolling stock and goodwill of the old company.

From January 1, 1917, Pullman services were greatly curtailed, and the 'Southern Belle' was withdrawn. This was in accordance with the general austerity of the latter part of the First World War. The train was restored (once daily) on October 1, 1919, but the 60-minute timing and twice-daily workings were not resumed until October 10, 1920. On January 1, 1925, the train was re-formed, with entirely new cars, which ran until they were displaced by electrification.

The last steam 'Southern Belle' from Victoria, the 3.05pm, on Saturday, December 31, 1932, was hauled by the ex-LBSCR Baltic tank No. 2333 *Remembrance* (the war memorial locomotive of the First World War). This made a fitting finale. Engines of this class had not been used for the 'Southern Belle' for some years. (The last regular steam train from Victoria to Brighton, the 12.05am on January 1, was hauled by another Baltic tank, No. 2329 *Stephenson*.)

For the electrified service to Brighton, which was inaugurated on January 1, 1933, the Pullman Car Company provided 38 new all-steel cars, of which 15 formed three units of five for 'The Southern Belle' and 23 were of the composite type for inclusion in other trains. The latter seated 12 first-class and 16 third-class passengers, and included kitchen and pantry. A 'Southern Belle' unit was composed of two first-class cars with kitchens, one third-class parlour car, and two third-class motor brakes. The unit seated 40 first-class and 152 third-class passengers. Either one or two units composed the train, as required, with the third unit spare.

All the new stock was built by the Metropolitan-Carnmell Carriage, Wagon & Finance Co Ltd. The cars were 68ft 8¾in long over buffers, 8ft 11½in wide, and 12ft 5in high from rail to top of roof. They were thus of greater length and width than any Pullman cars hitherto provided for service in this country. The new 'Southern Belle' became the first all-steel, all-electric Pullman express train in the world. It was the first to use electric cooking. Moreover, with electric

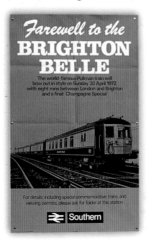

Farewell to the **BRIGHTON BELLE** The world-famous Pullman train will bow out in style on Sunday 30 April 1972 with eight runs between London and Brighton and a final 'Champagne Special'

For details, including special commemorative trains and viewing permits, please ask for folder at this station

≥ Southern

The farewell leaflet produced by BR announcing the end of the 'Brighton Belle' Pullman service, culminating in a champagne special on April 30, 1972.
COLOUR RAIL

traction, the daily service was triplicated, and, for the first time, third-class bookings became available on Sundays.

Early in 1934, it was announced that the famous name 'Southern Belle' was to be changed to 'Brighton Belle', to the regret of many, but the actual change took place on June 29, 1934, with a formal ceremony at Brighton, performed by the mayor (Miss Margaret Hardy). The occasion coincided with the opening of a new £100,000 swimming stadium at Brighton.

With the outbreak of war in 1939, the 'Brighton Belle' was discontinued, and Pullman cars for public service were withdrawn as from September 11. A week later, some of the electric cars were reinstated, and full lighting was used in these, as adequate black-out fittings, devised at the company's works, had been installed. This lighting was much appreciated by those compelled to travel during the dark days in severe black-out conditions. All Pullman cars on regular services were withdrawn on May 21, 1942, and a special joint announcement was issued to the public by the Southern Railway and the Pullman Car Company.

In October 1945, the company was able to report that it was ready to begin negotiations for the restoration of some of its former regular services. On April 24, 1946, the composite electric Pullman cars were re-formed in the ordinary Southern Railway units, and, on October 7, 1946, the 'Brighton Belle', then completely renovated after war damage, was reinstated. With effect from July 1, 1954, the British Transport Commission purchased the ordinary share capital of the company. ∎

Years Apart – Mansfield Town

A look at the changing railway scene

On August 3, 1962, Stanier 8F No. 48267 rumbles through Mansfield Town station (above) heading towards Kirkby Lane End Junction with a short rake of wagons, as a youngster tries to race the train along platform 2.

Opened in 1872, the station still had its overall roof and lattice footbridge, and handled considerable parcels traffic, but was a victim of the Beeching cuts and closed on October 12, 1964, when services from Nottingham to Worksop were withdrawn. The overall roof was due to the station's high and exposed position above the town.

At one time Mansfield had the distinction of being the largest town in England without a railway station, but Mansfield Town was reopened in 1995 as part of the Robin Hood line extension to Mansfield Woodhouse, and is now a key part of the line's success, handling around 370,000 passengers every year. There are services to Nottingham every 30 minutes, and Worksop every hour, during much of the day, as well as a Sunday service.

Contrasting the scene today, East Midlands Trains Class 156 No. 156410 (left) eases to a halt with the 08.38 Worksop-Nottingham service on October 19, 2013. The Grade II listed station building was once a restaurant, but has returned to its former use as a railway booking office and a waiting room, and blends nicely with the modern station furniture.

PICTURES: N CAPLAN/ROBIN STEWART-SMITH

Thameslink Class 319 No. 319183 carries a version of the NSE livery with light grey lower bodypanels, as it approaches East Croydon on April 18, 1993, forming the 12.56 Bedford to Brighton service.
All pictures: TRACKS NORTH COLLECTION

Network SouthEast remembered

Sectorisation of British Rail in 1982 created a London & South East sector, but in 1986, this was relaunched by chairman Chris Green as Network SouthEast, along with a patriotic livery of red, white and blue. Spanning from Essex right across the South East to Devon, stations were repainted and rebranded as part of an overall marketing strategy that endeared the NSE brand to the travelling public. It is a fondly remembered period on the railways, and surprisingly the popular livery lasted right up until September 2007 - well into the Privatisation era. It was a distinctive livery that worked well on both locos and units.

A King's Lynn to Liverpool Street service hauled by No. 47579 *James Nightall G.C.* approaches Cambridge station on May 8, 1989, and passes Class 321 No. 321313, showing two contrasting NSE livery styles.

Above: 'Networker' EMU No. 465219 approaches Wandsworth Road in the summer of 1997, with a Victoria to Dartford service.

Left: NSE Class 312 No. 312793 is one of a pair of units working from Liverpool St to St Botolphs in June 1990.

Below left: NSE also used 1938 Tube stock on the Isle of Wight and on July 31, 1997, Class 483 No. 007 slows for the new Smallbrook Junction station.

Below right: The NSE livery even suited older trains. Here No. 302210 approaches Dagenham Dock station with a Shoeburyness service in August 1997.

Non-Stop Again!

Crowds cheered *Flying Scotsman* every inch of the way on its 40th anniversary journey to Edinburgh – but for the crew, all thoughts were on the serious business of locomotive performance

By O S NOCK, BSc, C Eng, MICE, M I Mech E, M I Loco E

I N the May 1968 issue of *The Railway Magazine* I recalled the running of the summer non-stop expresses that ran between King's Cross and Edinburgh each season from 1928 to 1961, save for the intervention of the war years.

The inauguration of so celebrated a service is always worthy of commemoration, and with one of the two engines actually involved still available, and in first-class running trim, the temptation to try and do something special for the 40th anniversary must have been well-nigh irresistible.

But with steam traction to end completely on British Railways in the autumn of this year, it is not merely a case of having a locomotive of suitable calibre available. Servicing facilities have been dismantled, access points for loading of coal dispensed with, and the chances of having suitable young enginemen who could fire a Pacific on such a lengthy duty not exactly rosy.

It is not merely a question of stamina or firing skill; to keep a locomotive going, non-stop, over a run of nearly 400 miles, even with relays of firemen, needs the experience gained in years of hard training and regular footplate working.

Nevertheless, through the enthusiasm and enterprise of Alan Pegler, the owner of the Gresley Pacific engine No. 4472 *Flying Scotsman*, and the whole-hearted co-operation of British Railways and the Locomotive Club of Great Britain, No. 4472 once again left No. 10 platform at King's Cross at 10.00 on May 1, 1968, bound for Edinburgh – it was hoped, and planned for, non-stop.

The preliminary discussions, and detailed organisation that preceded this historic departure, would fill a whole volume of *The Railway Magazine*, let alone one article of mine. It is enough to say here that the best thanks of all railway enthusiasts are due to all those who took part in this planning, and who eventually had the great satisfaction of seeing No. 4472 enter Waverley station, without the wheels having stopped turning. I say this

> "The BBC television helicopters were in constant attendance."

rather than 'non-stop', because there were three moments on the journey when the speed was so reduced that a stop seemed absolutely inevitable.

The overriding problem was that of water supply. Three sets of troughs on the Great Northern line have been removed, those at Langley, Werrington and Newark. Three, at present, remain – namely Scrooby, Wiske Moor and Lucker. With a second tender and an initial supply of an extra 6,000 gallons, as compared with the conditions of 40 years ago, it might be thought that no further difficulties would be experienced once Scrooby was reached; because then things would be no different from those regularly met by the 'non-stop' in its long career with AI, A3 and A4 engines.

Today, however, with the troughs used to no more than a limited extent, the chances of getting a really good 'fill-up' at each were very much less than 100%, and as things turned out the dice seemed definitely loaded against us on May 1.

The train load was kept down to seven coaches, with a tare weight of 250 tons, while in comparing conditions with those of 40 years ago, the extra tender added 59 tons, making a tare load of 309 tons behind the first tender. Both tenders are of the corridor type.

As on the first 'non-stop' – May 1928 – the engine crews were from King's Cross and Gateshead sheds, although today of course King's Cross is no more than a nominal title now that 'Top Shed' is dismantled.

The crews in 1968 were: driver, J Hill; firemen, R Speller and A Ramage, from King's Cross; passed fireman, H Heron, driving; and passed fireman, S Whittaker, firing, from Gateshead. On the footplate in turn were: chief locomotive inspector, L Richards, Eastern Region; and headquarters locomotive inspector, G Harland. On these two, in particular, rested the responsibility for making important decisions at different stages in the journey, as will be told later.

It was a privilege to travel on the train that day, and to have as fellow passengers

Sir Nigel Gresley's elder daughter Mrs Godfrey, and her own son and daughter. Other old friends were Inspector A Dixon, now retired, with whom I have covered many hundreds of miles on the footplate, and driver E Hailstone, one of the most celebrated East Coast drivers of the post-war era, whose regular engine at 'Top Shed' was the pioneer Gresley-streamlined Pacific *Silver Link*.

Even before we had turned a wheel out of King's Cross it was evident that the occasion was to be made an outstanding one. The BBC television people had chartered one of the seven coaches of the train and their cheerful young director, cameramen, and continuity girls were preparing for a most

Running short of water, the 40th anniversary non-stop train crawls over the Royal Border Bridge into Berwick, where a stop was narrowly averted.
PHOTO: DEREK CROSS

comprehensive documentary film, in colour.

Crowds massed at every conceivable vantage point, at the platform ends, alongside the engine yard, and over the portals of Gasworks Tunnels. We left simultaneously with the present *Flying Scotsman*, recalling the regular procedure with the two 4pm departures of pre-war days, with the 'Coronation' and the 4pm Yorkshire express paralleling each other for the first hundred yards.

We took the slow line, duly slowing to cross over to the fast line at Finsbury Park, and in that exit from London we saw demonstrations of the extraordinary interest this run was arousing, in the almost ▶

"FLYING SCOTSMAN"—NON-STOP

Date					1928	1968
					Time (min.)	Time (min.)
Kings Cross	...	...	...	dep.	0	0
Peterborough		...	...	pass	84	83
Grantham	...	...	...	,,	118	112
Doncaster	...	...	...	,,	174	163
York	...	...	...	,,	217	205
Newcastle	...	...	...	,,	322	298
Berwick	...	...	...	,,	410	395
Edinburgh	...	...	...	arr.	483	465

continuous crowds of sightseers and well-wishers along the lineside. It would have been interesting to know the acreage of film exposed on us during the day, quite apart from all that the BBC television folks did.

I have dwelt rather on the accompaniments at the start, because they were all so deeply impressive; but by the time we passed Wood Green it was time to get down to the serious business of locomotive performance. The preliminaries were, however, enough to show the deep affection in which the steam locomotive is held, by an extraordinary number of people.

Time had been allowed for the slow, photographic start out of King's Cross, but we passed Wood Green at 55mph and went in fine style up the long 1-in-200 to Potters Bar, topping the summit at 57mph.

Then came a relaying slack at Hatfield, and thereafter the going was leisurely for a time to keep as close as possible to our timetable path. Any exuberance had to be restrained, because running ahead of time could easily have led to a signal stop, and with that all the prestige value of a non-stop run would have been lost.

The point-to-point time of 12min for the 14.8 miles from Sandy to Huntingdon was very sharp, however, and things were neatly judged by passing Sandy a minute early, and taking 13min on this stage. By this, inordinately hard work over a short section was avoided. The engine was clearly in splendid form from the way we stormed up Stukeley Bank, falling only from 68 to 63mph in this 3.1 miles of 1 in 200, and we touched 76mph at Connington South, before easing off for the stretch across the Fens.

Signals were all clear for us through Peterborough, and after passing Werrington on time we made a fine climb to Stoke,

Flying Scotsman passes Newcastle Central and crosses Castle Junction with the 40th anniversary non-stop special on May 1, 1968. V C K ALLEN

More crowds at Edinburgh Waverley on May 4, 1968 to see *Flying Scotsman* leave with the up 'East Coast Limited' non-stop to King's Cross. DEREK CROSS

averaging 64.2mph from Tallington to the summit box, with a minimum of 56mph. This climbing makes an interesting comparison with an ordinary run of my own with engine 4472 on the 5.45pm Newcastle express in 1936 when, with a gross load of 505 tons, we averaged 57.3mph.

We passed Grantham a little before time, but again this was intentional to offset another sharp allowance of 12min for the 14.6 miles on to Newark. Admittedly, this latter is mostly downhill; but it would have demanded an average of 73mph following recovery from the easy run through Grantham. Running as we did, a more even demand was kept on the boiler – a most important factor in securing economic performance, and minimum coal and water consumption. I need hardly add that the attainment of a maximum speed of 76mph near Claypole was achieved on the easiest of steaming.

After a quiet run across the Trent valley there came another excellent climb, with a minimum speed of 56mph at Markham summit (milepost 134). At this point we had covered 129 miles, from Wood Green, in 124min 53sec, at an average speed of 62mph. This was excellent in itself, having regard to the intermediate slacks at Hatfield and Peterborough, but also because no advantage whatever had been taken of the traditional racing stretch of the old GNR from Stevenage to Sandy.

So economically had the engine been working that by the time we passed Retford and were nearing the critical 'pick-up' at Scrooby troughs the crew had not yet begun to draw on the water supply in the second tender. A distance of 140 miles had been covered on less than 6,000 gallons – only 42gal to the mile. While this splendid

thermodynamic performance had been in progress, the train itself had been the object of extraordinary attention all along the line.

The BBC television helicopters were in constant attendance, often flying little higher than the tops of the trees; inside the train the cameramen, and others of the team, worked like Trojans, and in their frequent trips through the two corridor tenders, and their long vigils at open windows, got almost as begrimed as Alan Pegler and George Harland; while at every township and village organised parties of schoolchildren were waving ecstatically, old men doffed their caps, and toddlers were held high by their mothers to see the *Flying Scotsman* pass.

To some of us in the train the very smoothness of our progress seemed almost too good to last. It was indeed!

Although we recovered well from the Retford permanent-way check, there was consternation after Scrooby, where we scooped considerably less than 1,000gal. Speed had been carefully reduced to about 45mph, which is generally considered the optimum speed for a maximum pick-up; and although with the supply in the second tender to draw upon we had plenty to get to Wiske Moor, if the poor pickup at Scrooby was then repeated we should be in dire trouble.

Before leaving that smooth and exhilarating start to the long run, I should add that fireman Speller had done the firing as far as Grantham, and there he was relieved by fireman Ramage who continued to Aycliffe. Despite the Retford check we approached Doncaster well on time, and with clear signals throughout passed through some minutes to the good.

Then misfortune struck, good and hard. Bentley Colliery 'distant' was on. Speed was reduced to a crawl, and with continuous whistling we approached the box, where a crowd of platelayers were seen on the line. Obstinately, the home signal remained on, and with speed down to less than walking pace Inspector Harland jumped down from the engine and ran ahead to learn there was a broken rail. By this timely and unprecedented action he obtained authority to proceed before we had actually stopped, and having passed at dead-slow speed over the fracture we all breathed again as speed was regained, and we bowled along the level towards Selby.

This check had cost us five minutes in running, but there was no point in hurrying to regain the loss. There was an ample recovery margin between Selby and York, and to approach the latter the least fraction ahead of time would be asking for a stop. There was a very tight margin behind a Birmingham-Newcastle express. Actually, things worked out to perfection; all signals were green for us, and we passed through the great station within a few seconds of precise schedule time.

From the viewpoint of locomotive power output the continuation of the journey had few features of interest. The schedule allowed 94min for the ensuing 80.1 miles from York to Newcastle, and if there were some slight variations from that point-to-point allowance they were made in the interest of evening out the demands on the boiler.

As before, a major point of interest became the amount of water likely to be scooped at Wiske Moor. Here, we did much better than at Scrooby, collecting nearly 3,000gal, and with beautifully judged firing and driving, and clear signals, we passed King Edward Bridge Junction and wound our way through Newcastle Central a minute early. That minute, nevertheless, very nearly cost us the non-stop run, for we got signals 'on' at Manors, and only the most judicious crawling afterwards avoided a dead stand. Speed was down to 2mph before the line was cleared for us.

By this time the weather had sadly deteriorated, and we ran through Northumberland in pouring rain. Speed was kept at the moderate level demanded by the schedule, and despite the episode at Manors we were only a minute down at Alnmouth.

We were now approaching the critical point of this later part of the journey – Lucker troughs. The possibility of our running short of water had loomed large in all the preparations for the trip, and a road tanker, with 4,000gal, was standing in readiness in the goods yard, at Berwick. If we did not get enough at Lucker there was this emergency supply, though it would of course have meant stopping.

Lucker was passed, and shortly ▶

TABLE I
EAST COAST ROUTE
THE 40TH ANNIVERSARY NON-STOP: MAY 1, 1968
Load: 7 coaches, 250 tons tare behind second tender
330 tons gross behind first tender
Engine: 4-6-2 No. 4472, *Flying Scotsman*
Drivers: Hill (Kings Cross)
Heron (Gateshead)

Dist.		Sch.	Actual		Speeds
Miles		min.	m.	s.	m.p.h.
0.0	KINGS CROSS	0	0	00	—
2.6	Finsbury Park	7½	9	37	
5.0	Wood Green		13	37	55
12.7	Potters Bar	22	21	57	57
			p.w.s.		68/15*
17.7	HATFIELD	27	27	30	
25.0	Knebworth		35	32	70(max.)
31.9	HITCHIN	44	42	00	easy
44.1	Sandy	55	53	43	63½
47.5	Tempsford		56	43	75
51.7	St. Neots		60	28	68/72
58.9	Huntingdon	67	66	42	68
62.0	Milepost 62		69	32	63
69.7	Holme		75	45	76(max.
76.4	PETERBOROUGH ...	83	83	10	—
79.5	Werrington Junc.	88	87	44	60
88.6	Essendine	97	95	55	69(max.)
97.1	Corby Glen		103	55	57/63
100.1	Stoke Box	108	106	53	56½
105.5	GRANTHAM	113	112	10	easy
109.7	Barkston S. Junc. ...	117	116	02	72
115.4	Claypole		120	45	76½
120.1	NEWARK	125	124	43	eased
134.0	Milepost 134		138	30	56½(min.)
			p.w.s.		
—	Scrooby		—		69½/48
156.0	DONCASTER	164	163	05	—
—	Bentley Colliery		sigs.		broken rail
160.2	Shaftholme Junc.	169	171	50	—
174.4	SELBY	183	187	03	—
186.2	Chaloners Whin Junc. ...		201	06	—
188.2	YORK	205	204	45	—
197.9	Tollerton	217	217	04	57
210.4	Thirsk	228½	230	00	—
218.2	NORTHALLERTON ...	236	237	48	60/45
—			p.w.s.		15
227.1	Eryholme Junc.	248	248	50	—
232.3	DARLINGTON	256	257	40	—
245.2	Ferryhill	269½	271	05	68(max.)
254.3	DURHAM	279	280	51	—
264.5	Lamesley		291	32	73(max.)
267.7	King Edward Bridge Junc. ...	296	294	55	—
268.3	NEWCASTLE	299	297	55	—
—			sigs.		2
273.3	Forest Hall		308	45	—
284.9	Morpeth	323	323	25	slow
293.9	Chevington		335	37	easy
303.1	Alnmouth	344	345	10	56
307.7	Little Mill		350	32	49
319.9	Belford	364	365	03	—
333.9	Tweedmouth Junc.	387	386	55	—
—			sigs. prolonged		—
335.2	BERWICK-UPON-TWEED		394	50	—
340.8	Burnmouth		406	45	40
—			p.w.s.		20
351.5	Grantshouse	410	423	45	40
358.9	Innerwick		431	03	75
363.5	DUNBAR	424	435	08	60*
369.2	East Linton		440	48	64
374.9	Drem		445	37	73
378.5	Longniddry		449	39	66/69
386.6	Monktonhall Junc.	445	456	17	—
389.7	Portobello	449	459	15	—
392.7	EDINBURGH WAVERLEY	460	464	57	—

* Speed restrictions

TABLE II

EAST COAST ROUTE
THE UP NON-STOP: SATURDAY, MAY 4, 1968
Load: 7 coaches, 250 tons tars behind second tender
330 tons gross behind first tender
Engine: 4-6-2 No. 4472, *Flying Scotsman*
Drivers: Borlace (Gateshead)
Lunnis (Kings Cross)

Dist.		Sch.	Actual		Speeds
Miles		min.	m.	s.	m.p.h.
0.0	EDINBURGH WAVERLEY	0	0	00	—
3.0	Portobello	6	6	14	—
6.1	Monktonhall Junc.	10	11	02	—
17.8	Drem	21	23	51	62
29.2	DUNBAR	31	34	08	73/58*
33.8	Innerwick		39	17	64
41.2	Grantshouse	48	48	17	43
57.5	BERWICK-UPON-TWEED		65	19	easy
58.8	Tweedmouth Junc.	68	67	07	—
—	Goswick		72	32	71
72.8	Belford	88	84	33	eased
89.6	Alnmouth	108	106	28	—
107.8	Morpeth	126	129	38	40*
114.5	Cramlington		137	40	58/52
124.4	NEWCASTLE	150	151	35	—
125.0	King Edward Bridge Junc. ...	153	153	12	—
128.2	Lamesley		157	03	60
138.4	DURHAM	170	169	20	—
147.5	Ferryhill	182	180	44	62(max.)
160.4	DARLINGTON ...	198	199	58	easing
			p.w.s.		30
165.6	Eryholme Junc.		207	59	—
170.8	Danby Wiske		213	01	70/48
174.5	NORTHALLERTON ...	213	216	57	61
182.3	Thirsk	220	223	19	80
193.3	Alne		231	58	74/80
—			sigs.		2
194.8	Tollerton	230	239	16	—
202.9	Skelton Box		247	14	72(max.)
204.5	YORK	240	250	26	25*
214.2	Riccall		261	04	76
218.3	SELBY	256	265	44	40*
222.9	Templehirst		267	54	62
229.7	Moss		275	53	80
232.5	Shaftholme Junc.	273	278	16	58/73
236.7	DONCASTER	280	282	42	61
245.0	Bawtry		291	00	65(max.)
254.1	RETFORD	303	302	10	—
—			p.w.s.		30
272.6	NEWARK	322	324	30	easy
277.3	Claypole		329	14	60
283.0	Barkstone S. Junc.	334	334	55	57
287.2	GRANTHAM	339	339	14	63
292.6	Stoke Box	346	344	53	50
304.1	Essendine	357	356	33	78(max.)
316.3	PETERBOROUGH ...	372	370	24	15*
333.8	Huntingdon	393	390	22	easy
341.0	St. Neots		398	04	56
348.6	Sandy	405	405	37	71
360.8	HITCHIN	416	416	27	62
364.1	Stevenage		420	05	54
375.0	HATFIELD	432	431	19	70(max.)
—			p.w.s.		20
380.0	Potters Bar	439	438	29	56
383.5	New Barnet		441	51	68
387.7	Wood Green		445	17	—
390.1	Finsbury Park	452	448	48	—
392.7	KINGS CROSS	458	455	32	—

* Speed restrictions

afterwards Pegler came back from the footplate with a look on his face that told its own tale. We had scooped up less than 1,000gal and, as he put it, we had left the experts on the footplate to judge whether they had enough to get through. It had been decided that if we needed water at Berwick a warning whistle would be given as we passed Beal, and hearing no such whistle we assumed Les Richards had decided he had enough to get through.

Approaching Tweedmouth the brakes went on, and, although we passed there dead on time, we commenced an agonisingly slow crawl over the Royal Border Bridge.

The colour-light signals were on, and with the whole area northwards to Burnmouth remotely controlled from the Tweedmouth panel no amount of whistling or gesticulations from the footplate could hurry their clearance.

We could only crawl on, but when Berwick was approached it was seen that the points were set for us to go through the goods line, beside that road tanker, in which, to quote Pegler, there were "four thousand gallons of lovely water".

As we turned off the main line, heads were out from end to end of the train, despite the pouring rain, and then, to everyone's amazement and delight, old 4472 rode slowly, but determinedly, right past that tanker, and continued on her way. There was one last breathless moment in this episode: the signals to let us out onto the main line remained steadfastly on, but the track-circuit lights on Tweedmouth panel must have shown – just in time – that we were still on the move, and the outlet signal suddenly changed to green.

For the third time a dead stop had, by a hair's breadth, been avoided, and on this last occasion the loss of time had been serious. We got under way again once more, up the 1 in 190 over the border and into Scotland; but the 6.8 miles from Tweedmouth Junction to Burnmouth had taken no less than 19 min 50sec, and with a further permanent-way slack near Reston we topped the summit near Grantshouse nearly 14min late. There remained 41.2 miles to go and 38 min left for a punctual arrival. Assured of ample water supply it could have been done, in spite of the overall speed limit of 75mph throughout Scottish region. But Inspector Richards, above all people, knew that he was cutting things fine, for water, and the engine was not pressed.

On this last stage there was another hazard. Even in the open country of the East Lothians there was one tight timetable margin. A diesel multiple-unit train from North Berwick was due to take the main line at Drem four minutes after our scheduled passing time.

Crowds look on as newsreel cameramen record the scene under the watchful eye of a policeman, as *Flying Scotsman* prepares to leave platform 10 at King's Cross to repeat the non-stop run of 40 years earlier. G R MORTIMER

We passed Dunbar 11 min late, and those 'in the know' once again held their breaths until Drem 'distant' was sighted. It was clear. More than this, we dashed through Drem at 70mph to see, through steamed-up rain-slashed windows, that the DMU had been held for us, and we had a clear road right into Waverley.

With the help of a generous amount of recovery time from Portobello we were only five minutes late – in any case, half an hour faster than the schedule time of 40 years ago.

I must not dilate on the scenes that greeted our arrival. Waverley rang to the shrill welcoming notes of a pipe band; the Lord Provost was on the platform to meet us, with the Lady Provost; and later that evening Edinburgh Castle was floodlit in honour of the occasion.

This, however, is an article about locomotive performance, and a careful check-up on arrival showed that our total water consumption was a little under 14,000gal – only 35gal per mile. Of the checks experienced en route, I estimate that Bentley cost us 5min, Eryholme 3min, and Manors 3min. Of course, Berwick was by far the most severe, and cost about 14min. The remaining three permanent-way slacks cost about 3min between them, making up a total of 28 min. The net time can thus be set down as 437min, a splendid average of 54mph – NON-STOP! The engine was stabled for the night at Dunfermline, and on arrival there everything was found to be in perfect order, all bearings cool, and when being prepared for the next day's work, in all only two pints

of oil were needed to replenish all three big ends and all three small ends, together with the motion pins.

It is interesting to compare the actual times made on the inaugural journey in 1928 with our own times.

I was not able to participate in any more of the special running that week, and returned to King's Cross by the *Night Scotsman* on May 1. Imagine my astonishment, after the previous day's proceedings, to read next morning in *The Times*, of all newspapers, THIRSTY 'SCOT'

"For the third time, a dead stop had been avoided."

STOPS TO DRINK, heading a curiously ill-informed article in which readers were told that the *Flying Scotsman* had to make three halts to take on water.

From whom the Scottish correspondent of this usually most reliable newspaper gathered this nonsense is hard to imagine! Equally garbled was his reference to the record run on the last night of the 1895 race, which suggested that only one engine was then concerned.

It was learned afterwards that the water level in the troughs was at the lower level normally maintained for the diesels, and on Saturday, May 4, when the return trip was attempted non-stop, the water level was raised to full height, and with an ample water supply a very comfortable trip ensued.

Through the kindness of Mr C F Firminger of the LCGB, I have been furnished with a very detailed log, a summary of which is set out in Table II herewith. There was one anxious moment, when adverse signals cut short a grand piece of high-speed running south of Northallerton, but other than that it was a triumphantly smooth and punctual trip.

Once again, one notes the excellent hill-climbing, as in the minimum speed of 43mph up the Cockburnspath Bank, after four miles of 1-in-96, and the good going from Newark up to Stoke Box.

For the most part, however, skilful enginemanship was being displayed to keep as close as possible to the scheduled timetable path.

I am delighted to be able to set on record this splendid complementary run to the anniversary trip of May 1; the two together represent a triumph of organisation and enterprise, and yet another tribute to the work of Sir Nigel Gresley. It was delightful that his elder daughter and his grandchildren were able to participate, and to see for themselves and tremendously enjoy the manifestations of interest and enthusiasm displayed throughout the entire trip, on both days of non-stop running.

On arrival at King's Cross on May 4, they had 4,000gal of water and more than two tons of coal in hand, thus showing that so long as the three remaining water troughs exist, and are kept full, the 392.7 miles between King's Cross and Edinburgh does not by any means represent the limit of non-stop running with No. 4472.

King's Cross to Dundee next time? ∎

The 'Hiawatha' and its locomotives

By 'MERCURY'

OF all the high-speed express services in the world for the working of which steam is responsible, the 'Hiawatha', of the Chicago, Milwaukee, St Paul & Pacific Railroad of the USA, is probably the only one on which speeds up to 100mph are necessary every day for timekeeping.

The working timetables of that company contain the unique printed instruction that the speed of this express is "not to exceed 100mph", though, with the usual tolerances above and below a limit, speed often rises to 105mph.

The original 'Hiawatha' trains, introduced on May 29, 1935, leave Chicago and St Paul at 1pm. From January 21, 1939, they have been supplemented by new morning trains in each direction, which are not worked by the original 'Hiawatha' Atlantics, but by new 'general purpose' streamlined 4-6-4 locomotives.

The original 'Hiawatha' trains had intermediate stops only at Milwaukee, Portage, New Lisbon, and La Crosse. Now the 1pm 'Hiawatha' from Chicago calls also at Winona and Red Wing; the 1pm from St Paul has seven stops, Winona, Red Wing, and Watertown being added to the original halts; while the eastbound morning 'Hiawatha', at 8.25am, is required to stop seven times intermediately – at Red Wing, Winona, La Crosse, Sparta, Portage, Columbus, and Milwaukee – and still to complete the 410.5 miles from St Paul to Chicago in 390min, including 19min standing at these stations.

The westbound morning 'Hiawatha' is a slower train, however, as it makes 16 intermediate stops, and is allowed 7hr 35min from Chicago to St Paul, though even so many of the start-to-stop timings are extremely tight. Indeed, the time allowed for the 280.8 miles from Chicago to La Crosse is only 300min, and this includes 10min at Milwaukee; 5min at Portage, and eight other regular stops.

The schedules of the three 6½hr trains gives some indication of the locomotive work involved. Between Minneapolis and St Paul the distance is only 10.9 miles, but with a ruling grade of 1-in-80, and a restriction on speed of 25mph for some miles, the allowance from leaving Minneapolis to leaving St Paul, or, in the reverse direction, from reaching St Paul to reaching Minneapolis, is usually 30min with the fast trains. Out of St Paul there is a 25mph limit at Lower St Paul, then 60mph over both tracks for eight miles to Pulman Avenue, and the same limit continued over the westbound track to Langdon, another six miles. It should

Class F7 4-6-4 cab interior. PHOTO: MILWAUKEE ROAD

Class F7 No. 102 with train 6, the morning 'Hiawatha' between Minneapolis and Chicago, at Mayfair in Chicago, May 1941. E T HARLEY

here be explained that the Burlington and Milwaukee Companies have pooled their trackage between Hastings and St Paul; westbound trains use the Burlington line, which is one mile the longer of the two, for most of the distance, and eastbound trains the Milwaukee line. Through Hastings there is a 40mph limit for two miles, and eastbound trains have two other 50mph slowings before Red Wing. There is another 40mph limit through Red Wing; 30mph at Lake City, between there and Wabasha; 50mph at Wabasha; various other minor slowings; and then 35mph from River Jct over the drawbridge into La Crosse. This

explains the relative leisure-lines of the 'Hiawatha' schedules between St Paul and La Crosse.

But then the eastbound trains get away in tremendous style. From La Crosse to Chicago is a distance of 280.8 miles – 12.5 miles further than from Newcastle to King's Cross. The morning 'Hiawatha' is allowed 4hr 15min – 15 min more than the 'Silver Jubilee' – inclusive of 12min standing at four intermediate stops, that is, 4hr 3min actual running time, which works out at 69.3mph. Of this distance, 250 miles of pass-to-pass timings demand an average speed of 77.4mph.

In succession from La Crosse, the train has to run 24.6 miles to Sparta in 20min start-to-stop (73.8mph); 78.3 miles from Sparta to Portage in 62min (75.8mph and the fastest run with steam in the world); 28.2 miles from Portage to Columbus in 24min (70.5mph); 64.7 miles from Columbus to Milwaukee in 62min (62.8mph); and 85 miles from Milwaukee to Chicago in 75min (68mph). These last two bookings include the customary American margins for recovery of lost time, amounting to about 3min from Brookfield into Milwaukee, and 4min from Tower A20 into Chicago. ▶

Three miles out of Sparta, on the 74.6mph run, there begins a grade of 1-in-200, which continues with slight intermissions for 7¼ miles to Raymore; here, there is a 40mph slack to enter the only stretch of single line on the route, and a steepening of the grade to 1-in-150 for 2¾ miles to Tunnel City, where a second 40mph slack is enforced, prior to resuming double track. There are also minor slowings at Camp Douglas and New Lisbon, with the result that intermediate speeds must be extremely high if time is to be kept. A 25mph slack through Watertown affects the Columbus to Milwaukee run, and from Wauwatosa into Milwaukee the speed limit gradually narrows from 50 to 30mph, necessitating a very cautious approach for 5½ miles.

The eastbound 'Afternoon Hiawatha' is booked over the 59.8 miles from La Crosse to New Lisbon in 51min (70.4mph start-to-stop), the 43.1 miles from New Lisbon to Portage in 35min (73.9mph); the 46.9 miles from Portage to Watertown in 39min (72.2mph); and from Milwaukee to Chicago, like the morning train, in 75min. Both these flyers are expected to run the 57.6 miles from Lake, outside Milwaukee, to Signal Tower A20, where the reduced speed into Chicago begins, in 40min, at a pass-to-pass average of 86.4mph.

In the reverse direction, the 'Afternoon Hiawatha' has the even more extraordinary allowance of 38min for the same distance, demanding an average of 90.9mph (which includes a booked average of 96.6mph over

the 16.1 miles from Sturtevant to Lake), but the Lake-Milwaukee time includes about 6min recovery margin for delays. This train is duplicated in summer at 1.05pm by another daily express on the same timing from Chicago to Milwaukee, continuing as a relief train to New Lisbon with North Woods passengers. From Milwaukee there are runs of 92.9 miles to Portage in 83min (67.2mph); Portage to New Lisbon, 43.1 miles in 36min (71.8mph); and New Lisbon to La Crosse, 59.8 miles in 51min (70.4 mph); together with a margin of about 7min from Hastings into St Paul, to ensure a punctual arrival.

The first streamlined 'Hiawatha' trains were six-car formations weighing 313 English tons tare, and seating 376 passengers; the sets now in use are nine-car trains weighing 430 tons, and each seating 499 passengers. Extra vehicles are attached as traffic requires, and time has been kept with 15-car trains up to 700 tons in weight.

The new cars average only 48 tons apiece, and were introduced in 1938. By the use of Cor-Ten high tensile steel and welded construction it is reckoned that 40 per cent in weight has been saved as compared with normal riveted steel construction. Special measures have been taken in the design of coaches and bogies to absorb shocks and damp out vibrations, in order to give perfectly smooth riding. Each set of cars as normally run includes a combined baggage and buffet car, four luxury cars for 'coach' passengers (the equivalent of third class), a café-dining car, two parlour cars, and a parlour-observation car. A striking external feature of the last-mentioned vehicle is the beaver tail, which has a central vertical projecting fin, with four transverse horizontal fins, three above and one below the window level. Not only is there decorative value in this form of construction, but the upper fins shield the rear windows from the sun, and the whole device adds strength to the tail of the train and offers protection in the event of rear-end impact.

All the internal decoration and fittings of these vehicles are of a striking description. They were built in the Milwaukee Company's own shops at Milwaukee.

The original Atlantics used on the 'Hiawatha' trains were two in number, built by the American Locomotive Company at Schenectady in 1934, and two more were added shortly afterwards. They were notable by reason of their 7ft driving wheels – then an unusually large diameter for American practice – and their small 19in x 28in cylinders relatively to a heating surface of 3,245sq ft, a superheating surface of 1,029sq ft, and a grate area of 69sq ft. The high working pressure of 300lb per sq in was adopted, and out of a total engine weight of

Original *Hiawatha* departing Chicago, bound for Minneapolis on its inaugural run, May 29, 1935. HOWARD CHRISTIANSEN

The interior of *Hiawatha* parlour-observation car, 1937. PHOTO: MILWAUKEE ROAD

Class A 4-4-2 No. 3 at Milwaukee, Wisconsin, in 1939. R H KINDIG

125k tons, 62½ tons – equal to the adhesion weight of most modern British six-coupled designs – was available for adhesion.

On further locomotive power becoming necessary, Mr C H Bilty, the chief mechanical engineer of the C M St P & P RR, decided to introduce a much more powerful design which could be used when desired on the 'Hiawatha' trains, but would be available also for the heavy 'Pioneer Limited' and 'Olympian' sleeping car services between Chicago, Milwaukee, St Paul, and Minneapolis, and westwards without change of engine over the 914 miles between Minneapolis and Harlowton, Montana.

This resulted in the introduction in 1938 of a 4-6-4 type, of which six have been built by the American Locomotive Company. These magnificent locomotives have the same spread-wing streamlining at the front end which gives distinction to the Atlantics, and of which, incidentally, the sloping nose, inclined at 16 degrees from the vertical, is found very effective in winter as a snow plough, but in order to keep the weight within permissible limits, the later engines have not been fully streamlined at the sides.

As compared with the Atlantics, which are oil-fired, the 4-6-4s are arranged for coal firing, with automatic stokers; they have the same 7ft diameter driving wheels and 300lb pressure as the former. A multiple-jet type of exhaust is fitted.

The customary procedure is to work the 'Morning Hiawatha' in each direction with a 4-6-4 locomotive, and the 'Afternoon Hiawatha', as from its inception, with an Atlantic. The North Woods section of the 'Hiawatha', already referred to, leaves the main line at New Lisbon, and is worked over a secondary line through the Wisconsin valley to Star Lake. In order that locomotive power may be available, harmonising in appearance with the stock, an old 4-6-0 locomotive, built by Baldwin in 1900 as one of a series of 25 Vauclain compounds, and rebuilt in 1926 as a two-cylinder Simple, has received a streamlined casing and is painted similarly to the new 4-4-2 and 4-6-4 engines.

As regards the performance of the Atlantics, it may be recalled that on the run on the 'Hiawatha' streamliner described in the April 1938 issue, which was timed from the footplate by Baron Vuillet, speed first reached 100mph out of Chicago at a point between Rondout and Wadsworth; then, after two severe permanent way checks, one to 18 and the other to 27mph, speed rose in just over 8min from 60 to 100mph, and successive miles were covered at 103, 106, 103, and 103mph, with five further miles at 97 and 102mph, and an average of 100.7 for nine miles continuously.

The load was 465 tons gross, and the tendency of the gradients over this stretch, where the cut-off was 28 per cent, boiler pressure the full 300lb, steam-chest pressure 285lb, and superheat temperature 700deg F, was slightly in favour of the engine. The 85 miles from Chicago to Milwaukee were run in 76min 10 sec, or 67¾min net (75.5mph). Milwaukee to Portage, 92.9 miles, took 85min 18sec, including a dead stand of 2½min for adverse signals, or 75½min net (73.8mph), with a maximum of 100mph near Oconomowoc. Portage to New Lisbon, 43.1 miles, 32min 30sec (79.6mph start-to-stop), averaged 97.8mph for 10.9 miles, with a maximum of 102mph. The 59.8 miles from New Lisbon to La Crosse, with three 40mph slacks and one 50mph slack, took 49min 5sec, or 46min net (78mph). Overall, the net running time for the 411.5 miles from Chicago to St Paul was 342¾min, representing an average of 72mph throughout.

Such complete details are not yet available of the performance of the new 4-6-4s, but some significant feats have already been performed. The 'tape' off the self-recording indicator of one of these locomotives, on a certain journey from Chicago to Milwaukee, showed that a speed ▶

Class A No. 2 with 'Hiawatha' cars on display at Milwaukee before launch of service, May 23, 1935. PHOTO: MILWAUKEE ROAD

of over 100mph was maintained for more than 19 miles continuously; for five miles, including a three-quarter mile fall at 1-in-150, half-mile level, three-quarter mile up at 1-in-300, a mile level, and two miles at 1-in-250 up, speed was round about 120mph, the maximum to which the indicator will record.

A remarkable heavy load demonstration was also given on November 28 last, when the 'Pioneer Limited' and the 'Olympian' were combined into one vast train of 26 cars, weighing 1,904 tons behind the tender, which was accelerated to 70mph on the level in a distance of 12 miles from starting.

It may finally be emphasised that the high speed is by no means confined alone to the 'Hiawatha' streamliners. Apart from the four 75min services over the 85 miles between Chicago and Milwaukee, there are four trains in 80min, six in 85min, and four in 90min.

Allowing for the slow running in the vicinity of both Chicago and Milwaukee, the working timetable shows two of these expresses timed over the 68.9 miles between Mayfair and Lake in 53min, at 78mph; two in 56min, at 73.8mph; four in 58min, at 71.3mph; two in 59min, at 70.1mph; one in 61min, at 67.8mph; two in 62min, at

66.7mph; and one in 63min, at 65.6mph.

The 'Hiawatha' trains, with their 48min westbound (86.1mph), and 49min eastbound (84.4mph) for the same distance, together with their tremendous speeds throughout their journeys over all sections where conditions permit, can certainly claim the distinction of being the fastest long-distance steam-hauled expresses in the world. Further, the value of a high-speed facility such as this, both to the travelling public and to the owners of the train, may be measured by the fact that the net earnings of the original 'Hiawatha', during the first four years that it has been running, have been $2,929,435, or more than three times the cost of the 18 cars and two Atlantic locomotives required for the maintenance of an each-way service daily, and this despite the competition of the Burlington 'Zephyr' trains and 'The 400' of the Chicago & North Western between Chicago and the 'Twin Cities'. This is striking evidence that high speed pays.

So much is this the case, indeed, that from January 28 last, three of the 'Hiawatha' trains had 15min cut from their schedule; this news arrived too late for incorporation in the article. The westbound 'Afternoon Hiawatha' has its

schedule unchanged to Milwaukee, and thence runs the 92.9 miles to Portage in 76min (73.3mph); another fast run is from New Lisbon to La Crosse, 59.8 miles, in 49min (73.2mph), and the remaining 6min are economised at various points.

Eastbound the 'Afternoon Hiawatha' has its principal speed-up after La Crosse, running the 280.8 miles thence to Chicago, with four intermediate stops totalling 6min, in 4hr 1min. The fastest runs are from La Crosse to New Lisbon, 59.8 miles, in 46min (78mph); New Lisbon to Portage, 43.1 miles, in 33min (78.4mph); and Portage to Watertown, 46.9 miles, in 37min (76mph) – a magnificent sequence for a steam-hauled express.

The eastbound 'Morning Hiawatha', with seven stops, has to cover the 24.6 miles from La Crosse to Sparta in 20min (73.8mph), then the 78.3 miles from Sparta to Portage in the extraordinary time of 59min (79.6mph and easily the fastest booking with steam in the world), following that with 28.2 miles from Portage to Columbus in 22min (77.2 mph).

Both trains still take 75min for the final run from Milwaukee into Chicago. ∎

∎ **ALL PHOTOGRAPHS COURTESY OF** *CLASSIC TRAINS* **MAGAZINE.**

PILGRIMS

Keith Sugden

Avebury is a 'superhenge', a prehistoric temple not only older but far larger than Stonehenge. Its sarsen stones were dragged to the site from nearby Fyfield Down; the largest weighs 45 tons.

Pagan Sites

Two of Britain's most evocative and popular shrines are pagan in origin. The Isle of Avalon in Celtic mythology is the mystical land of the dead. For centuries, this paradise has been identified as a magical hill rising out of the Somerset Levels – Glastonbury Tor.

For the Romans and their British subjects, the hot springs of *Aquae Sulis* (modern Bath), unique in Britain, held an even greater attraction. A genuine little shrine-town developed there by the 3rd century AD, now beautifully excavated and explained in the Roman Baths Museum.

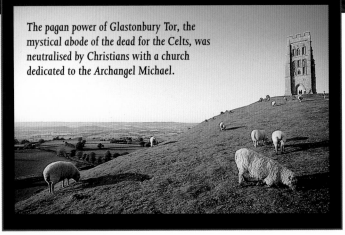

The pagan power of Glastonbury Tor, the mystical abode of the dead for the Celts, was neutralised by Christians with a church dedicated to the Archangel Michael.

ABOVE: Suppliants at the Romano-British sacred spring of Aquae Sulis (now called Bath) would sometimes cast curses into the steaming water. Inscribed on lead, they were rolled up to keep their power secret.

The temple of Stonehenge, a shrine of the moon and later of the sun, was a focus for prehistoric religion in Wessex for 1,700 years. Bronze Age chieftains sought to be buried within sight of it.

BELOW: *St Augustine's cross.*

pilgrimage is by no means the sole domain of Christians. Think of the *Hadj* to Mecca, one of the five pillars of Islam; or consider those pagan supplicants at the Delphic Oracle or the great shrine to Aphrodite in Asia Minor. Naturally, ancient philosophy influenced the early Christians. Evangelists generally found it prudent to adapt the pagan beliefs to the new religion rather than simply destroy them, taking on board the old myths and sacred sites. A famous letter from Pope Gregory the Great to St Augustine instructs the 6th-century missionary to build his churches on ancient places of worship. Of course many Britons had been Christians under the Roman Empire, and at a few places in Britain, tradition or modern research claims that Christianity never died out during the pagan invasions of the Dark Ages – Glastonbury in Somerset and Deerhurst in Gloucestershire are among them.

St Augustine and his followers began their mission in England by converting the Saxon royal families; from that point the faith of the individual kings led to the replacement of the pagan beliefs. Some rulers became so devout that their own souls took precedence over the kingdom. Such was King Ina of Wessex, who gave his throne to a kinsman and made the 'perma-nent pilgrimage' to Rome, founding there the English Hospice in AD727 (which still exists close to the Vatican). Many wealthy Englishmen of the day followed suit, trusting that by dying at Rome, close to the bearer of the keys of heaven, St Peter, they would stand the best possi-ble chance on the Day of Judgement.

RIGHT: *The Gorgon's head from the pediment of the temple in Bath, found in 1790 when the Pump Room was being built, also represents Sul, god of the sacred spring.*

✚ Motives & Means

In early Christian times only the wealthy could afford the pilgrimage to Rome and common Englishmen had to rest content with visiting a local shrine. Even then the choice of shrines must have been wide, with the memory of the foundation of their churches still fresh in the minds of the people, and the relics of hundreds of founders ('saints') close at hand, especially in Wales and Cornwall. By the time pilgrimage reached its heyday in the 14th century the phenomenon was enormous. The recorded numbers of pilgrims to Canterbury for many years exceeded 200,000, out of a total population in England estimated at just under four million on the outbreak of the Black Death in 1348.

The number of famous shrines grew and grew as monks and prelates vied to attract more pilgrims. Every single church was supposed to have a relic of some kind. Many judged the fame of towns, not on the size of the population or the quality of their products, but on the number and reputation of their relics. Some shrines had connections with numerous saints: 13 at Glastonbury. Other monasteries and churches possessed more relics than they knew what to do with – over 400 were said to exist at Canterbury, where 250 miracles were described in the six years after St Thomas's death.

The pilgrim, who had a home to return to, was distinct from the palmer, who had none. He was a professional pilgrim, living on nothing but alms and perpetually journeying from

ABOVE: *Pilgrims contemporary with Geoffrey Chaucer make their way to the Holy Land in this illumination from a 14th-century manuscript on the Crusades.*

shrine to shrine. Men knew him by the palm or branch brought back from the Holy Land itself. Of course being a palmer was a most convenient cover for all kinds of escaped villeins and criminals, or those who found a settled existence or their fellow men too much to bear. In a word, some of them were tramps, adept at putting the evil eye on those common souls who shunned them.

If a man was too sick, or busy, or lazy to go on pilgrimage for himself, it was common to employ a proxy to do the journey on his behalf, and the Church prudently recognised this as just as effective as making the journey himself. More commonly the proxy pilgrimage took place after death to gain some favour on the Day of Judgement; funds would be specified by will for the purpose.

People had many different motives for going on a pilgrimage. Mostly they went for religious reasons, but often the dominant factor was more secular. The most common motive was to pray at the shrine, appealing directly to the saint for success in a venture, which might be business, love, war or an attempt to throw off an illness or

disability. Vows made at home, in a church or even in the heat of battle often obliged the believer to make long journeys as a thanksgiving for safe deliverance.

The obligatory gifts to the shrine gave the Church a truly vast income, and such was the prestige and wealth conferred on a church by the major miracle-working relics that theft of relics and outright fraud by monks were widespread in the Middle Ages.

ABOVE: A 12th-century stained-glass window of St Thomas Becket in Canterbury Cathedral, made a few years after the archbishop's martyrdom.

LEFT & RIGHT: A group of monks (left) and crusaders on horseback, from the 14th-century Chronicle of St Denis.

✠ The Celtic Saints

The Celtic Church was a bastion of learning and artistic endeavour in a barbarous Europe and its contacts were international. The early monks moved at will around the seaways of western Britain – Dumnonia (the Cornish peninsula), Wales and Dalriada (the west of Scotland) – Ireland and Brittany, exploiting their common language. In those times any learned man who successfully founded a new church was likely to be canonised after a decent interval by his congregation – St Carantoc in Cornwall is an example. Such was the independence of each community under the Celtic rule. Energetic monks like Patrick, Columba, David or Piran were held in such esteem by their brethren and spiritual children that their churches soon became shrines to their memory and pilgrims braved every hardship to gain wisdom, guidance, comfort or healing from their physical remains. Among these inspiring figures, some are remembered for their extraordinary spirituality and some for the strangeness of their legends.

Columba is famous as the monk who evangelised Scotland, but this happened almost by accident. He was an Irish prince, born about 521,

LEFT: *St John, seen in the Lindisfarne Gospels (c. AD 698), the most precious work of art to survive from early Christian England.*

who became a follower of St Patrick. His character might be considered unsaintly: his actions show that he was forceful, stubborn and ambitious. In about 563 Columba's refusal to give up a manuscript, the Vulgate Gospels, culminated in vast bloodshed at the Battle of Cul Dremne. Regretting his stubbornness, he vowed to leave Ireland and never return. Columba sailed to Iona and was soon taking the word across the sea to the pagans of Mull and beyond into Argyll. There he converted the ruling house of Dalriada and then carried his mission all over Scotland. Following his death on Iona in 597, pilgrims came to venerate his relics in the church there.

Cuthbert was a shepherd boy from the Lammermuir Hills in the Scottish Lowlands. In 651, at the age of about 16, he entered the Celtic monastery of Melrose. Later in life he was prior of Lindisfarne (Holy Island) but wherever he served he was to go on long missionary journeys, preaching in remote villages and farmsteads in the hills. Returning to Lindisfarne, he would retire to the solitude of a hermitage on the bare slab of rock in the sea near the priory which still bears the name

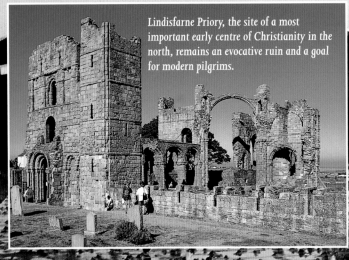

Lindisfarne Priory, the site of a most important early centre of Christianity in the north, remains an evocative ruin and a goal for modern pilgrims.

St Cuthbert's Isle. In 676, as a result of his 'long and spotless active life', he was allowed by his abbot and monks the special privilege of retiring to 'the stillness of divine contemplation' on one of the Farne Islands off the Northumbrian coast. In about 698, eleven years after his death and burial at Lindisfarne, the monks elevated his body to a new shrine and discovered its incorruption: the body had not decayed and the saint appeared as if asleep. From that time onward, it was an object of

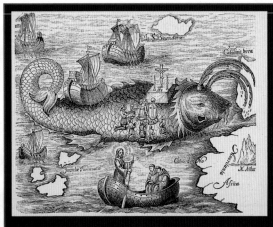

Brendan's Voyage and Patrick

There are many legends about St Patrick and his conversion of Ireland in the 5th century (see pages 26–7). As a youth, he was enslaved by raiders in Ireland but he escaped, and spent many years in France. Patrick, impelled by recurrent dreams, was over 60 when he began his mission to Ireland. Later, an Irish monk called Brendan (c.486–575) made a voyage by coracle (a light boat covered in skins), perhaps even reaching North America. The Voyage of St Brendan enjoyed great popularity in the Middle Ages. It is a curious allegory of discovery combined with mysticism, sometimes describing nature in minute detail.

ABOVE: *An early Christian monastery was founded at Glendalough in County Wicklow by St Kevin, who died in 618. The remains include a round tower used for refuge in times of danger.*

BELOW: *The 8th-century St John's Cross stands outside Iona's restored church, on the site of the monastery used by St Columba as a base for converting Scotland to Christianity.*

special veneration. Cuthbert's cult was already well established by the end of the 7th century and he has remained Northumbria's favourite saint ever since. The body, its shrine and the famous Lindisfarne Gospels began a long journey to a new home when the Vikings threatened Lindisfarne in 875. Only in 995 did they find a permanent home at Durham, where a Saxon church was specially built for them and consecrated three years later.

Pilgrims walking across the mudflats to the tidal island of Lindisfarne (Holy Island), once the retreat of St Cuthbert and his monks.

✠ The Celtic Saints

David, or **Dewi Sant** in Welsh, is the patron saint of Wales who gave his name to the peninsula, Dewisland, containing his shrine, cathedral and city. The historical David is difficult to pin down because we are unsure how much written about his life by later chroniclers is distortion or sheer invention. As with the life of St Patrick, there is an almost complete lack of contemporary witness. We know for certain that David was a native Welshman who lived in the 6th century, and a great missionary and founder of monasteries in his country. He is said to have come from a royal line. According to legend, his mother was St Non, a nun at Ty Gwyn near Whitesands Bay, Pembrokeshire, who was seduced by Prince Sant and then spent the rest of her life in prayer and self-mortification. However, it is possible that she became a nun in widowhood after David's birth.

At David's baptism a fountain of the purest water burst forth spontaneously for the rite (this is now St Non's Well, a mile from St Davids Cathedral), while a blind monk holding the infant received his sight. After founding monasteries all over the land, David chose Vallis Rosina for his main community, which grew into the influential

RIGHT: *St David's shrine, in his cathedral at the remote end of Pembrokeshire, is graced by his restored reliquary, found walled up during 19th-century restoration work.*

BELOW: *The peace and simplicity of St Non's Chapel, restored in the local early Christian style, evokes the spirit of St David, born at this place on the Pembrokeshire coast in the 6th century.*

monastery and diocese of St Davids. David died and was buried in his own monastery. It is believed that his relics still exist in an ancient oak and iron casket which is now displayed in a stone niche behind the high altar – the very place, in fact, where the clergy hid them in the 16th century. A beautiful wrought-iron screen thwarts latter-day relic thieves. To see this shrine resplendent with daffodils, pilgrims should visit the cathedral on St David's Day (1 March).

In the 7th century, according to the myth, a young Welsh prince called Caradoc tried to seduce the virgin **Winefrede**. Failing in his objective but still inflamed with lust, he cut off her head 'which falling to the earth, deserved of God to have a fountain of water to spring in the place, which to this day continueth'. Her tutor, Beuno, came out of

Who would true valour see,
Let him come hither;
One here will constant be,
Come wind, come weather.
There's no discouragement
Shall make him once relent
His first avowed intent
To be a pilgrim.

THE PILGRIM'S PROGRESS, JOHN BUNYAN

St Michael's Mount, a mystical island off the coast of Cornwall, was the scene of two visions of the Archangel Michael and site of a Benedictine monastery.

the nearby church and discovering the calamity, cursed Caradoc so that the ground swallowed him up. Then taking Winefrede's head into Mass and calling on his people for their prayers, Beuno joined the head back with the body. Not only did Winefrede miraculously survive but she lived on for another 15 years.

This legend was only written down by an unknown monk in the 12th century. Six centuries later, in the Age of Reason, Dr William Fleetwood, Bishop of St Asaph, loathed this pilgrimage in his diocese and condemned it, declaring that he could not believe a story recorded 500 years after the subject's death. On the other hand, Winefrede seems very much like a pagan legend in a Christian dress. The story of a severed head miraculously rejoined to a body which springs back to life is typical of the often dark Celtic imagination and occurs several times in Celtic mythology.

ABOVE: The annual pilgrimage to St Winefrede's Well, the site of the saint's martyrdom at Holywell in Flintshire, north Wales. Winefrede's is the only pilgrimage to have survived unchecked through the Reformation. Her sacred well is the most complete medieval shrine in Britain.

9

✠ The Pilgrim Routes
Canterbury † Rome † Jerusalem † Santiago

The greatest pilgrimage in medieval times was to Jerusalem. After the Muslim conquest of Palestine in the 7th century, genuine pilgrims continued to travel to the Holy Sepulchre, the traditional site of Christ's burial. But the journey was difficult and dangerous, not to say expensive. During the Crusades, the few pilgrims who ventured on the journey needed the Knights Hospitaller to succour them and the Knights Templar to defend them.

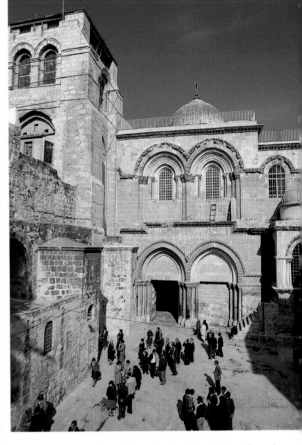

Crowds throng the Plaza de Obradoiro, dominated by the riotous 18th-century façade of the famous shrine of St James the Greater at Santiago de Compostela. Since medieval times the faithful have worn the cockleshell (inset) to symbolise their successful completion of this pilgrimage.

ABOVE: The south door of the Holy Sepulchre in Jerusalem, the traditional site of Christ's crucifixion, burial and resurrection. This shrine, the most rewarding of all possible Christian pilgrimages, is now shared between the many denominations.

Many pilgrims preferred a safer and cheaper option. For those willing to travel beyond their own country the most popular destinations were to the seven pilgrimage churches of Rome and the shrine of the apostle, St James the Greater, at Santiago de Compostela in Galicia (north-west Spain). Sometimes the Pope decreed, in a Papal Bull, the relative value of shrines to the pilgrim's soul; for example, Pope Calixtus II granted that two pilgrimages to St Davids in Pembrokeshire were equal to one pilgrimage to Rome; or in Latin, *Roma semel quantum, Dat bis Menevia tantum.*

The most popular pilgrimage during the Middle Ages was along the Pilgrims' Way from Winchester to Canterbury, to the shrine of England's most famous saint and martyr, St Thomas Becket. The archbishop's brutal and shocking murder, after his quarrel with King Henry II, led to his canonisation on Ash Wednesday in 1173. The largest number of medieval miracles in Britain occurred in the name of St Thomas.

Geoffrey Chaucer's *Canterbury Tales*, composed in about 1390, describes with wry humour the journey of a group of worldly pilgrims from London to Canterbury. Chaucer reveals a lack of esteem for the monastic life and the cult of relics, an increasingly common attitude in his day.

The main roads to major medieval shrines achieved quite a high degree of organisation, with pilgrims forming convoys to travel from one hospice or inn to another.

The best-known account of life on the road and a specific pilgrimage is the *Codex Calixtenus*, edited by Aymery Picaud in about 1150. In five books he describes three routes from France which all combine at the Pyrenees to conduct the faithful to the shrine of St James of Compostela. This hallowed route across northern Spain to Santiago offers the modern traveller, whether as a pilgrim or as an historian, the most satisfying experience of any of the old pilgrimages.

Less well-known than Picaud's work is the itinerary of Sigeric, an Anglo-Saxon Archbishop of Canterbury who went on a pilgrimage to Rome in 990 to collect his pallium (mantle of office) from Pope John XV. A clerk or cleric in his retinue recorded all 80 stages of their journey. So it is possible to trace the exact route the 10th-century pilgrim followed from England to Rome. Following Sigeric's route today leads to the discovery of numerous relics of the roads and their medieval traffic in the form of wayside crosses, especially elaborate wayside shrines, old street names and accommodation built for the faithful by religious orders or town guilds.

ABOVE: *A medieval map of Christendom showing Jerusalem at the centre of the world. Pilgrims to the Holy Land faced many dangers and were protected on the journey by the knights of the Crusades.*

LEFT: *Medieval pilgrims in front of the Holy Sepulchre in Jerusalem, from the Book of Marvels, on the travels of Marco Polo. They wear traditional costume and one of them makes a donation to the shrine.*

✠ The Pilgrim's Journey

The first stage in the medieval pilgrim's journey was usually the ceremony of leaving his home parish. After Mass and special prayers, the priest consecrated the pilgrim's scrip (a wallet similar to a modern fishing bag) and bourdon (his tall staff), sprinkling each with holy water. Then his friends and relatives led him out of the village with the cross borne high before them and gave him their blessing at the parish boundary. He would also carry a letter from his priest or his temporal lord to act as a recommendation of his genuine status to the pious and charitable.

How would he be recognised on the road? To wear the pilgrim's costume was both an honour and a penance, which served to identify him and help in begging for alms along the way. He wore a long and coarse woollen robe, brown or russet in colour and big enough to wrap around him for sleeping. A cross decorated the sleeve. His large round hat had a broad brim, usually turned up at the front to display his pilgrim badges – the symbolic shell and leaden images from the shrines he had already visited. Slung on lanyards around his neck he carried a scrip, a large knife, a flask for water and a rosary. The scrip was for spare pairs of hosen (stockings), two day's food and essential ointment for the feet. Finally, he carried a long stout staff, used for vaulting over streams, climbing hills and as defence against outlaws. It might be tipped with a hollow metal ball, the jangling 'Canterbury bell'.

Pilgrimage was largely a summer occupation and presumably people often slept under hedges or in barns. The accommodation which survives in England from the heyday of pilgrimage varies from hospices run by monks or a dedicated charity, to monasteries whose rules obliged the brethren to offer hospitality to any traveller, and common inns. The Hospital of Newark at Maidstone was a fine example of a hospice supported by a charity. Archbishop Boniface built it in 1261 to receive pilgrims to

ABOVE: *White Hart Cottage at Compton, in Surrey, is by tradition a former pilgrims' hospice.* INSET: *Geoffrey Chaucer.*

Pilgrim Crosses

Wayside crosses served as waymarks to reassure travellers that they were on the right road and as roadside shrines, where they could offer prayers for a safe journey. Old maps and records indicate where some of them once stood. They were often sited where they could be seen from a great distance, at old crossroads on a pilgrim route. Most of these have disappeared but two fine examples survive on the route to the shrine of Our Lady at Walsingham: Binham Cross on the road from the miraculous Holy Rood of Bromholme, and Hockley cum Wilton Cross on the road from Ely.

LEFT: *A Canterbury pilgrim leaves the city past the great Benedictine Abbey of St Augustine, from the 15th-century Poetry of John Lydgate.*

BELOW RIGHT: *A leaden pilgrim badge in the form of the head of St Thomas Becket, of the type sold to visitors as tokens of their pilgrimage to Canterbury. The badge (on view in the Canterbury Heritage Museum ©) was a vital part of the medieval pilgrim's costume.*

The Pilgrim's Progress

John Bunyan rose from humble origins as a tinker to become one of the world's best-known and popular Christian writers. His *Pilgrim's Progress*, first published in 1678, is now read in more than 200 languages. Bunyan found that he had a gift for preaching, as well as free-thinking. His activities, however, landed him in Bedford County Gaol for 12 years. There he 'dreamed a dream' and wrote his famous book about a pilgrimage through the Slough of Despond, Vanity Fair, the Hill of Difficulty and onwards to the Celestial City.

BELOW: *A pilgrim travels with the customary scrip (pouch) and staff, in an illustration from John Bunyan's famous tale.*

Canterbury, although it is several miles from the Pilgrims' Way. Now only its Early English chapel survives and is in use as the chancel of St Peter's church.

Canterbury had many hospices, such as the Hospital of St Thomas the Martyr, now known as the King's Bridge Hospital and founded, according to its charter, by the 'glorious St Thomas the Martyr to receive poor wayfaring men'. The Norman crypt and later refectory and chapel can still be seen. Other pilgrims lodged in the great priory of Christ Church (the cathedral), where a 15th-century extension known as Chillenden Guest Chamber survives as part of the Bishop of Dover's house. Smaller numbers dispersed to the Hospital of St John in Northgate, the great Augustinian abbey or guest houses run by the mendicant friars.

The motley group of worldly pilgrims in Geoffrey Chaucer's Canterbury Tales, shown on the road in The Canterbury Pilgrims by Thomas Stothard, RA in The Royal Museum & Art Gallery, Canterbury ©.

✣ Walking the Pilgrim Ways

Stand at the crossroads and look,
Ask for the ancient paths,
Ask where the good way is,
And walk in it,
And you will find rest for your souls.

HOLY BIBLE, JEREMIAH 6:16

The wide expanses of the
Wiltshire Downs, close to the
prehistoric Harrow Way, an
ancient route across southern
Britain.

Modern pilgrims often travel by car or coach to a popular shrine such as St Thomas at Canterbury or Our Lady at Walsingham, yet there are many who still prefer to go on foot. They are to be seen, especially, on the Way of St James in the north of Spain. In Britain, our inspiration comes from the writer Hilaire Belloc, who wore the three mantles of faithful pilgrim, observant local historian and incorrigible trespasser. He trudged from Alsace to the Vatican and left us a witty account in *The Path to Rome* (1902). Then he muddied his boots on our own Pilgrims' Way from Winchester to Canterbury, describing what remained to be seen from medieval times and merrily theorising as only he could in *The Old Road* (1904). Since then there have been several other guidebooks to The Pilgrims' Way and plenty of authors have written about miracles, relics and the architecture of pilgrimage.

TOP: *Walkers who follow the old pilgrim routes will discover the many joys of the British countryside, such as this ancient Cotswold bridge, which marks the spot where the Roman Fosse Way crosses the infant River Avon.*

LEFT: *Chaucer's much-married Wife of Bath, who told a bawdy story during her ride to the shrine of St Thomas. An illumination from the Ellesmere Manuscript.*

✠ Saints & Shrines

Beverley † Canterbury † Chester

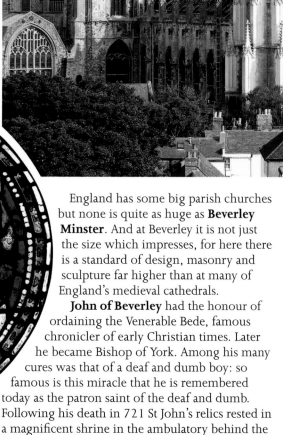

Medieval beliefs about relics are central to pilgrimage. Relics inspired the medieval faithful with a sense of power and mystery. The power suffused the physical remains that a holy person left behind on earth, and the supplicants could, by adoring the relics, gain the intercession of the saint in their lives. So the saints were simultaneously present in heaven and in their earthly relics. If a saint's relics were divided and dispersed to other churches, their power was not diminished; a finger bone was as precious as a whole body.

A relic was kept for its own security, and for its greater glory, in a shrine, a term which refers specifically to its receptacle (*scrinium*). More generally, the term means the shrine-base with its elaborate superstructure and cover which surround the small jewelled reliquary. More widely, shrine refers to a holy place, such as Canterbury Cathedral.

ABOVE: *A 13th-century stained-glass window in the Trinity Chapel at Canterbury Cathedral shows pilgrims worshipping at the splendid shrine to St Thomas Becket.*

England has some big parish churches but none is quite as huge as **Beverley Minster**. And at Beverley it is not just the size which impresses, for here there is a standard of design, masonry and sculpture far higher than at many of England's medieval cathedrals.

John of Beverley had the honour of ordaining the Venerable Bede, famous chronicler of early Christian times. Later he became Bishop of York. Among his many cures was that of a deaf and dumb boy: so famous is this miracle that he is remembered today as the patron saint of the deaf and dumb. Following his death in 721 St John's relics rested in a magnificent shrine in the ambulatory behind the high altar at Beverley, the most usual place in a large medieval church. Pilgrims would have approached along the choir aisles. The relics were moved to the nave after the shrine's destruction at the Reformation.

Pilgrims to the medieval shrine of **St Thomas Becket** in **Canterbury Cathedral** found themselves

The twin west towers and the great central tower ('Bell Harry') still rise above the city of Canterbury to welcome pilgrims to Britain's most famous shrine.

RIGHT: Modern medallion showing St John of Beverley's cure of a dumb and diseased youth, as described by the Venerable Bede.

RIGHT: A 14th-century bench-end in Chester Cathedral's splendid choir shows a pilgrim with his staff and characteristic hat.

well organised. Monks met them, marshalled them into orderly groups and conducted them into the cathedral through the very same door in the north transept used by both Becket and his attackers on 29 December 1170. The first station was the spot where Thomas was brutally cut down, the whole scene no doubt vividly described by the practised guide, as the pilgrims knelt on the cold flags and looked in horror on the tip of de Brito's sword, shattered by the mighty blow that had split the martyr's skull in two.

The second station was the high altar where the body lay throughout the fatal night. Finally the pilgrims descended to the Norman crypt and prayed at the miraculous tomb itself. On 7 July 1220 the relics were translated (moved) to their new shrine behind the high altar in the new Gothic cathedral. As it was the most famous shrine in the kingdom, Henry VIII's commissioners took special care to destroy everything at the Reformation.

St Werburgh, whose shrine is found in the Lady Chapel in **Chester Cathedral**, was the daughter of Wulfere, the Saxon king of Mercia. She became a nun and, through her piety, an abbess noted for her reforms. After she died, in the early 8th century at her nunnery of Trentham, many miracles were reported from her tomb at Hanbury in Staffordshire. Her relics came to Chester to protect them from ravages by the Danes. The church was then a minster, specially enlarged to house her relics. After the Norman Conquest it was rebuilt again, following its conversion to a Benedictine abbey. Werburgh's shrine remained a great centre of pilgrimage until the Reformation; part of its stone base survives in today's cathedral. Her main emblem in art is a goose, which, according to Goscelin's Life, she was supposed to have restored to life.

Marc Chagall's 1978 stained-glass window in the north of the retrochoir, illustrating Psalm 150, greets modern pilgrims to Chichester Cathedral, site of the shrine of St Richard until the Reformation.

Richard of Wych, bishop of **Chichester** 1245–53, was born at Droitwich in 1197, the son of a yeoman farmer. He studied in the universities of Oxford, Paris and Bologna. In 1235 he returned to Oxford to lecture in canon law and soon became chancellor. Following his ordination in 1242, he became priest in the Kent parishes of Charing and Deal. In 1244 he was elected bishop of Chichester, but Henry III and part of the chapter refused to accept him. After an appeal to the authority of Rome, Pope Innocent IV consecrated Richard bishop at Lyons. Besides being a model diocesan bishop, Richard enthusiastically preached the crusades, not as a political expedition, but as a means of making access to the Holy Land easier for pilgrims. He was canonised in 1262 and his relics were translated to a splendid new shrine behind the high altar in his cathedral in 1276. The shrine was despoiled by Henry VIII's commissioners in 1538, when Richard's body was reburied secretly. In art, he is depicted with a chalice at his feet, in memory of the occasion when he dropped the chalice at Mass, but the wine miraculously remained unspilt.

The cult and fame of **St Cuthbert** was responsible for the rebuilding of **Durham Cathedral** in the magnificent Norman style. In about 1140 an attempt by Bishop de Puiset to build a Lady Chapel at the east end failed due to subsidence but this was attributed to the displeasure of St Cuthbert, buried nearby. As a result, the bishop built at the west end the Romanesque Galilee Chapel. In these surroundings, unique in England, the cult of St Cuthbert flourished. A huge catalogue of wealth accumulated but it was all surrendered to the crown in 1540, along with the monastery. Following the destruction of his shrine, St Cuthbert was reburied on the same spot beneath a plain marble slab.

The Venerable Bede describes the life of the saint who founded **Ely Cathedral**. Despite two noble marriages, **Etheldreda** remained a virgin and retreated to an island in the Fens which had been part of the dowry of her first marriage. There she founded a nunnery in 673 and died in 679. Sixteen years after Etheldreda's burial, her body was found free from decay – then seen as the surest sign of sanctity. In the 13th century the east end of the great cathedral was rebuilt to honour her tomb – before the Reformation her shrine was in the place of honour immediately in front of the high altar.

BELOW: *The tomb of St Cuthbert, the north of England's most popular saint, behind the high altar of Durham Cathedral, where he was reburied during the Reformation.*

LEFT INSET: *Cuthbert's precious garnet-and-gold Pectoral Cross, dating from the 7th century.*

Fragments from the base of the shrine can still be seen next to the tomb of Bishop Hugh de Northwold who extended the cathedral. The translation of her body to its new shrine is observed on 17 October, St Etheldreda's Fair, vulgarly called St Awdry's Fair. So cheap and showy was the finery, especially lace, sold there that the contraction of 'St Awdry' gives us the English word 'tawdry'. But there is nothing tawdry about the marvellous cathedral, with its famous 'Octagon' tower, which rises like a huge ship above the Fens and the little buildings of this well-preserved old market town.

ABOVE: *The choir at Ely Cathedral, rebuilt in honour of the founder, St Etheldreda, in the 13th century. Her shrine stood, rather unusually, in front of the high altar between the choir stalls.*

✠ Saints & Shrines

Hereford † Lichfield † Lincoln

Thomas Cantelupe, known as St Thomas of **Hereford**, was born in 1218 at Hambledon in Buckinghamshire into a noble and powerful Norman family. His uncle, the bishop of Worcester, supervised his education and prepared Thomas for high office in both church and state. He went to study in Oxford, Paris and Orleans, returning, like St Richard of Chichester before him, to be chancellor at Oxford. Following the defeat of Henry III at the Battle of Lewes, Thomas became chancellor of England for a year until Simon de Montfort's defeat at the Battle of Evesham. He left the country and returned to Paris as lecturer in canon law. In 1275 the canons of Hereford elected him their bishop but Thomas soon quarrelled violently with John Pecham, Archbishop of Canterbury. He found himself excommunicated and resorted to the papal court at Orvieto in central Italy, but died on 25 August 1282 at Montefiascone. He was buried at Orvieto but his heart and bones were returned to Hereford Cathedral. How the shrine survived the Reformation is a mystery.

Chad, a much-loved monk, was brought out of retirement in his monastery to be Bishop of Mercia in 669. The Venerable Bede recounts, in his History of the English Church and People, written in 731, that Chad died of disease on 2 March 672,

an event foretold by a choir of angels seven days earlier at **Lichfield**, where his cult has since remained. Bede says that he was first buried in St Mary's Church, then in St Peter's. At both shrines frequent miracles of healing attested to Chad's virtues. In 1148 the relics were translated to a shrine at the high altar of the Norman cathedral. The cult was so popular that in 1330, at a cost of £2000, Bishop Langton built another shrine, placed behind the high altar for easier access to pilgrims. The site is still marked today.

ABOVE: St Chad preferred to make his missionary journeys around Mercia on foot. In this Victorian roundel at Lichfield Cathedral, Archbishop Theodore instructs him to ride a horse around his diocese.

LEFT: Few medieval shrines escaped destruction by Henry VIII's commissioners, though St Thomas Cantelupe's survived, in the north transept of Hereford Cathedral. Set on a pedestal of Purbeck marble, the niches at the base of the shrine contain statues of fourteen Knights Templar. The saint was their provincial grand master.

Lincoln Cathedral's glorious Angel Choir, built for the growing number of pilgrims attracted to St Hugh's shrine, takes its name from the 30 carved angels in the triforium spandrels. Queen Eleanor attended its consecration in 1280.

Such a fine cathedral also acquired other relics: the Sacrist's Roll for 1345 lists 'the relics of divers saints...some of the bones of St Laurence, some of Golgotha...part of the sepulchre of the Blessed Virgin Mary...part of the finger and cowl of St William, some of the bones of St Stephen...'. Episodes in Chad's life are shown in six panels of stained glass in the Chapter House and in a Victorian tiled floor by Minton in the presbytery.

Hugh was a strong-minded and zealous bishop at **Lincoln** who survived an argument with Henry II over the excommunication of a royal forester. Hugh was conspicuous by his unbounded charity, especially towards lepers, and his efforts in rebuilding the cathedral. His funeral was held during a council of state at Lincoln in 1200: among the bearers were King John of England and King William of Scotland. In 1280 Hugh's body was translated in splendour to a golden shrine in the place of honour in the glorious Angel Choir. The head graced a separate golden *chef* (reliquary in the shape of a head) nearby. The scale of the pilgrimage to his shrine was then second only to St Thomas at Canterbury. Lincoln also boasted three other shrines, those of Little St Hugh and two more bishops, Robert Grosseteste and John of Dalderby.

✠ Saints & Shrines

Ripon † St Alban's † St Edmundsbury † Salisbury

A new Anglican diocese was created in 1836 at an attractive market town in rural Yorkshire. Only then did **Ripon** Minster become a cathedral. Today it is a mixture of styles. It has a Saxon crypt and displays in its parts the development of the Romanesque and Gothic styles. The cathedral contains the shrine of **St Wilfrid**. He was the robust protagonist whose arguments defeated the Celtic partisans, or followers of St Columba, at the Synod of Whitby in 664. Elected Bishop of York, he converted the Northumbrian church to the Roman custom and introduced the Benedictine rule to northern monasteries. After an argument over the division of his see, he fell from power, appealed to the Pope (the first time an English bishop did this) and was finally restored to

BELOW: A detail of the modern window in the Pilgrim Chapel at Ripon Cathedral commemorates the cult of St Wilfrid, which flourished in the former minster. The crypt of Wilfrid's church is a rare survival.

RIGHT: The shrine of St Alban, destroyed in the Reformation and now reconstructed from 2,000 fragments. Behind it is the rare oak watching loft, used by monks who guarded the shrine and relics.

his monastery at Ripon, where he was buried in 709.

St Alban is honoured as Britain's first martyr (c.209), suffering his fate for sheltering a Christian priest fleeing the persecution of Septimus Severus. According to legend the executioner's eyes fell out as his sword struck off the head. Passionate debates arose about St Alban's bones. In the two centuries between the Norman Conquest and the account by the monk Matthew Paris so many lies had been told about the saint's relics that it became difficult for anyone to claim that they had the bones of the protomartyr if, indeed, they had ever been preserved. The elaborate and richly bejewelled shrine of c.1302–08 was destroyed in 1539 but two thousand fragments of its tall pedestal of Purbeck marble were discovered in 1872, built into a wall blocking off the east end of the church. Painstakingly reassembled then, and again in 1991, it still gives a hint of the richness of this most worldly of medieval abbeys, although its canopy was destroyed at the Reformation.

Edmund, a Saxon prince, inherited the throne of the East Angles at the age of 15, at a time when the incursions of the Danes were increasing. According to tradition, the young Edmund fought the Danes in 869 at the battle of Thetford. Dismayed by the carnage of his people, he surrendered himself to the enemy in the hope that the sacrifice of his own life might save his subjects. After a severe beating, he was tied naked to a tree, scourged with whips, riddled with arrows and finally beheaded. A legend says that the discarded head was found by a wolf, who followed the funeral procession at Hoxne until the head was rejoined to the body. Thirty-three years later, following a series of miracles, the relics were translated to a shrine at Bury, where the cult of the last king of East Anglia flourished. Although the arms

ABOVE: *This detail from a hanging embroidered by Sybil Andrews in 1975 shows Edmund, king and martyr, shot by Danish bowmen during their invasion. Also depicted is the legendary wolf who guarded Edmund's head.*

BELOW: *This tomb is traditionally identified as part of the medieval shrine of St Osmund, whose body was moved from Old Sarum and reinterred at the new Salisbury Cathedral in 1226.*

of the city of Bury St Edmunds incorporate a wolf's head to this day, the site of the shrine is now lost and very little remains of the once gigantic abbey.

According to a 15th-century document, **Osmund**, bishop of Old Sarum 1078–99, was a nephew of William the Conqueror and came to England as chaplain with the Duke's army in 1066. This may well be true, as he was employed by the king in a civil capacity to prepare part of the Domesday Book. He was also present at the consecration of Battle Abbey. He perhaps even held the chancellorship before being consecrated bishop of Old Sarum in 1078. He himself consecrated the new **Salisbury** cathedral on the hilltop in 1092 and was active in establishing a Norman chapter and hierarchy. Later, his *Use of Sarum*, a service book, met with almost universal acceptance in Britain and Ireland. Osmund was canonised in 1457.

✠ Saints & Shrines

Westminster † Winchester † Worcester † York

Westminster Abbey still venerates the shrine of King **Edward the Confessor**, builder of the late Saxon abbey. The well-documented reconstruction by Henry III further elevated the status of this royal shrine. In 1241 he ordered a new monument to be made of gold and marble. Both king and queen presented jewels or money for the extremely lavish work. This great shrine survives, stripped of valuables but surrounded by the tombs of most of England's medieval kings. Nearby in the abbey, the tomb of Henry VII was almost an official shrine. The tomb of this king, a usurper who defeated Richard III at the Battle of Bosworth, serves the purpose of legitimising his Tudor regime.

RIGHT: *The shrine of Edward the Confessor in Westminster Abbey was briefly dismantled during the Reformation. It probably escaped destruction because Henry VIII claimed kinship with Edward. The tombs of England's medieval kings and queens surround the shrine.*

Winchester became the focus for trade and travellers through Southampton, and by late Saxon times the city was the capital of England. The Normans, too, favoured Winchester, which continued to be the land's royal and administrative centre until about 1250. This is reflected in the magnificence of **Winchester Cathedral**, which was the longest and finest church in Norman England.

A distant view of Winchester Cathedral, begun by Bishop Walkelin in 1079. It rained for 40 days when St Swithun's relics were translated into the previous church, starting the legend of the saint's control over the English summer climate.
RIGHT: *Pilgrims at Winchester observe a prayerful tradition.*

Quite apart from its strategic and political importance, the 12th-century city had famous 'workshops' of carving and manuscript illumination. The Winchester School was one of the great triumphs of English artistic genius. It was also esteemed for the shrine of **St Swithun**, its 9th-century bishop during the period of the great monastic reforms under St Dunstan. This pilgrimage site was highly popular long before the murder of Thomas Becket in 1170. Only a few fragments remain of the medieval shrine but the cathedral continues to be the starting point for the Pilgrims' Way to Canterbury.

As an esteemed novice, **Wulfstan** was admitted as a monk to **Worcester** cathedral-monastery before the Norman Conquest. Rising to be prior under the bishop, he travelled about baptising the children of the poor because, it is said, the secular clergy refused to do this without a fee. Wulfstan made himself useful to King Harold but then swiftly made submission to William the Conqueror at Berkhampstead. In 1088, he denounced English and Welsh rebels marching on Worcester, thereby, according to tradition, securing their defeat. He was buried at Worcester and immediately regarded as a saint, although he was not formally canonised until 1203. King John on his deathbed commended his soul to God and St Wulfstan and was buried next to the shrine.

William Fitzherbert was of noble birth, the son of Herbert, Henry I's treasurer, and had a luxurious upbringing, probably at the Norman royal court in Winchester. When the Archbishop of York, Thurstan, died in 1140, a furious and prolonged dispute arose about the succession, involving King Stephen, the Cistercians at Fountains

LEFT: Wulfstan offering his church. Parts of Wulfstan's cathedral at Worcester, built in the Romanesque style, still survive, and include the largest Norman crypt in England.

Abbey, the Archbishop of Canterbury, the great St Bernard of Clairvaux and Pope Innocent II. When William finally became archbishop, tragedy struck within a month. He was seized with a sudden illness while celebrating Mass in his own minster. Poisoning was suspected and antidotes were administered at once but to no avail. William died eight days later, with Archdeacon Osbert accused of poisoning the eucharistic chalice. William was admitted to the calendar of saints in 1227.

RIGHT: St William of York, a minor figure promoted in life beyond his abilities and in death beyond his miracles, from the Bolton Hours, c.1420, in York Minster Library.

✠ Survival and Revival

Holywell in North Wales is a shrine where the adherents of the old faith never let go. During the Middle Ages this ancient pagan well became one of the most popular Christian places of pilgrimage due to the legend of St Winefrede. During the Reformation, for reasons which remain obscure, it also became a focus of activity by Catholic recusants (nonconformists). Pilgrims never stopped coming to the shrine, despite the best efforts of the Anglican bishop and the civil authorities. Today the shrine is still visited by thousands of pilgrims every year; not too many to destroy the peace of this most ornamental of Gothic chapels, but enough to keep the candles burning constantly.

At Walsingham, during the 20th century, both Anglicans and Catholics revived the pilgrimage of medieval kings, each maintaining a separate shrine, but neither on the original sacred site. The pilgrimages at Glastonbury, begun in 1924 as a small celebration of faith, now involve some 3,000 people (Catholics, Anglicans and Orthodox Christians), many travelling from far afield to take part. Canterbury, too, has benefited from this modern enthusiasm for an old custom. A greater number of genuine pilgrims now arrive at the shrine of

ABOVE: *The annual procession to the Anglican shrine of Our Lady of Walsingham in Norfolk, a medieval pilgrimage vigorously revived in the 20th century by Catholic, Protestant and Orthodox Christians.*

St Thomas Becket than at any time since 1500.

In the far west of Ireland, there are three shrines with an even stronger hold on their devotees. Nowhere else in the British Isles is pilgrimage taken more seriously than at Lough Derg in county Donegal, where pilgrims assemble on St Patrick's Island on the saint's day for an extremely rigorous three-day penance to commemorate his fast.

St Patrick's Island in Lough Derg, County Donegal, is the scene of the most rigorous pilgrimage in Britain or Ireland, where devotees assemble for a strict three-day penance on the saint's day.

Our Lady at Lourdes

A picturesque French town nestling at the foot of the Pyrenees receives five million visitors a year. They come here because of the most famous vision of modern times. On 11 February 1858, a poor girl aged 14 years, Bernadette Soubirous, met and later spoke with the Virgin Mary in a cave called Massabielle. The vision said, among other things, 'I am the Immaculate Conception' and 'I do not promise to make you happy in this world but the other'. The story spread like wildfire, Bernadette was canonised in 1933, crutches now hang at the grotto and the little town hosts the most impressive Marian cult in Europe.

ABOVE: 21st-century piety at Lourdes: A statue of St Bernadette in front of an apse mosaic showing the schoolgirl's famous vision of the Virgin Mary.

LEFT: Pilgrims at Lourdes.

Croagh Patrick is a mountain of rock and scree on the Atlantic coast of county Mayo, where St Patrick meditated for 40 days and prayed that Ireland should remain forever Christian. On the last Sunday in July, 'Reek Sunday' as it is known, some 60,000 Roman Catholics commemorate Patrick's devotion. It has been described as 'an extraordinary, almost medieval sight. Above you, the line stretches along the brow of Ireland's Holy Mountain till it disappears in the thickening cloud. Below you, hundreds more are on their way up or down.

At Knock, also in County Mayo, pilgrims visit the site of a vision that was witnessed by the entire village in 1879. St Joseph, the Blessed Virgin Mary and the *Agnus Dei* appeared over the gable of the modest church. In 1979 the villagers persuaded Pope Paul to bless the site on its centenary. On that occasion no fewer than one million Irish men and women, nearly one third of the population of the Republic of Ireland, converged on Knock. Such is the continuing power of miracles, holy places and the spirit of pilgrimage.

It is this enduring spirit which inspires people today, as of old, to set out to walk the ancient ways, visit the holy places and explore the roots of their faith. Whatever the motive for setting out, whatever the hardships encountered along the way, the pilgrim's reward is the secret joy of spiritual discovery.

LEFT: Pilgrims at Knock pay their respects to stones from the simple church where the triple vision appeared in 1879 to the people of this remote village in County Mayo.

✛ Saints & Shrines

Beverley Minster	St John of Beverley
Bromholme, Norfolk	The Holy Rood
Canterbury Cathedral	St Thomas Becket
Chester Cathedral	St Werburgh
Chichester Cathedral	St Richard
Croagh Patrick, County Mayo	St Patrick
Dorchester Abbey, Oxfordshire	St Birinus
Durham Cathedral	St Cuthbert
Ely Cathedral	St Etheldreda
Glastonbury Abbey	St Dunstan
Hailes Abbey, Gloucestershire	The Holy Blood
Hereford Cathedral	St Thomas Cantelupe
Holywell, Flintshire	St Winefrede
Ilam, Staffordshire	St Bertelin
Iona Abbey	St Columba
Knock, County Mayo	St Joseph, Virgin Mary, *Agnus Dei*
Lichfield Cathedral	St Chad (and holy well)
Lincoln Cathedral	St Hugh and Little St Hugh
Lindisfarne Priory	St Cuthbert, Oswald, Aidan
Llandaff Cathedral	St Teilo
Lough Derg, County Donegal	St Patrick
Ripon Cathedral	St Wilfrid
Salisbury Cathedral	St Osmund
St Alban's Cathedral	St Alban
St David's Cathedral	St David (*Dewis*)
St Edmundsbury Cathedral	St Edmund
St Michael's Mount	Archangel Michael
Walsingham, Norfolk	Our Lady
Waltham Abbey, Herts	The Miraculous Cross
Westminster Abbey	Edward the Confessor
Winchester Cathedral	St Swithun
Whitchurch Canonicorum, Dorset	St Candida or Wita
Worcester Cathedral	St Wulfstan
York Minster	St William of York

ATLANTIC

OCEAN

Iona ✛

Lough Derg ✛

NORTHERN
IRELAND

✛ Knock

✛
Croagh Patrick

IRI

EIRE

St Davids

Most of the saints and shrines on the map
are mentioned in this guidebook; however
space does not permit a comprehensive list.